Marx Refuted

The Verdict of History

Edited by
RONALD DUNCAN
and
COLIN WILSON

ASHGROVE PRESS, BATH

First published in Great Britain by
ASHGROVE PRESS LIMITED
19 Circus Place, Bath, Avon BA1 2PW

ISBN 0 906798 71 X (*hardcover*)
ISBN 0 906798 72 8 (*paperback*)

First published 1987

Typeset in 10/11½ Bembo
by Ann Buchan (Typesetters), Surrey
Printed and bound by Billings, Worcester

CONTENTS

ACKNOWLEDGEMENTS

The editors are grateful to the B.B.C. for permission to print an edited transcript of Bernard Levin's interview with Vladimir Bukovsky; to the Index on Censorship for permission to reprint Section 6 of Solzhenitsyn's *Letter to Soviet Leaders* (1973) and the interview with Swedish Radio and Television given by Andrei Sakharov to Olle Stenholm (1973), both excerpts translated by Hilary Sternberg; to Hamish Hamilton Ltd for permission to reprint part of *Testimony – The Memoirs of Shostakovich* as related to and edited by Solomon Volkov; to Andre Deutsch for permission to reprint the paragraph from Bukovsky's *To Build a Castle* translated by Michael Scammell.

The editors also wish to express their gratitude to Diana Johnson for the considerable research and editing she has contributed to this book.

INTRODUCTORY NOTE

This book has taken a long time to see the light of day.

It was conceived by Ronald Duncan in 1981, as a sequel to his *Encyclopaedia of Ignorance* and *Lying Truths*, both edited in collaboration with Miranda Weston-Smith, and published by Pergamon Press. Pergamon Press also contracted to publish *Marx Refuted*. Its owner, Robert Maxwell, had been a friend of Ronald Duncan's for many years.

But for some reason, Pergamon Press changed its mind. Whereupon, Ronald Duncan had the idea of placing an advertisement in a newspaper – I think it was the *Times* – in which he listed the contributors to the book, and asked publishers to contact him. To his astonishment, it was Pergamon Press who wrote to him and offered to publish the book.

The typescript was handed over some time early in 1982, and was duly copy-edited. Then there was a long, unexplained delay. Months went by, and still no proof was forthcoming. On June 3rd, 1982, Ronald Duncan died of lung cancer. Shortly thereafter, I received a letter from Pergamon Press saying they had decided not to publish the book after all. It would, of course, have been possible to hold them to their legal contract, but there seemed no point. In fact, I was sympathetic about the feelings of a millionaire socialist who had committed himself to publishing a book attacking Karl Marx. But I could have wished that he had made up his mind sooner.

The book is now published under the auspices of the Ronald Duncan Literary Foundation.

C.W.

An Interview with Lenin

By 1917, Lenin himself had already outgrown Marxism, as becomes plain from his interview with George Solomon extracted from David Shub's biography of Lenin

LENIN You are smiling? You mean to say that it is all a fantasy, a dream? I know what you are going to say. I know the whole stock of those stereotyped, threadbare Marxist phrases which in reality are *petit-bourgeois* futilities which you cannot for a moment discard. By the way I remember Vorovsky wrote to me about your conversation with him and that you had called it all a dream and all that. Let me tell you, we are past all that. All that has been left behind. All that is nothing but Marxist hairsplitting. We discarded that as one of those inevitable children's diseases which every society and every class must go through and with which they part when they see a new dawn gleaming on the horizon. . . . Don't even attempt to contradict me! It's no use. You and your Krassin with his theory of natural evolution are not going to convince me. We are turning more and more towards the Left.

Yes, we will destroy everything and on the ruins we will build our temple! It will be a temple for the happiness of all. But we will destroy the entire bourgeoisie, grind it to a powder. Remember this – you and your friend Nikitich (Krassin) that the Lenin whom you knew ten years ago no longer exists. He is dead.

I will be merciless with all counter-revolutionists, and I shall employ Comrade Uritsky (chief of the Petrograd Secret Police) against all counter-revolutionists, no matter who they are. I do not advise you to make his acquaintance.

No, let them protest. Let them boil a little, rage a little, drink a lot of tea, split intellectual hairs till dawn then fall into their vodka. They're fit for nothing else.

VOICE	(FROM AUDITORIUM) You've no majority here.
ANOTHER	You're anti Marxist!
LENIN	(SHOUTING) Yes, I am. I know the whole stock of those stereotyped threadbare Marxist phrases which in reality are petty bourgeois futilities which you cannot for a moment discard. But let me tell you all Marxist hairsplitting has now been left behind, discarded as those inevitable children's diseases which every society and class have to suffer at some time or other.

(*Lenin* at The Tauride Palace, Moscow – Jan. 18th 1918)

PREFACE
RONALD DUNCAN

The purpose of this book is to re-examine the dogma of Marx. The ideas of Dialectical Materialism now plague a third of the world. It claims to be a science: so might astrology. It behaves like a religion, being evangelical, dogmatic and cruel. As a theory of economics it has reduced Russia, which before 1917 used to have a grain surplus, to be dependent on imports of wheat from the USA. The Tsars freed the serfs. Communism has imposed servitude on the entire nation.

If poverty has been diminished, its method has been to liquidate the poor. The aristocracy were beheaded or banished and yet the classless society failed to materialise. Bureaucracy spreads over all. The Monarchy has been replaced by the all powerful State, which is not so easily assassinated.

As these pages reveal, science has been perverted, and artistic endeavour frustrated. Choice, the essence of an invidual's being, has been reduced to the minimum. The Soviet citizen cannot leave his country, he fears to converse or make a telephone call. Whole races are being subjugated by an imperialism more ruthless than Genghis Khan.

To substantiate these views, the editors have invited current philosophers and economists to scrutinise the fundamental tenets of Marxism and to invite those who have endured this regime and managed to escape from it to describe their experiences.

Ronald Duncan

PART ONE

In Theory

INTRODUCTION

Marx Refuted

COLIN WILSON

Half a century ago it would probably have been true to say that most western 'intellectuals' were sympathetic to Russia and the 1917 Revolution. They may have had their doubts about Lenin and Stalin and Trotsky, and they may, in practice, have preferred to live in the West; but they nevertheless felt that Capitalism is fundamentally rather wicked, and that the Russians probably did the right thing in overthrowing it. They had that slightly guilty attitude that most of us feel when we hear a television appeal for starving refugees; that perhaps we *ought* to sell the colour TV and second car but that in practice we are too weak and lazy, and it wouldn't make much difference anyway . . .

Since those early days, the west has had the chance to see communism in practice in many countries in the world, and to observe that it always seems to result in oppression and totalitarianism. From the Stalin purges to the Vietnam boat people and the takeover of Cambodia, the face of Communism seems invariably brutal. So there are nowadays far fewer people ready to argue — as Shaw did in the 1930s — that you cannot make an omelette without breaking eggs. Yet there is still a widespread feeling that the *principles* of socialism are probably good, and that for some odd reason, it is the practice that always seems to go wrong. After all, the history of Christianity is nearly as horrific, but no one lays the blame on its founder.

But *is* Marxism a sound theory that is betrayed by its practitioners? Would it actually work if human beings were less imperfect? Since the 1930s, doubts have been growing steadily. *In The Open Society and Its Enemies*, Karl Popper argued that oppression was inherent in the whole socialist theory from the moment Plato decided that poets were too dangerous to live in his ideal Republic. Camus scandalised French intellectuals by asserting, in *L'Homme Revolté*, that terror is an inevitable consequence of revolutionary socialism, and that all such revolutions are bound to degenerate into tyranny. His most passionate opponent, Sartre — that romantic anti-authoritarian — attempted to create a form of Marxism based on individual freedom, but abandoned the attempt after the first volume. And most Marxist commentators are now willing to admit that Marx was wrong about many central issues, and that some of his most important prophecies — like the increasing alienation of the workers, the polarisation of the social classes, and the 'withering away of the State' — were simply unrealistic guesses.

In spite of which, a great many 'men of goodwill' continue to feel that there is something fundamentally wrong with Capitalism, and therefore fundamentally right about Socialism. This is not an issue to which they devote much thought; but it seems to be based on a vague conviction that the continued existence of the poor and underprivileged somehow proves that Marx was correct.

Now, in fact, although the poor and underprivileged remain the chief propaganda weapon of the Marxists, a little reflection shows that Capitalism is no more responsible for them than is Communism. Both Capitalism and Communism are theories about the distribution of wealth. But wealth has to exist before it can be distributed. According to Marx, this was no problem. Once the workers took over the means of production, there would be more than enough wealth to go round. Yet, in practice, this has never happened. From Russia to China, Poland to Cuba, from Angola to Mozambique, the hallmark of every Marxist state in the world is low productivity, which is due in turn to bureaucratic centralism with its inevitable inefficiency and corruption. Ex-Communists like Bukovsky and Koliakovsky assert that these are inherent in the nature of Marxism.

All socialist systems are based upon this pleasing notion that there is plenty of wealth, and that the only problem is to distribute it fairly and prevent the greedy from taking more than their share. This is contradicted by the fact that the creation of wealth — or anything else — is always an individual enterprise. Give a man an aim, an objective, and tell him he can achieve it by effort, and he will work until he drops. Tell a man he is part of a group, and that everything he earns belongs by right to 'society', and you destroy his mainspring of purpose. Marxism fails to grasp — or prefers to ignore — the most basic psychological truth about human beings: that their 'productivity' depends upon an essentially *individual* creativity — the urge to 'self-actualisation'. It cannot, by its nature, be socialised or mechanised.

How is it possible for intelligent individuals to overlook anything so fundamental? The answer can be found in a passage from the Communist historian of science, J.D. Bernal: ". . . we have in the practice of science the prototype for all human common action. The task which the scientists have undertaken — the understanding and control of nature and of man himself — is merely the conscious expression of the task of human society . . . In science men have learned to subordinate themselves to a common purpose without losing the individuality of their achievements . . . In science men collaborate not because they are forced to by superior authority or because they blindly follow some chosen leader, but because they realise that only in this willing collaboration can each man find his goal."[1]

In spite of the slip of the tongue about the control of human beings, this may be taken as a good example of woolly-minded liberal thinking about communism: he fixes his mind firmly upon an idealised picture of scientists collaborating on some great enterprise, and tells us that this ought to apply to all human society. He takes care not to fix his sights on the actuality of modern society, with its millions of workers streaming into factory gates or football matches; that would reveal to him that his picture of scientists collaborating on atomic research is inapplicable. Scientists belong to the tiny percentage of people whose work is truly 'individual' and therefore satisfying. In a modern technological society, it is inevitable that the work of the majority should be repetitive and not particularly fulfilling. But this does not mean that the worker is bound to be 'alienated'. If labour relations are good, if his life outside the factory or office fulfills his personal needs, then repetitive labour is no hardship — just as, in my own case, the repetitive labour of pounding on a typewriter for several hours a day is no hardship when compared to the satisfaction of being allowed to say what I like. Marx was mistaken to believe that the labourer in a capitalist society will become more and more alienated. What has happened is that the labourers have become increasingly middle class, with cars and colour televisions to provide a degree of fulfilment that is not to be found in the factory. This is the truth of the matter, the 'law' of capitalist society, and Marx was quite simply wrong about it. (He was wrong for the same reason as Bernal — because he preferred to fix his eyes on his own abstractions, instead of observing human beings.) It is the business of any reasonable society to offer its citizens as much 'fulfilment' as possible. But nothing can ever turn them into scientists working together on a great enterprise. The scientist belongs, of necessity, to a very small class whose work produced individual fulfilment.

The passage from Bernal is quoted in a paper by Paul Ostreicher,[2] who, having based his argument on this false analogy, goes on to assert: "Economic injustice is the fundamental problem. Without economic justice a call for population control . . . is unrealistic and lacks credibility". So the picture of an ideal society as an assemblage of scientists leads to a proposition about what is wrong with capitalist society: that the average worker cannot play his creative and individualistic role because he is too poor. So the wicked rich must be stopped from grabbing more than their share, and the surplus value be distributed among the workers, permitting them all to become creative individuals. Ostreicher is frank enough to admit that a worker in Eastern Europe is likely to be just as alienated as one in the West, and that communism has not yet found the practical answers. But he goes on hopefully to suggest that the "Chinese experiment", with the "devolution of power on the commune pattern, with local people *in touch with nature* (his italics), can lead to a genuinely organic development". This was written in 1975, before the workers of China began to show the same dissatisfaction with communist ideology as the workers of Poland, and before Mao's successors found it necessary to dilute the pure Marxist doctrine with infusions of democracy and individual freedom.

It is easy enough to see how a bored worker might feel deprived of his rightful freedom in an assembly line, but more difficult to understand how 'intellectuals' like Bernal and Ostreicher — who, after all, themselves belong to the 'individualist elite' — can deceive themselves with false analogies about scientists or artists. The answer seems to be that intellectuals are inclined to identify their own vaguely idealistic aims with any theory that promises revolutionary change. The existentialist philosopher, Berdyaev, describes in his autobiography how he became an early convert to Marxism: "What struck me above all was the prospect of a spiritual revolution: a rising of the spirit, of freedom and meaning, against the deadly weight, the slavery and meaninglessness of the world". And he adds: "When I was a small boy, the sight of a government building or state-institution filled me with abhorrence, and I desired its immediate destruction". We can understand how a child would feel this way about large buildings (particularly schools), but it is less easy to understand how an intelligent person can carry this attitude into adulthood. We simply have to recognise that few human beings ever grow-up emotionally. Many intellectuals start off from a position of anti-authoritarianism because they personally feel threatened by people in authority who are more stupid than they are. The sensible solution would be to use their intelligence to rise to a position from which stupid people cease to be a threat; but vagueness and incompetence may prevent this from happening; in which case, the 'revolutionary' attitude may persist for life. It was Berdyaev's own experience of the actual revolution — of 1917 — that finally taught him what many intellectuals fail to grasp: that while capitalism may show inadequate regard for the individual, socialism regards him with suspicious hostility. Capitalism tolerates its intellectual rebels and even gives them academic appointments; socialism suppresses them.

Socialism, of course, existed long before Marx, in St Simon, Fourier, Proudhon and the rest. This was liberal socialism, idealistic socialism, based upon a vaguely rebellious attitude to authority and a vague idealism of the kind we have noted in Bernal and Ostreicher. Oddly enough, Marx spent much of his life exploding this kind of socialism, denouncing it as a dream, a wish-fulfilment fantasy based on emotion — in short as unrealistic. Many non-socialists find it hard to understand why Marx devoted so much energy and fury to attacking fellow socialists. The answer is that he believed that bad doctrine drives out good. He claims to have replaced this vague, emotional socialism with a scientific variety based upon ineluctable laws of social development. His opponents objected that Marx's socialism was just as unworkable as the previous kind because it was just as unrealistic, and prophesied that in practice, a Marxian state would turn out to be just as authoritarian, just as repressive, as the old regime. A rigid social theory requires a centralised bureaucracy to impose it and co-ordinate its activities. And centralised bureaucracy tends to be sluggish and inefficient by nature — because it *is* centralised, and reacts too slowly to economic needs — and corrupt because it requires bribery to oil the wheels.

Marx rejected these accusations as reactionary libels, and there can be no doubt that he was sincere. He genuinely believed that the triumph of the proletariat would bring about an increase in individual freedom and the eventual withering away of the state.

History has shown him to be wrong. It has shown him to be as vague, idealistic and woolly-minded as the colleagues he attacks so bitterly. At the moment (1985), it seems unlikely that the outcome will be the total destruction of communism and its sudden replacement by a system that permits more individual freedom. Communism may be suffering from hardening arteries, but it is clearly not dying. No doubt the communist state would suffer the same fate as those it replaced if it stayed around long enough. What seems to be happening is a gradual, cautious swing back towards capitalism. Some of the most successful countries in the Eastern bloc have mixed economies. China has experienced its own revulsion against Maoism. The Soviet Union itself seems to be slowly recognising that efficiency is more important than Marxist doctrine. *The Economist* reports that a decree of January 17, 1981 calls for the encouragement of more private plots of land, and that although Russian's 'private plots' are only 3% of the total farming land, they produce one quarter of the country's agricultural output.

So, in a sense, it is superfluous to try and refute Marx: his work has already been refuted by the actuality of Communism.

NOTES

1. 'The Social Function of Science' pp 415–6.
2. 'Marxism, Nature and Work', in *Man and Nature*, edited by Hugh Montefiore, Collins, 1975.

KARL POPPER

Introduced by
COLIN WILSON

It could be argued that Popper's life work as a philosopher owed its original impetus to Marxism. Excited and impressed by Edward Bellamy's *Looking Backward*, which he read at the age of twelve, Popper was converted to socialism by a friend named Arthur Arndt, who had been one of the student leaders during the Russian revolution of 1905. 'He found me very willing to listen to socialist ideas', says Popper. 'Nothing, I felt, could be more important than to end poverty.' At the end of the first world war, when he was sixteen, Popper became a member of the association of socialist pupils of secondary schools, and attended meetings at which communist speakers talked about the horrors of war. Before the age of seventeen he was a communist convert. But he was 'deconverted' almost immediately. Several young socialist and communist workers were killed when shooting broke out at a demonstration in Vienna. As a communist, Popper recognised that he ought to regard this with equanimity since, according to Marxist doctrine, incidents like this intensify the class struggle and bring the revolution nearer.

> By the time I was seventeen I had become an anti-Marxist. I realised the dogmatic character of the creed, and its incredible intellectual arrogance. It was a terrible thing to arrogate to oneself a kind of knowledge which made it a duty to risk the lives of other people for an uncritically accepted dogma, or for a dream which might turn out not to be realizable. It was particularly bad for an intellectual, for one who could read and think. It was awfully depressing to have fallen into such a trap.
>
> Once I had looked at it critically, the gaps and loopholes and inconsistencies in the Marxist theory became obvious. Take its central point with respect to violence, the dictatorship of the proletariat: who were the proletariat? Lenin, Trotsky and the other leaders? The communists had never formed a majority.

He was also struck by the vague and unrealistic attitude of his Marxist friends, who confidently expected to become the future leaders of the working class, although they had no special intellectual qualifications, and were not even well-acquainted with Marxist literature. That is to say, their Marxism was simply a vague emotional adherence to the idea of an 'equitable distribution of wealth.' A bridge builder with an equally vague knowledge of applied mathematics would undoubtedly be courting disaster; yet the young Marxists had no doubt that they were building a bridge into the future. The confidence of Marxists is based on Marx's assertion that his ideas constitute a scientific system, and that the historical result they predict is inevitable. Popper found himself reflecting on this matter of the 'inevitability' of history, and on how a science – like physics – can be distinguished from a pseudo-science like Marxism. It was the germ of his future work in philosophy.

> I remained a socialist for several years, even after my rejection of Marxism; and if there could be such a thing as socialism combined with individual liberty, I would be a socialist still. For nothing could be better than living a modest, simple and free life in an egalitarian society. It took some time before I recognised this as no more than a beautiful dream; that freedom is more important than equality; that the attempt to realise equality endangers freedom; and that, if freedom is lost, there will not even be equality among the unfree.

Popper's remarks about the delights of living a modest, simple and free life in an egalitarian society may be taken literally. He himself became apprenticed to a cabinet maker; and then, when it became clear that he would never make a good cabinet maker, became a schoolmaster. The doctrines of logical positivism, as formulated by the Vienna Circle, stimulated him to formulating his own ideas on scientific method. These, cast to some extent in the form of a critique of logical positivism, form the backbone of his first book *The Logic of Scientific Discovery*, published in 1934. In Popper's most influential work, *The Open Society and Its Enemies*, we find Popper's basic objection to 'historicism':

> While the ordinary man takes the setting of his life and the importance of his personal experiences and petty struggles for granted, it is said that the social scientist or philosopher has to survey things from a higher plane. He sees the individual as a pawn, as a somewhat insignificant instrument in the general development of mankind.

For Popper, such an attitude is a denial of human freedom. He insists that advances in human knowledge occur as a result of attempts to solve our problems; and these problems must be solved piecemeal. At any point in history, man is faced with a thousand possible choices, and there is no royal road to an ideal society. Popper's pragmatism springs out of a deep sense of human freedom, and the way in which we exercise this freedom from moment to moment.

Popper's 'refutation of Marxism' occupies almost 150 pages of *The Open Society and Its Enemies*, and is therefore too long to quote in full; the close-knit nature of its argument also makes it peculiarly difficult to anthologise. In his book on Popper, Bryan Magee offers an admirable summary of its achievement:

> A crucial consequence of Marxism's claim to be a science is that it must defend itself successfully at a scientific level of argument or else lapse into incoherence. And if it suffers defeat at any point on this level, it has no recourse to other forms of argument: it must, in short, submit itself to tests and accept the consequences. And what Popper is thought to have done is to demolish its claims to scientific truth beyond any serious possibility of their reconstitution. He has not done this by showing Marx's theory to be unfalsifiable. Vulgar Marxism is unfalsifiable, but Popper does not make the mistake of attributing vulgar Marxism to Marx. Karl Marx's own theory, treated with the intellectual seriousness it deserves, yielded a considerable number of falsifiable predictions, the most important of which have now been falsified. For instance, according to the theory, only fully developed Capitalist countries could go Communist, and therefore all societies would have to complete the capitalist stage of development first: but in fact, except for Czechoslovakia, all the countries to have gone Communist have been pre-industrial – none has been a fully developed Capitalist society. According to the theory the revolution would have to be based on the industrial proletariat: but Mao Tse-Tung, Ho Chi-Minh and Fidel Castro explicitly rejected this and based their successful revolutions on the peasantries of their different countries. According to the theory there are elaborate reasons why the industrial proletariat must inevitably get poorer, more numerous, more class-conscious and more revolutionary: in fact, in all industrial countries since Marx's day, it has become richer, less numerous,

less class-conscious and less revolutionary. According to the theory Communism could be brought about only by the workers themselves, the masses: in fact, in no country to this day, not even Chile, has the Communist party managed to get the support of the majority in a free election. Where they have achieved full power it has been imposed on the majority by an army, usually a foreign one. According to the theory, ownership of the Capitalist means of production was bound to become concentrated in fewer and fewer hands: in fact, with the development of the joint-stock company, ownership has become so widely dispersed that control has passed into the hands of a new class of professional managers. And the emergence of this class is itself a refutation of the Marxist prediction that all other classes would inevitably disappear and be polarised into two, an ever shrinking Capitalist class which owned and controlled but did not work, and an ever expanding proletariat which worked but did not own or control.

Magee also emphasises Popper's impressive fair-mindedness, his refusal to 'score', his determination to make the fullest possible concessions to Marx, to give the benefit of every possible doubt. He never attacks Marx at his weakest, but at his strongest. This spirit of fair-mindedness is conveyed by this paragraph from the first page of Popper's section on Marx:

> It is tempting to dwell upon the similarities between Marxism, the Hegelian left-wing, and its fascist counterpart. Yet it would be utterly unfair to overlook the difference between them. Although their intellectual origin is nearly identical, there can be no doubt of the humanitarian impulse of Marxism. Moreover, in contrast to the Hegelians of the right-wing, Marx made an honest attempt to apply rational methods to the most urgent problems of social life. The value of the attempt is unimpaired by the fact that it was, as I shall try to show, largely unsuccessful. Science progresses through trial and error. Marx tried, and although he erred in his main doctrines, he did not try in vain. He opened and sharpened our eyes in many ways. A return to pre-Marxian social science is inconceivable. All modern writers are indebted to Marx, even if they do not know it. This is especially true of those who disagree with his doctrines, as I do. . .

The same fair-mindedness can be seen in Popper's presentation of Marx's central arguments, taken from his chapter on Capitalism and its Fate:

CAPITALISM AND ITS FATE

According to Marxist doctrine, capitalism is labouring under inner contradictions that threaten to bring about its downfall. A minute analysis of these contradictions and of the historical movement which they force upon society constitutes the first step of Marx's prophetic argument. This step is not only the most important of his whole theory, it is also the one on which he spent most of his labour, since practically the whole of the three volumes of *Capital* (over 2,200 pages in the original edition) is devoted to its elaboration. It is also the least abstract step of the argument since it is based upon a descriptive analysis, supported by statistics, of the economic system of his time – that of unrestrained capitalism. As Lenin puts it: 'Marx deduces the inevitability of the transformation of capitalist society into socialism wholly and exclusively from *the economic law of the movement of contemporary society*.'

Before proceeding to explain in some detail the first step of Marx's prophetic argument, I shall try to describe its main ideas in the form of a very brief outline.

Marx believes that capitalist competition forces the capitalist's hand. It forces the capitalist to accumulate capital. By doing so, he works against his own long-term economic interests (since the accumulation of capital is liable to bring about a fall of his profits). But although working against his own personal interest, he works in the interest of the historical development; he works, unwittingly, for economic progress, and for socialism. This is due to the fact that accumulation of capital means (*a*) increased productivity; increase of wealth; and concentration of wealth in a few hands; (*b*) increase of pauperism and misery; the workers are kept on subsistence or starvation wages, mainly by the fact that the surplus of workers, called the 'industrial reserve army', keeps the wages on the lowest possible level. The trade cycle prevents, for any length of time, the absorption of the surplus of workers by the growing industry. This cannot be altered by the capitalists, even if they wish to do so; for the falling rate of their profits makes their own economic position much too precarious for any effective action. In this way, capitalist accumulation turns out to be a suicidal and self-contradictory process, even though it fosters the technical, economic, and historical progress towards socialism.

I

The premises of the first step are the laws of capitalist competition, and of the accumulation of the means of production. The conclusion is the law of increasing wealth and misery. I begin my discussion with an explanation of these premises and conclusions.

Under capitalism, competition between the capitalists plays an important rôle. 'The battle of competition', as analysed by Marx in *Capital*, is carried out by selling the commodities produced, if possible at a lower price than the competitor could afford to accept. 'But the cheapness of a commodity', Marx explains, 'depends in its turn, other things being equal, upon the productivity of labour; and this, again, depends on the scale of production.' For production on a very large scale is in general capable of employing more specialized machinery, and a greater quantity of it; this increases the productivity of the workers, and permits the capitalist to produce, and to sell, at a lower price. 'Large capitalists, therefore, get the better of small ones. . . Competition always ends with the downfall of many lesser capitalists and with the transition of their capital into the hands of the conqueror.' (This movement is, as Marx points out, much accelerated by the credit system.)

According to Marx's analysis, the process described, *accumulation due to competition*, has two different aspects. One of them is that the capitalist is forced to accumulate or concentrate more and more capital, in order to survive; this means in practice investing more and more capital in more and more as well as newer and newer machinery, thus continually increasing the *productivity* of his workers. The other aspect of the accumulation of capital is the *concentration* of more and more wealth in the hands of the various capitalists, and of the capitalist class; and along with it goes the reduction in the number of capitalists, a movement called by Marx the *centralization*of capital (in contra-distinction to mere accumulation or concentration).

Now three of these terms, competition, accumulation, and increasing productivity, indicate the fundamental tendencies of all capitalist production, according to Marx; they are the tendencies to which I alluded when I described the *premise* of the first step as 'the laws of capitalist competition and of accumulation'. The fourth and the fifth terms, however, concentration and centralization, indicate a tendency which form one part of the *conclusion* of the first step; for they describe a tendency towards a continuous increase of wealth, and its centralization in fewer and fewer hands. The other part of the conclusion, however, the law of increasing misery, is only reached by a much more complicated argument. But before beginning an explanation of this argument, I must first explain this second conclusion itself.

The term 'increasing misery' may mean, as used by Marx, two different things. It may be used in order to describe the extent of misery, indicating that it is spread over an increasing number of people; or it may be used in order to indicate an increase in the intensity of the suffering of the people. Marx undoubtedly believed that misery was growing both in extent and in intensity. This, however, is more than he needed in order tto carry his point. For the purpose of the prophet's argument, a wider interpretation of the term 'increasing misery' would do just as well (if not better); an interpretation, namely according to which the extent of misery increases, while an intensity may or may not increase, but at any rate does not show any marked decrease.

But there is a further and much more important comment to be made. Increasing misery, to Marx, involves fundamentally an *increasing exploitation of the employed workers; not only in numbers but also in intensity*. It must be admitted that in addition it involves an increase in the suffering as well as in the numbers of the unemployed, called by Marx the (relative) 'surplus population' or the "industrial reserve army'. But the function of the unemployed, in this process, is to exert pressure pon the employed workers, thus assisting the capitalists in their efforts to make profit out of the employed workers, to exploit them. 'The industrial reserve army', Marx writes, 'belongs to capitalism just as if its members had been reared by the capitalists at their own cost. For its own varying needs, capital creates an ever-ready supply of exploitable human material. . . During periods of depression and of semi-prosperity, the industrial reserve army keeps up its pressure upon the ranks of the employed workers;

and during periods of excessive production and boom, it serves to bridle their aspirations.' Increasing misery, according to Marx, is essentially the increasing exploitation of labour power; and since labour power of the unemployed is not exploited, they can serve in this process only as unpaid assistants of the capitalists in the exploitation of the employed workers. The point is important since later Marxists have often referred to unemployment as one of the empirical facts that verify the prophecy that misery tends to increase; but unemployment can be claimed to corroborate Marx's theory only if it occurs together with increased exploitation of the employed workers, i.e. with long hours of work and with low real wages.

This may suffice to explain the term 'increasing misery'. But it is still necessary to explain the *law* of increasing misery which Marx claimed to have discovered. By this I mean the doctrine of Marx on which the whole prophetic argument hinges; namely, the doctrine that capitalism cannot possibly afford to decrease the misery of the workers, since the mechanism of capitalist accumulation keeps the capitalist under a strong economic pressure which he is forced to pass on to the workers if he is not to succumb. This is why the capitalists cannot compromise, why they cannot meet any important demand of the workers, even if they wished to do so; this is why 'capitalism cannot be reformed but can only be destroyed'. It is clear that this law is the decisive conclusion of the first step. The other conclusion, the law of increasing wealth, would be a harmless matter, if only it were possible for the increase of wealth to be shared by the workers. Marx's contention that this is impossible will therefore be the main subject of our critical analysis. But before proceeding to a presentation and criticism of Marx's arguments in favour of this contention, I may briefly comment on the first part of the conclusion, the theory of increasing wealth.

The tendency towards the accumultion and concentration of wealth, which Marx observed, can hardly be questioned. His theory of increasing productivity is also, in the main, unexceptionable. Although there may be limits to the beneficial effects exerted by the growth of an enterprise upon its productivity, there are hardly any limits to the beneficial effects of the improvement and accumulation of machinery. But in regard to the tendency towards the centralization of capital in fewer and fewer hands, matters are not quite so simple. Undoubtedly, there is a tendency in that direction, and we may grant that under an unrestrained capitalist system there are few counteracting forces. Not much can be said against this part of Marx's analysis as a description of an unrestrained capitalism. But considered as a prophecy, it is less tenable. For we know that now there are many means by which legislation can intervene. Taxation and death duties can be used most effectively to counteract centralization, and they have been so used. And anti-trust legislation can also be used, although perhaps with less effect. To evaluate the force of Marx's prophetic argument we must consider the possibility of great improvements in this direction; and as in previous chapters, I must declare that the argument on which Marx bases this prophecy of centralization or of a decrease in the number of capitalists is inconclusive.

Having explained the main premises and conclusions of the first step, and having disposed of the first conclusion, we can now concentrate our attention entirely upon Marx's derivation of the other conclusion, the prophetic law of increasing misery. Three different trends of thought may be distinguished in his attempts to establish this prophecy. They will be dealt with in the next four sections of this chapter under the headings: II: the theory of value; III: the effect of the surplus population upon wages; IV: the trade cycle; V: the effects of the falling rate of profit.

II

Marx's *theory of value*, usually considered by Marxists as well as by anti-Marxists as a corner-stone of the Marxist creed, is in my opinion one of its rather unimportant parts; indeed, the sole reason why I am going to treat of it, instead of proceeding at once to the next section, is that it is generally held to be important, and that I cannot defend my reasons for differing from this opinion without discussing the theory. But I wish to make it clear at once that in holding that the theory of value is a redundant part of Marxism, I am defending Marx rather than attacking him. For there is little doubt that the many critics who have shown that the theory of value is very weak in itself are in the main perfectly right. But even if they were wrong it would only strengthen the position of Marxism if it could be established that its decisive historico-political doctrines can be developed entirely independently of such a controversial theory.

The idea of the so-called *labour theory of value*, adapted by Marx for his purposes from suggestions he found in his predecessors (he refers especially to Adam Smith and David Ricardo), is simple enough. If you need a carpenter, you must pay him by the hour. If you ask him why a certain job is more expensive than another one, he will point out that there is more work in terminology, means increased surplus labour; it means both an increased number of hours available to the capitalist, and on top of this, an increased number of commodities produced per hour. It means, in other words, a greatly increased profit. This is admitted by Marx. He does not hold that profits are dwindling; he only holds that the total capital increases much more quickly than the profits, so that the *rate* of profit falls.

But if this is so, there is no reason why the capitalist should labour under an economic pressure which he is forced to pass on to the workers, whether he likes it or not. It is true, probably, that he does not like to see a fall in his rate of profit. But as long as his income does not fall but, on the contrary, rises, there is no real danger. The situation for a successful average capitalist will be this: he sees his income rise quickly, and his capital still more quickly; that is to say, his savings rise more quickly than the part of his income which he consumes. I do not think that this is a situation which must force him to desperate measures, or which makes a compromise with the workers impossible. On the contrary, it seems to me quite tolerable.

It is true, of course, that the situation contains an element of danger. Those capitalists who speculate on the assumption of a constant or of a rising rate of profit may get into trouble; and things such as these may indeed contribute to the trade cycle, accentuating the depression. But this has little to do with the sweeping consequences which Marx prophesied.

This concludes my analysis of the third and last argument, propounded by Marx in order to prove the law of increasing misery.

VI

In order to show how completely wrong Marx was in his prophecies, and at the same time how justified he was in his glowing protest against the hell of an unrestrained capitalism as well as in his demand, 'Workers, unite!', I shall quote a few passages from the chapter of *Capital* in which he discusses the General Law of Capitalist Accumulation'. 'In factories . . . young male workers are used up in masses before they reach the age of manhood; after that, only a very small proportion remains useful for industry, so that they are constantly dismissed in large numbers. They then form part of the floating surplus population which grows with the growth of industry. . . Labour power is so quickly used up by capital that the middle-aged worker is usually a worn-out man. . . Dr Lee, medical officer of health, declared not long ago "that the average age at death of the Manchester upper middle class was 38, while the average age at death of the labouring class was 17; while at Liverpool those figures were represented as 35 against 15. . ." . . . The exploitation of working-class children puts a premium upon their production. . . The higher the productivity of labour . . . the more precarious become the worker's conditions of existence. . . Within the capitalist system, all the methods for raising the social productivity of labour . . . are transformed into means of domination and of exploitation; they mutilate the worker into a fragment of a human being, they degrade him to a mere cog in the machine, they make work a torture . . . and drag his wife and children beneath the wheels of the capitalist Juggernaut. . . *It follows that to the degree in which capital accumulates, the worker's condition must deteriorate, whatever his payment may be* . . . the greater the social wealth, the amount of capital at work, the extent and energy of its growth, . . . the larger is the surplus population. . . The size of the industrial reserve army grows as the power of wealth grows. But . . . the larger the industrial reserve army, the larger are the masses of the workers whose misery is relieved only by an increase in the agony of toil; and . . . the larger is the number of those who are officially recognized as paupers. *This is the absolute and general law of capitalist accumulation*. . . The accumulation of wealth at the one pole of society involves at the same time an accumulation of misery, of the agony of toil, of slavery, ignorance, brutalization, and of moral degradation, at the opposite pole. . .'

Marx's terrible picture of the economy of his time is only too true. But his law that misery must increase together with accumulation does not hold. Means of production have accumulated and the productivity of labour has increased since his day to an extent which even he would hardly have thought possible. But child labour, working hours, the agony of toil, and the precariousness of the worker's existence, have not increased; they have declined. I do not say that this process must continue. There is no law of progress, and everything will depend on ourselves. But the actual situation is briefly and fairly summed up by Parkes in one sentence: 'Low wages, long hours, and child labour have been characteristic of capitalism not, as Marx predicted, in its old age, but in its infancy.'

Unrestrained capitalism is gone. Since the day of Marx, democratic interventionism has made immense advances, and the approved productivity of labour – a consequence of the accumulation of capital – has made it possible virtually to stamp out misery. This shows that much has been achieved, in spite of undoubtedly grave mistakes, and it should encourage us to believe that more can be done. For much remains to be done and to be undone. Democratic interventionism can only make it possible. It rests with us to do it.

I have no illusions concerning the force of my arguments. Experience shows that Marx's prophecies were false. But experience can always be explained away. And, indeed, Marx himself, and Engels, began with the elaboration of an *auxiliary hypothesis* designed to explain why the law of increasing misery does not work as they expected it to do. According to this hypothesis, the tendency towards a falling rate of profit, and with it, increasing misery, is counteracted by the effects of *colonial exploitation*, or, as it is usually called, by 'modern imperialism'. Colonial exploitation, according to this theory, is a method of passing on economic pressure to the colonial proletariat, a group which, economically as well as politically, is weaker still than the industrial proletariat at home. 'Capital invested in colonies', Marx writes, 'may yield a higher rate of profit for the simple reason that the rate of profit is higher there where capitalist development is still in a backward stage, and for the added reason that slaves, coolies, etc., permit a better exploitation of labour. I can see no reason why these higher rates of profit . . ., when sent home, should not enter there as elements into the average rate of profit, and, in proportion, contribute to keeping it up.' (It is worth mentioning that the main idea behind this theory of 'modern' imperialism can be traced back for more than 160 years, to Adam Smith, who said of colonial trade that it 'has necessarily contributed to keep up the rate of profit'.) Engels went one step further than Marx in his development of the theory. Forced to admit that in Britain the prevailing tendency was not towards an increase in misery but rather towards a considerable improvement, he hints that this may be due to the fact that Britain 'is exploiting the whole world'; and he scornfully assails 'the British working class' which, instead of suffering as he expected them to do, 'is actually becoming more and more bourgeois'. And he continues: 'It seems that this most bourgeois of all nations wants to bring matters to such a pass as to have a bourgeois aristocracy and a bourgeois proletariat *side by side* with the bourgeoisie. Now this change of front on Engels' part is at least as remarkable as that other one of his which I mentioned in the last chapter and like that, it was made under the influence of a social development which turned out to be one of decreasing misery. Marx blamed capitalism for 'proletarianizing the middle class and the lower bourgeoisie', and for reducing the workers to pauperism. Engels now blames the system – it is still blamed – for making bourgeois out of workers. But the nicest touch in Engels' complaint is the indignation that makes him call the British who behave so inconsiderately as to falsify Marxist prophecies 'that most bourgeois of all nations'. According to Marxist doctrine we should expect from the 'most bourgeois of all nations' development of misery and class tension to an intolerable degree instead, we hear that the opposite takes place. But the good Marxist's hair rises when he hears of the incredible wickedness a capitalist system that transforms good proletarians into bad bourgeois; quite forgetting that Marx showed that the wickedness of the system consisted solely in the fact that it was working the other way round. Thus we read in Lenin's analysis of the evil causes and dreadful effects of modern British imperialism 'Causes: (1) exploitation of the whole world by this country; (2) its monopolistic position in the world market; (3) its colonial monopoly. Effects: (1) *bourgeoisification of a part of the British proletariat*; (2) a part of the proletariat permits itself to be led by people who are bought by the bourgeoisie, or who are at least paid by it.' Having given such a pretty Marxist name, 'the bourgeoisification of the proletariat', to a hateful tendency – hateful mainly because it did not fit in with the way the world should go according to Marx – Lenin apparently believes that it has become a Marxist tendency. Marx himself held that the more quickly the whole world could go through the necessary historical period of capitalist industrialization, the better, and he was therefore inclined to support imperialist developments. But Lenin came to a very different conclusion. Since Britain's possession of colonies was the reason why the workers at home followed 'leaders bought by the bourgeoisie' instead of the Communists, he saw in the colonial empire a potential trigger or fuse. A revolution there would make the law of increasing misery operative at home, and a revolution at home would follow. Thus the colonies were the place from which the fire would spread. . .

I do not believe that the auxiliary hypothesis whose history I have sketched can save the law of increasing misery; for this hypothesis is itself refuted by experience. There are countries, for instance the Scandinavian democracies, Czechoslovakia, Canada, Australia, New Zealand, to say nothing of the United States, in which a democratic interventionism secured to the workers a high standard of living, in spite of the fact that colonial exploitation had no influence there, or was at any rate far too unimportant to support the hypothesis. Furthermore, if we compare certain countries that 'exploit' colonies, like Holland and Belgium, with Denmark, Sweden, Norway, and Czechoslovakia which do not 'exploit' colonies, we do not find that the industrial *workers* profited from the possession of colonies, for the situation of the working classes in all those countries was strikingly similar. Furthermore, although the misery imposed upon the natives through colonization is one of the darkest chapters in the history of civilization, it cannot be asserted that their misery has tended to increase since the days of Marx. The exact opposite is the case; things have greatly improved. And yet, increasing misery would have to be very noticeable there if the auxiliary hypothesis and the original theory were both correct.

ARTHUR KOESTLER

Introduced by
COLIN WILSON

Arthur Koestler was converted to Communism at the age of fourteen – in 1919 – by Chopin's funeral march. In the first volume of his autobiography, he speaks of the enormous funeral procession of a number of Communists who had been killed during a demonstration, with fifty thousand sturdy proletarians marching slowly behind the coffins. 'Chopin's March made a romantic Communist of me long before I knew what that word meant.'

Koestler was born in Budapest, son of a Hungarian father and Viennese mother. As a child, he was obsessed by science and mathematics, and, with a less mercurial temperament, he would probably have gone on to become an engineer or research chemist. But at college he became a member of a Jewish duelling fraternity and was converted to Zionism. One night, after a long philosophical discussion on free will, Koestler decided to burn his boats, and became a 'drop out'. He went to Palestine and lived on a Kibbutz; but a few months were enough to convince him that this almost monastic life was not what he was looking for. He became a jack-of-all trades, experienced semi-starvation, then became the Middle East Correspondent for a German chain of newspapers. He was posted to Paris, as cultural correspondent, then moved on to Berlin, arriving on the day of the Reichstag elections in 1930. As a result of his knack for popularising science, he became science editor for the Ullstein newspaper chain. Again, he seemed set for a successful and respectable career; again, his revolutionary impulse won the day. In a disintegrating society – the Berlin later described by Christopher Isherwood – his quest for intellectual certainty led to the study of Marxist literature.

> By the time I had finished with Engel's *Feuerbach* and Lenin's *State and Revolution*, something had clicked in my brain and I was shaken by a mental explosion. To say that one had 'seen the light' is a poor description of the intellectual rapture which only the convert knows (regardless to what faith he has been converted).

> The new light seems to pour from all directions across the skull; the whole universe falls into pattern like the stray pieces of a jigsaw puzzle. . .

In *Arrow in the Blue*, Koestler speaks of the stages of his conversion. First, there was an increasing enthusiasm for all things Russian:

> Every comparison between the state of affairs in Russia and in the Western world seemed to speak eloquently in favour of the former. In the West, there was mass unemployment; in Russia, a shortage of manpower. In the West, chronic strikes and social unrest. . .; in Russia, where all factories belonged to the people, the workers vied in socialist competitions for higher production output. . . The contrast between the downward trend of capitalism and the simultaneous steep rise of the planned Societ economy was so striking and obvious that it led to the equally obvious conclusion: they are the future – we are the past.
> The next stage was my falling in love with the Five Year Plan. On one-sixth of our sick planet, the most gigantic constructive effort of all times had begun; there Utopia was being built in steel and concrete. Steeped in the Soviet literature of the period whose one and only subject was the building of factories, power stations, tractors, silos and the fulfillment of the Plan, I half-seriously considered writing a modern version of the Song of Songs: 'The eyes of my beloved shine like the blast furnaces in the steppe; her lips are boldly drawn like the White Sea Canal; her shoulder is slenderly curved like the Dnieper Dam. . .'

Koestler applied for membership of the German Communist Party at the end of December 1931. He applied by writing direct to the Central Committee; a Comrade had advised him that if he did it by the usual method – of joining a 'cell' – his membership would quickly become known and he would lose his job with the Ullsteins, which was a distinct advantage to the Party. He was interviewed by a Party official, and when he mentioned that he would like to become a tractor driver in the Soviet Union, was told that he could be more useful by staying where he was. He was given the Party-name Ivan Steinberg.

His first lesson in the Marxist approach to politics came when he asked why the Party could not come to an understanding with the Socialists, instead of attacking them as 'Social Fascists'. Surely they ought to unite in the face of the common danger – Hitler? His mentor argued convincingly that the Social Democrats were traitors who would only betray them. True to Marx's principle of treating all other socialists as enemies, the German Party had no intention of collaborating with anyone. Within a year, history had proved Koestler right, and the German Communist Party lay in ruins.

His usefulness to the Party ended when he was sacked: a fellow-employee, whom he had converted, began to experience pangs of conscience, and confessed to the Ullsteins that they were passing on political information to the Communists; Koestler was politely dismissed.

Koestler now became a member of a cell in what was known as the Red Block. The psychologist Wilhelm Reich was another member. The Party instructed its members in how to think:

> Not only our thinking, but also our vocabulary was reconditioned. Certain words were taboo – for instance 'lesser evil' or 'spontaneous': the latter because 'spontaneous' manifestations of the revolutionary class-consciousness were part of Trotsky's theory of the Permanent Revolution. Other words and turns of phrase became favourite stock-in-trade. I mean not only the obvious words of Communist Jargon like 'the toiling masses'; but words like 'concrete' or 'sectarian' ('You must put your question into a more concrete form, Comrade'; 'you are adopting a Left-sectarian attitude, Comrade'); and even such abstruse words as 'herostratic'. In one of his works Lenin had mentioned Herostratus, the Greek who had burnt down a temple because he could think of no other way of achieving fame. Accordingly, one often heard and read phrases like 'the criminally herostratic madness of the counter-revolutionary wreckers of the heroic efforts of the toiling masses in the Fatherland of the Proletariat to achieve the second Five Year Plan in four years.'

In 1933, Hitler set out to smash the German Communist Party, and succeeded with an ease that startled the other Communist Parties of Europe. Fortunately, Koestler was no longer in Berlin by that time; he had received a visa to travel in the Soviet Union. He had been invited to write a book, which was to tell how a bourgeois journalist, Mr K, travels around Russia with strong anti-Soviet prejudices, but is gradually converted until he becomes Comrade K. Koestler saw hordes ravaged by famine in the Ukraine, industrial towns resembling one vast slum, old men with frostbitten noses who were described as 'enemies of the people' because they had refused to be 'collectivised'. He admits: 'My faith had been badly shaken, but thanks to the elastic shock-absorbers, I was slow in becoming conscious of the damage'. Since Hitler had now come to power, Koestler joined other Party friends in exile in Paris, and worked with Willi Munzenberg, the 'Red Eminence of the international anti-Fascist movement', and helped to prepare the influential *Brown Book of the Hitler Terror and the Burning of the Reichstag*. Their aim was to demonstrate that the Nazis themselves had organised the burning of the Reichstag as an excuse for repression. Koestler admits 'We had, in fact, no idea of the concrete circumstances,' and later investigation has revealed that the arsonist, Van der Lubbe, acted alone. But the book was translated in many languages and 'became the Bible of the anti-Fascist crusade.'. Koestler mentions that Munzenberg was murdered in the summer of 1940 by unknown assassins; 'there are only indirect clues, all pointing in one direction like magnetic needles to the pole.' It seems grimly typical that Munzenberg should be 'liquidated' by his own people.

In 1936, Koestler began to move towards the final stage of his disillusion with Marxism.

THE GOD THAT FAILED

On July 18, 1936, General Franco staged his *coup d'état*. I went to see Willi and asked him to help me to join the Spanish Republican Army; this was before the International Brigades were formed. I had brought my passport along; it was a Hungarian passport. Willi looked at it absentmindedly; as an inveterate propagandist he was not enthusiastic about writers wasting their time digging trenches. In the passport was my press card as a Paris Correspondent of the *Pester Lloyd*. I had never written a word for the *Pester Lloyd*, but every self-respecting Hungarian emigré in Paris was equipped with a press card from one Budapest paper or another, to obtain occasional free theater and movie tickets. Willi's eyes suddenly brightened, he had an idea.

'Why don't you rather make a trip to Franco's headquarters for the *Pester Lloyd*?' he suggested. 'Hungary is a semi-Fascist country; they will welcome you with open arms.'

I too thought it was an excellent idea, but there were some hitches. Firstly, the *Pester Lloyd* would never agree to sending me; but then why bother to inform them of my going? In the middle of a civil war, nobody was likely to take the trouble to check my accreditation. Secondly, other foreign correspondents might think it fishy that a poor Hungarian paper was sending a special correspondent to Spain. That difficulty too was overcome. I had friends on the *News Chronicle* in London; the *News Chronicle* was violently anti-Franco and stood no chance of having a staff correspondent of its own admitted to rebel territory; so the Foreign Editor gladly agreed that I should act as his special correspondent provided that I ever got into Franco Spain.

I did get in, via Lisbon to Seville, but my sojourn was short. On the second day in Seville, which was then Franco's headquarters, I was recognized and denounced as a Communist; but thanks to the incredible Spanish muddle, managed to get out in the nick of time via Gibraltar. Even during that short visit however, I had seen the German pilots and German airplanes of Franco's army; I published the facts in the *News Chronicle* and in a pamphlet, and thereby incurred the special hostility of the Franco regime. Accordingly, when I was captured six months later, as a correspondent with the Republican Army, by Franco's troops, I was convinced that to be shot without unpleasant preliminaries was the best I could hope for.

I spent four months in Spanish prisons, in Málaga and Seville, most of the time in solitary confinement and most of the time convinced that I was going to be shot. When, in June, 1937, thanks to the intervention of the British Government, I was unexpectedly set free, my hair had not grayed and my features had not changed and I had not developed religious mania; but I had made the acquaintance of a different kind of reality, which had altered my outlook and values, and altered them so profoundly and unconsciously that during the first days of freedom I was not even aware of it. The experiences responsible for this change were fear, pity and a third one, more difficult to describe. Fear, not of death, but of torture and humiliation and the more unpleasant forms of dying – my companion of patio exercises, Garcia Atadell, was garroted shortly after my liberation. Pity for the little Andalusian and Catalan peasants whom I heard crying and calling for their *madres* when they were led out at night to face the firing squad; and finally, a condition of the mind usually referred to in terms borrowed from the vocabulary of mysticism, which would present itself at unexpected moments and induce a state of inner peace which I have known neither before nor since.

The lesson taught by this type of experience, when put into words, always appears under the dowdy guise of perennial commonplaces: that man is a reality, mankind an abstraction; that men cannot be treated as units in operations of political arithmetic because they behave like the symbols for zero and the infinite, which dislocate all mathematical operations; that the end justifies the means only within very narrow limits; that ethics is not a function of social utility, and charity not a petty-bourgeois sentiment but the gravitational force which keeps civilization in its orbit. Nothing can sound more flat-footed than such verbalizations of a knowledge which is not of a verbal nature; yet every single one of these trivial statements was incompatible with the Communist faith which I held.

If this story were fiction, it would end here; the chief character, having undergone a spiritual conversion, takes leave of his comrades of yesterday and goes his own way with a serene smile. But when I was liberated I did not know that I had ceased to be a Communist. The first thing I did after the Guardia Civil put me across the frontier at Gibraltar was to send a cable to the Party. It started with the line from Schiller, '*Seid umschlungen, Millionen*' – 'I embrace thee, ye millions.' And, even more strange, I added the words 'am cured of all belly-aches' – 'belly-ache' being our slang expression for qualms about the Party line.

It was a short euphoria. I spent three quiet months with friends in England, writing a book on Spain; then, after a short trip to the Middle East for the *News Chronicle*, which offered no points of friction with the Party, the conflict began. There was nothing dramatic about it. I made a lecture tour through England for the Left Book Club; whenever a questioner, in the predominantly Communist audiences, asked for details about the treasonable activities of the POUM – an independent Left-Wing splinter group of Trotskyite leanings in Spain, whom the Party accused of being 'agents of Franco' – I answered that their fractional policy might be bad for the cause, but that they were certainly not traitors. Surprisingly enough, I got away with that; the British CP was notoriously lax in denouncing deviations to higher quarters.

Then I learned that, in the Russian mass-purges, my brother-in-law and two of my closest friends had been arrested. My brother-in-law, Dr Ernst Ascher, was a doctor who worked in a State hospital in the Volga German Republic. Though a member of the German CP, he was politically naïve and indifferent. The accusation against him, as I later learned, was that he was a saboteur who had injected syphilis into his patients,[1] that he had demoralized the people by pretending venereal diseases were incurable, and thirdly, as a matter of course, that he was the agent of a foreign power. He has never been heard of since his arrest twelve years ago.

The other two were Alex Weissberg and his wife Eva. For reasons which will appear later, I have to tell their story in some detail. Alex, a physicist, was employed at the Ukrainian Institute for Physics and Technology (UFTI); I had known them both for many years and had stayed with them in Kharkov. When I left Russia, in 1933, Alex had seen me to the train; his farewell words had been: 'Whatever happens, hold the banner of the Soviet Union high'. He was arrested in 1937 on the charge (as I learned much later) of having hired twenty bandits to ambush Stalin and Kaganovitch on their next hunting trip in the Caucasus. He refused to sign a confession, was kept in various prisons for three years, then, after the Ribbentrop-Molotov Pact, was handed over by the GPU to the Gestapo, in 1940, at Brest Litovsk, together with a hundred-odd other Austrian, German and Hungarian Communists. (Among them Grete Neumann Buber, wife of the German Communist leader Heinz Neumann and sister-in-law of Willi Münzenberg, and the physicist Fiesl Hautermans, a former assistant of Professor Blackett.) He survived the Gestapo, took part in the Warsaw Revolt, and has written a book which will shortly be available to English readers.

Alex's wife Eva, was a ceramist; she was arrested about a year before Alex and was at first accused of having inserted swastikas into the pattern on the teacups which she designed for mass production; then, of having hidden under her bed two pistols which were to serve to kill Stalin at the next Party Congress. She spent eighteen months in the Lubianka, where the GPU tried to brief her as a repentant sinner for the Bukharin show-trial. She cut her veins, was saved, and was released shortly afterwards thanks to the extraordinary exertions of the Austrian Consul in Moscow, who happened to be a friend of her mother.

I met Eva after she had been released and expelled from Russia, in the spring of 1938. Her experiences in Russian prisons, and particularly of the GPU's methods of obtaining confessions, provided me with part of the material for *Darkness at Noon.* I promised her to do what I could to save Alex. Albert Einstein had already intervened on his behalf; so I wrote a carefully worded cable to Stalin, for which I obtained the signatures of the three French Nobel Prize physicists, Perrin, Langevin and Joliot-Curie. The cable, a copy of which was sent to State Attorney Vishinsky, requested that the charges against Weissberg, if any, be made public, and that he be given a public trial. It is characteristic that although both Langevin and Joliot-Curie were Soviet sympathizers who shortly afterward became members of the Party, they obviously did not set great store by the methods of Soviet justice – for, though they had never heard of Alex before, and knew me only slightly, they at once took it for granted that he was innocent. The cable was also signed by Polanyi in Manchester; the only prominent physicist whom I approached and who refused to sign was Professor Blackett. I mention this fact because Blackett did his best to save his former assistant, Hautermans, a close friend of Weissberg's. He was probably afraid that, by signing two protests, he might spoil the chance of saving at least one victim from the mortal embrace of the Socialist Fatherland.

The moral of this story is that Joliot-Curie, Blackett, and the rest of our nuclear Marxists cannot claim starry-eyed ignorance of the goings-on in Russia. They know in detail the case-history of at least these two of their colleagues, both loyal servants of the Soviet Union, arrested on grotesque charges, held for years without trial, and delivered to the Gestapo. They further know that these cases are not exceptional; reliable, second-hand reports of hundreds of similar cases in Russian academic circles are available to them. And the same is true of all Communists or fellow-travelling authors, journalists and other intellectuals. Every single one of us knows of at least one friend who perished in the Arctic subcontinent of forced labor camps, was shot as a spy or vanished without trace. How our voices boomed with righteous indignation, denouncing flaws in the procedure of justice in our comfortable democracies; and how silent we were when our comrades, without trial or conviction, were liquidated in the Socialist sixth of the earth. Each of us carries a skeleton in the cupboard of his conscience; added together they would form galleries of bones more labyrinthine than the Paris catacombs.

At no time and in no country have more revolutionaries been

killed and reduced to slavery than in Soviet Russia. To one who himself for seven years found excuses for every stupidity and crime committed under the Marxist banner, the spectacle of these dialectical tight-rope acts of self-deception, performed by men of good will and intelligence, is more disheartening than the barbarities committed by the simple in spirit. Having experienced the almost unlimited possibilities of mental acrobatism on that tight-rope stretched across one's conscience, I know how much stretching it takes to make that elastic rope snap.

About the time when I learned of Alex' arrest, a comrade escaped to Paris from Germany where he had served a term of five years' hard labor. Before his arrest, he had worked for a certain branch of the Apparat whose leaders had meanwhile been liquidated as spies. So, without being given a hearing, without a chance of defending himself, my friend and his wife were denounced as agents of the Gestapo, and their photographs were printed in the Party Press accompanied by a warning not to have any truck with them. Such cases I had heard of before; I had shrugged them off and continued on the tight-rope. Now these two individuals had become more real to me than the cause in the name of which they were to be sacrificed, and I took their side.

The Party did not react. While I had been in jail, they had used me as a martyr for propaganda purposes; some time must be allowed to lapse before I could be denounced as an agent of Franco and the Mikado.

The end came as a curious anticlimax. Some time during the spring of 1938, I had to give a talk on Spain to the German Emigrë Writers' Association in Paris. Before the talk, a representative of the Party asked me to insert a passage denouncing the POUM as agents of Franco; I refused. He shrugged, and asked me whether I would care to show him the text of my speech and 'to discuss it informally.' I refused. The meeting took place in the hall of the Societé des Industries Françaises in the Place St Germain des Près, before an audience of two or three hundred refugee intellectuals, half of them Communists. I knew it was my last public appearance as a member of the Party. The theme of the speech was the situation in Spain; it contained not a single word of criticism of the Party or of Russia. But it contained three phrases, deliberately chosen because to normal people they were platitudes, to Communists a declaration of war. The first was: 'No movement, party or person can claim the privilege of infallibility.' The second was' 'Appeasing the enemy is as foolish as persecuting the friend who pursues your own aim by a different road.' The third was a quotation from Thomas Mann: 'A harmful truth is better than a useful lie.'

That settled it. When I had finished, the non-Communist half of the audience applauded, the Communist half sat in heavy silence, most of them with folded arms. This was not done by order, but as a spontaneous reaction to those fatal commonplaces. You might as well have told a Nazi audience that all men are born equal regardless of race and creed.

A few days later I wrote my letter of resignation to the Central Committee of the Party.

[1] Cf the charge against Jagoda, former head of the OGPU, and three physicians that they had poisoned Maxim Gorky by quicksilver fumes.

[2] They have now entered on a new existence, under a different name, in a British Dominion. Incidentally, it was this girl who was caught out by the Gestapo on the word 'concrete.'

FRIEDRICH von HAYEK

Introduced by
COLIN WILSON

It was in the spring of 1944 that Friedrich von Hayek's book *The Road to Serfdom* achieved its notoriety. Russia was now on the side of the Allies; and, since Hitler detested Communism, it seemed to follow that it must be, in principle, diametrically opposed to Fascism and not so far removed from democracy. Even extreme Conservatives seemed to agree that it was time to call a truce and give Stalin the benefit of the doubt. Hayek's book declared uncompromisingly that there is almost no intellectual difference between Communism and Fascism because both spring out of the collectivist mentality. George Orwell summarised its theme in a sympathetic review:

> Professor Hayek's thesis is that Socialism inevitably leads to despotism, and that in Germany the Nazis were able to succeed because the Socialists had already done most of their work for them, especially the intellectual work of weakening the desire for liberty. By bringing the whole of life under the control of the State, Socialism necessarily gives power to an inner ring of bureaucrats, who in almost every case will be men who want power for its own sake and will stick at nothing in order to retain it. Britain, he says, is now going the same way as Germany, with the left-wing intelligentsia in the van and the Tory Party a good second. The only salvation lies in returning to an unplanned economy, free competition, and emphasis on liberty rather than on security.

Orwell then reviews another book which he describes as a vehement denunciation of *laissez faire* capitalism, and goes on:

> Between them these two books sum up our present predicament. Capitalism leads to dole queues, the scramble for markets, and war. Collectivism leads to concentration camps, leader worship, and war. There is no way out of this unless a planned economy can be somehow combined with freedom of

> the intellect, which can only happen if the concept of right and wrong is restored to politics.

The Americans were far more shocked by the book when it appeared there a few months later, their attitude towards socialism being more idealistic and more enthusiastic than in England. Yet it was an American Leftist, Max Eastman, who provided Hayek with one of his most telling quotations:

> It seems obvious to me now [writes Eastman] . . . that the institution of private property is one of the main things that have given man that limited amount of free and equalness that Marx hoped to render infinite by abolishing the institution. Strangely enough Marx was the first to see this. He is the one who informed us, looking backwards, that the evolution of private capitalism with its free market had been a precondition for the evolution of all our democratic freedom. It never occurred to him, looking forward, that if this was so, these other freedoms might disappear with the abolition of the free market.

Like Popper and Koestler, Hayek began as what he calls a 'mild socialist.' He was converted by the 'very attractive books' of Walther Rathenau, the industrialist who had been in charge of the Raw Materials Department in Germany during the first world war, and who, as a result of this experience, decided that it would benefit society if economic planning was carried over into peacetime. Rathenau's books led Hayek to study economics at the University of Vienna, where his teachers were Ludwig von Mises and Friedrich von Wieser, both members of the influential 'Austrian school' of economists. And although Wieser himself was a mild socialist, he and Mises had soon convinced Hayek that State interference was not the answer to society's problems.

It is necessary to speak briefly of the ideas of the Austrian school, founded by Carl Menger. The 'classical' economists, from Adam Smith onward, accepted the 'labour theory of value' that Marx later made the foundation of his own theory. This stated that goods derive their value from the amount of labour that has gone into them; so, as Adam Smith said, if it costs twice as much for a hunter to kill a beaver as to kill a deer, then one beaver is worth two deer. But then, it is an obvious fact of economics that value is also determined by demand. And in 1871, W.S. Jevons and Carl Menger advanced simultaneously an alternative value theory – the 'utility' theory, which states simply that the 'value' of a thing is how much *satisfaction* it gives me, not how much labour has gone into it. The second-hand value of an out-of-print book does not depend on how much it cost to produce; it depends solely on how widely it is in demand and how much those individuals are willing to give for it.

This 'subjective' theory of value could be said to demolish Marxism in one sweep – since Marx's 'rigid demonstration' of the collapse of capitalism is based on the 'objective' theory. According to Marx, the capitalists keep the workers poor by gobbling up the 'surplus value' they create; and since a machine (according to Marx) cannot create this surplus value (because it cannot be overworked), increasing mechanisation will undermine capitalism. The 'marginal utility' theory of value destroys the foundation of Marxism. Understandably, Marxist critics hotly deny this. At all events, Hayek's exposure to the subjective theory of value, and to the ideas of the Austrian school in general, convinced him that socialism was simply founded upon false premises.

The basic socialist notion is that man has created society, and that it is now up to him to improve on his creation by planning and controlling it for the greatest good of its members. The best way of doing this is to study the history of society and try to apply its lessons. Those who hold these doctrines – like Gustav Schmoller – are known as historicists. But Hayek, like Popper, is fundamentally opposed to 'historicism', holding that history teaches us about the past, but can tell us nothing about the future, which is determined by individual choice, not by rigid laws. He also holds that men did *not* 'create' society; it developed as a result of human action, but not of human design. Hayek likes to cite Mandeville's *Fable of the Bees*, which demonstrates that the selfish action of individuals produces order even though they are not aiming for it, and that this order is beneficial for everyone. Conversely, when governments begin to interfere in the country's economic activities – particularly through nationalisation – they start a process that results in a downhill slide. As a hostile critic (Robert Heilbroner) puts it:

> [Hayek] believed, in fact, that once a government had interfered enough with the market mechanism it had no alternative but to embrace the economy in a top-to-bottom rigid grip.

Hayek is not against all planning; he states clearly in *The Road to Serfdom*:

> It is of the utmost importance . . . for the reader to keep in mind that the planning against which all our criticism is directed is solely the planning against competition – the planning which is to be substituted for competition.

(In his review of the book, Orwell remarked gloomily that 'the trouble with competitions is that somebody wins them' – but he seems to have no real alternative to offer.)

Hayek never discusses Karl Marx at length, although he has some pungent asides – such as his remark in *Individualism and Economic Order* (p. 128) that Marx positively discouraged any enquiry into the actual organisation and working of the socialist society of the future. Marx never describes what his future society will be like; he only makes occasional comments on what it will *not* be like. His notions about this future society are obviously extremely blurred.

But although Hayek devotes very little space to Marx, it is clear that Marxism contains the essence of all that he opposes under the name of socialism. The following chapter (the second) from *The Road to Serfdom* conveys some of the flavour – as well as the vigour – of his attack on the principles of socialism.

THE GREAT UTOPIA

> What has always made the state a hell on earth has been precisely that man has tried to make it his heaven.
>
> *F. Hoelderlin*

That socialism has displaced liberalism as the doctrine held by the great majority of progressives does not simply mean that people had forgotten the warnings of the great liberal thinkers of the past about the consequences of collectivism. It has happened because they were persuaded of the very opposite of what these men had predicted. The extraordinary thing is that the same socialism that was not only early recognised as the gravest threat to freedom, but quite openly began as a reaction against the liberalism of the French Revolution, gained general acceptance under the flag of liberty. It is rarely remembered now that socialism in its beginnings was frankly authoritarian. The French writers who laid the foundations of modern socialism had no doubt that their ideas could be put into practice only by a strong dictatorial government. To them socialism meant an attempt to 'terminate the revolution' by a deliberate reorganisation of society on hierarchical lines, and the imposition of a coercive 'spiritual power'. Where freedom was concerned, the founders of socialism made no bones about their intentions. Freedom of thought they regarded as the root-evil of nineteenth-century society, and the first of modern planners, Saint-Simon, even predicted that those who did not obey his proposed planning boards would be 'treated as cattle'.

Only under the influence of the strong domocratic currents preceding the revolution of 1848 did socialism begin to ally itself with the forces of freedom. But it took the new 'democratic socialism' a long time to live down the suspicions aroused by its antecedents. Nobody saw more clearly than de Tocqueville that democracy as an essentially individualist institution stood in an irreconcilable conflict with socialism:

> Democracy extends the sphere of individual freedom [he said in 1848], socialism restricts it. Democracy attaches all possible value to each man; socialism makes each man a mere agent, a mere number. Democracy and socialism have nothing in common but one word: equality. But notice the difference: while democracy seeks equality in liberty, socialism seeks equality in restraint and servitude.[1]

To allay these suspicions and to harness to its car the strongest of all political motives, the craving for freedom, socialism began increasingly to make use of the promise of a 'new freedom'. The coming of socialism was to be the leap from the realm of necessity to the realm of freedom. It was to bring 'economic freedom', without which the political freedom already gained was 'not worth having'. Only socialism was capable of effecting the consummation of the agelong struggle for freedom in which the attainment of political freedom was but a first step.

The subtle change in meaning to which the word freedom was subjected in order that this argument should sound plausible is important. To the great apostles of political freedom the word had meant freedom from coercion, freedom from the arbitrary power of other men, release from the ties which left the individual no choice but obedience to the orders of a superior to whom he was attached.

The new freedom promised, however, was to be freedom from necessity, release from the complusion of the circumstances which inevitably limit the range of choice of all of us, although for some very much more than for others. Before man could be truly free, the 'despotism of physical want' had to be broken, the 'restraints of the economic system' relaxed.

Freedom in this sense is, of course, merely another name for power[2] or wealth. Yet, although the promises of this new freedom were often coupled with irresponsible promises of a great increase in material wealth in a socialist society, it was not from such an absolute conquest of the niggardliness of nature that economic freedom was exptected. What the promise really amounted to was that the great existing disparities in the range of choice of different people were to disappear. The demand for the new freedom was thus only another name for the old demand for an equal distribution of wealth. But the new name gave the socialists another word in common with the liberals and they exploited it to the full. And although the word was used in a different sense by the two groups, few people noticed this and still fewer asked themselves whether the two kinds of freedom promised really could be combined.

There can be no doubt that the promise of greater freedom has become one of the most effective weapons of socialist propaganda and that the belief that socialism would bring freedom is genuine and sincere. But this would only heighten the tragedy if it should prove that what was promised to us as the Road to Freedom was in fact the High Road to Servitude. Unquestionably the promise of more freedom was responsible for luring more and more liberals along the socialist road, for blinding them to the conflict which exists between the basic principles of socialism and liberalism, and for often enabling socialists to usurp the very name of the old party of freedom. Socialism was embraced by the greater part of the intelligentsia as the apparent heir of the liberal tradition: therefore it is not surprising that to them the idea should appear inconceivable of socialism leading to the opposite of liberty.

In recent years, however, the old apprehensions of the unforeseen consequences of socialism have once more been strongly voiced from the most unexpected quarters. Observer after observer, in spite of the contrary expectation with which he approached his subject, has been impressed with the extraordinary similarity in many respects of the conditions under 'fascism' and 'communism'. While 'progressives' in this country and elsewhere were still deluding themselves that communism and fascism represented opposite poles, more and more people began to ask themselves whether these new tyrannies were not the outcome of the same tendencies. Even communists must have been somewhat shaken by such testimonies as that of Mr Max Eastman, Lenin's old friend, who found himself compelled to admit that 'instead of being better, Stalinism is worse than fascism, more ruthless, barbarous, unjust, immoral, anti-democratic, unredeemed by any hope or scruple', and that it is 'better described as superfascist'; and when we find the same author recognising, that, 'Stalinism *is* socialism, in the sense of being an inevitable although unforeseen political accompaniment of the nationalisation and collectivisation which he had relied upon as part of his plan for erecting a classless society',[3] his conclusion clearly achieves wider significance.

Mr Eastman's case is perhaps the most remarkable, yet he is by no means the first or the only sympathetic observer of the Russian experiment to form similar conclusions. Several years earlier Mr W.H. Chamberlin, who in twelve years in Russia as an American correspondent had seen all his ideals shattered, summed up the conclusions of his studies there and in Germany and Italy in the statement that 'Socialism is certain to prove, in the beginning at least, the road NOT to freedom, but to dictatorship and counter-dictatorships, to civil war of the fiercest kind. Socialism achieved and maintained by democratic means seems defintely to belong to the world of utopias.'[4] Similarly a British writer, Mr F.A. Voigt, after many years of close observation of developments in Europe was a foreign correspondent, concludes that 'Marxism has led to Fascism and National-Socialism, because, in all essentials, it is Fascism and National Socialism'.[5] And Dr Walter Lippmann has arrived at the conviction that

> the generation to which we belong is now learning from experience what happens when men retreat from freedom to a coercive organisation of their affairs. Though they promise themselves a more abundant life, they must in practice renounce it; as the organised direction increases, the variety of ends must give way to uniformity. That is the nemesis of the planned society and the authoritarian principle in human affairs.[6]

Many more similar statements from people in a position to judge might be selected from publications of recent years, particularly from those by men who as citizens of the now totalitarian countries have lived through the transformation and have been forced by their experience to revise many cherished beliefs. We shall quote as one more example a German writer who expresses the same conclusion perhaps more justly than those already quoted.

> The complete collapse of the belief in the attainability of freedom and equality through Marxism [writes Mr Peter Drucker[7]] has forced Russia to travel the same road towards a totalitarian, purely negative, non-economic society of unfreedom and inequality which Germany has been following. Not that communism and fascism are essentially the same. Fascism is the stage reached after communism has proved an illusion, and it has proved as much an illusion in Stalinist Russia as in pre-Hitler Germany.

No less significant is the intellectual history of many of the Nazi and Fascist leaders. Everybody who has watched the growth of these movements in Italy[8] or Germany has been struck by the number of leading men, from Mussolini downwards (and not excluding Laval and Quisling), who began as socialists and ended as Fascists or Nazis. And what is true of the leaders is even more true of the rank and file of the movements. The relative ease with which a young communist could be converted into a Nazi or *vice versa* was generally known in Germany, best of all to the propagandists of the two parties. Many a University teacher in this country during the 1930s has seen English and American students return from the Continent, uncertain whether they were communists or Nazis and certain only that they hated Western liberal civilisation.

It is true, of course, that in Germany before 1933 and in Italy before 1922 communists and Nazis or Fascists clashed more frequently with each other than with other parties. They competed for the support of the same type of mind and reserved for each other the hatred of the heretic. But their practice showed how closely they are related. To both, the real enemy, the man with whom they had nothing in common and whom they could not hope to convince, is the liberal of the old type. While to the Nazi the communist, and to the communist the Nazi, and to both the socialist, are potential recruits who are made of the right timber, although they have listened to false prophets, they both know that there can be no compromise between them and those who really believe in individual freedom.

Lest this be doubted by people misled by official propaganda from either side, let me quote one more statement from an authority that ought not to be suspect. In an article under the significant title of 'The Rediscovery of Liberalism', Professor Eduard Heimann, one of the leaders of German religious socialism, writes:

> Hitlerism proclaims itself as both true democracy and true socialism, and the terrible truth is that there is a grain of truth for such claims – an infinitesimal grain, to be sure, but at any rate enough to serve as a basis dor such fantastic distortions. Hitlerism even goes so far as to claim the rôle of protector of Christianity, and the terrible truth is that even this gross misinterpretation is able to make some impression. But one fact stands out with perfect clarity in all the fog: Hitler has never claimed to represent true liberalism. Liberalism then has the distinction of being the doctrine most hated by Hitler.[9]

It should be added that this hatred had little occasion to show itself in practice merely because, by the time Hitler came to power, liberalism was to all intents and purposes dead in Germany. And it was socialism that had killed it.

While to many who have watched the transition from socialism to fascism at close quarters the connection between the two systems has become increasingly obvious, in this country the majority of people still believe that socialism and freedom can be combined. There can be no doubt that most socialists here still believe profoundly in the liberal ideal of freedom, and that they would recoil if they became convinced that the realisation of their programme would mean the destruction of freedom. So little is the problem yet seen, so easily do the most irreconcilable ideals still live together, that we can still hear such contradictions in terms as 'individualist socialism' seriously discussed. If this is the state of mind which makes us drift into a new world, nothing can be more urgent than that we should seriously examine the real significance of the evolution that has taken place elsewhere. Although our conclusions will only confirm the apprehensions which others have already expressed, the reasons why this development cannot be regarded as accidental will not appear without a rather full examination of the main aspects of this transformation of social life. That democratic socialism, the great utopia of the last few generations, is not only unachievable, but that to strive for it produces something so utterly different that few of those who now wish it would be prepared to accept the consequences, many will not believe till the connection has been laid bare in all its aspects.

Postscript by Colin Wilson

The Road to Serfdom was intended as warning rather than prophecy; nevertheless, when Hayek wrote a foreword to the American paperback edition in 1956, he felt that the British experience under the post-war Labour government had confirmed his fears; he felt that the 'progressive destruction of the cherished foundation of British liberty' had been 'carried to a point which makes it doubtful whether it can be said that the Rule of Law still prevails in Britain'. The change, he emphasised, was psychological, and therefore not obvious – a change in the character of the people. One of the chief dangers, he felt, was of an increasing passivity on the part of the young as they grappled with endless regulations and tighter government control. In fact, it took another ten years or so – until the mid-sixties – for this to become apparent, as two decades of the Welfare State and creeping bureaucracy led to students' revolts all over Europe. One of the most striking things about the Baader-Meinhof revolutionaries or Britain's Angry Brigade is that they were recruited largely from the children of the comfortable middle classes. The group who called themselves Situation International – whose ideas were largely responsible for the Students' Revolt of 1968 that brought down De Gaulle – were less concerned about poverty and deprivation than about too much comfort and security. Guy Debord, who coined the phrase 'Society of the Spectacle', objected that television, computers, advertisements, consumer goods, cheap travel, were turning most people into passive spectators, with no desire for control over their own existence. Vandalism was a reaction against the *boredom* of the welfare society. The aim of the Situationists, said another of their spokesmen, Raoul Vaneigem, was 'to make the world a sensuous extension of man rather than to have man remain an instrument of an alien world'. He was clearly unaware of the latent irony of the situation – that he should be blaming 'alienation' on too much comfort, not on the exploitation of workers on starvation wages. This was certainly a development that would have bewildered Marx and Lenin. It did not bewilder Hayek: it is what he had been predicting all along.

NOTES

1. 'Discours prononcé à 'assemblé constituante le 12 Septembre 1848 sur la question du droit au travail.' (*OEuvres complètes d'Alexis de Tocqueville*, vol. IX, 1866, p. 546.)
2. The characteristic confusion of freedom with power, which we shall meet again and again throughout this discussion,, is too big a subject to be thoroughly examined here. As old as socialism itself, it is so closely allied with it that almost seventy years ago a French scholar, discussing its Saint-Simonian origins, was led to say that this theory of liberty 'est à elle seule tout le socialisme' (P. Janet, *Saint-Simon et le Saint-Simonisme*, 1878, p. 26, note). The most explicit defender of this confusion is, significantly, the leading philosopher of American left-wingism, John Dewey, according to whom 'liberty is the effective power to do specific things' so that 'the demand for liberty is demand for power' ('Liberty and Social Control', *The Social Frontier*, November 1935, p. 41).
3. Max Eastman, *Stalin's Russia and the Crisis of Socialism*, 1940, p. 82.
4. W.H. Chamberlin, *A False Utopia*, 1937, p. 202–3.
5. F.A. Voigt, *Unto Caesar*, 1939, p. 95.
6. *Atlantic Monthhly*, November 1936, p. 552.
7. *The End of Economic Man*, 1939, p. 230.
8. An illuminating account of the intellectual history of many of the Fascist leaders will be found in R. Michels (himself an ex-Marxist Fascist), *Sozialismus und Faszismus*, Munich 1925, vol. II, pp. 264–6, and 311–12.
9. *Social Research* (New York), vol. VIII, No. 4, November 1941. – It deserves to be recalled in this connection that, whatever may have been his reasons, Hitler thought it expedient to declare in one of his public speeches as late as February 1941 that 'basically National Socialism and Marxism are the same' (Cf. *The Bulletin of International News* published by the Royal Institute of International Affairs, vol. XVIII, no. 5, p. 269.)

HEGEL AND MARX

E.W.F. TOMLIN

I

> 'He (Hegel) is not an informant about the universe; he is its mouthpiece.'[1]

Like Nietzsche after him, Hegel deliberately assumed this role of cosmic interpreter; and it was not uncommon for his contemporaries to acknowledge it with awe and reverence. Moses Hess, the German socialist who was led to communism on philosophical grounds, held that 'Hegel's system represented the ultimate in philosophy; he considered it 'the absolutely highest point in the philosophy of spirit'.[2] In the Afterword of the second German edition of *Das Kapital*, Marx refers to Hegel as 'that mighty thinker'. The two Hegelian schools which flourished on the morrow of the Master's death – the right wing and the left wing – brought Hegelianism into the social and political domain. In fact, 'all the wings of the Hegelian school variously participated in the revolutions of the 19th century, and especially that of 1848'.[3] To-day, a great part of the world officially adheres to a philosophy or ideology derived from Hegel.

Such a development is new, at least to the western world. Both Plato and Aristotle were for a time court philosophers; but neither Dionysius II of Syracuse nor Alexander the Great called their realms Platonic or Aristotelian. In the Orient, the nearest parallel to the Marxist ideological domination was the hold of the Confucian ethic over the Chinese empire, which lasted for 25 centuries. We are talking of philosophies: the Roman Empire from the time of Constantine was officially Christian and the empire of Ashoka was officially Buddhist, but a religious revelation with its church and priesthood is a very different matter from a philosophy or ideology which is at best humanist.

Nevertheless, a philosophy or ideology which claims to explain the nature of the world, and the development of human society within that world, is clearly a substitute for religion; for a religion is something which men seek to live by and for which they are prepared finally to sacrifice themselves. We have only to read some of the literature published during the Stalinist or Maoist era to find a language of spiritual fervour ('Stalin, our Saviour', etc.,) borrowed directly from the devotional literature of the Higher Religions, especially Judaeo-Christianity. A materialist philosophy such as Marxism needs its own spiritual vocabulary, and quickly engenders it; and this transformation of materialism into idealism, on the ideological plane, took place immediately after the Russian Revolution of 1917, and it has been perpetuated by our contemporary neo-Marxians.

> *Cette philosophie matérialiste ne méconnait donc pas le spirituel, même si elle l'exprime autrement. A voir les choses sous l'angle de l'idéal, disait Plekhavnov, le marxisme est la plus idéaliste des théories qu'ait connus l'histoire de la pensée humaine.*[4]

Tell that, we may say, to the inhabitants of the Gulag Archipelago.

The human need for the ideal, even in philosophies claiming to be anti-idealist and in which there is by definition no place for values, makes itself felt in this unremitting elaboration of ideologies. Although the importance of ideology was stressed by both Marx and Engels, they were at variance in their definition of the term. Here is Marx:

> In studying revolutions, one must always distinguish between the material transformation in the economic conditions essential to production – which can be established with the exactitude of a natural science – and the juridical, political, religious, artistic and philosophical, in short ideological, forms in which men become *conscious* of this conflict and fight it out. *Critique of Political Economy*, 1859)

Here is Engels:

> An ideology is a distorted reflection which is *unconscious* of the fact that it is a reflection of economic conditions (*Anti-Dühring*: italics mine).

What is the cause of this ambivalent attitude to ideology? It stems from the most ambivalent of philosophical distinctions, that between appearance and reality. For the reflection and that which is reflected repeatedly undergo a change of status, the first being at one moment unreal and the second real, and at another moment the first becoming real (what we fight about) and the second unreal (a mere inert cause, which, being inert, is not really a cause). The Marxians are officially committed to the view that only matter is real – so that Trotsky, who was not anti-Marx but only anti-Stalin, could write that 'all the social illusions that mankind has raved about in religion, poetry, morals, or philosophy, serve only the purpose of deceiving and blinding the oppressed [to the basic material causes of their plight]'. But in practice men need a world of appearance, even of illusion, in which they can enlist the emotions and passions of their fellows and so *act* to effect the necessary social transformation, even if for really effective action they need more than that. Ideology for a materialistic society is therefore the indispensable dynamic of action, mobilizing in its cause all the old bourgeois virtues. The Russian resistance to Hitler was known as the Great Patriotic War. Had it been called the Great Dialectical Materialistic War, no one could have been inspired to fight.

II

This at once brings us back to the Hegelian dialectic, and its so-called transformation or reversal by Marx. For it is precisely in the Marxist interpretation of Hegel that the ambivalence of the notion of ideology originates, and in which matter itself, by a subtle mental conjuring-trick, ceases to be an inert substratum and becomes creative.

Fortunately, we do not need to enter into a detailed analysis of the Hegelian metaphysic in order to grasp the nature of the dialectic. To Hegel, the structure of reality was *thought*; but whereas thought was often regarded as inherently abstract, Hegel contended that the highest form of thought was, according to his own definition, *concrete*. To demonstrate this was the purpose of his first major work – his so-called 'voyage of discovery' – the *Phenomenology of Spirit* (1807). Here he made a journey from sense-perception to what he called 'absolute thinking'. But the most complete exposition of his view was contained in *Logic* (1812–1816). Hegel's *Logic*, it must be emphasized, was not the logic of textbooks, a science of 'how we think', it was a metaphysical process, a process of 'thought thinking itself', a conceptual passage whereby one concept was shown to generate another out of itself. Now the basic but most indeterminate concept was that of pure being; but because pure being was so completely featureless and undifferentiated, it inevitably passed over (one of Hegel's favourite terms, *aufgehoben*) into nothing, an antithetical concept. The two concepts, though apparently opposed, needed each other; and out of this fruitful opposition of thesis and antithesis arose a third concept, a synthesis of the other two, namely the concept of becoming. This was the first concrete concept. From this a new set of triadic concepts dialectically arose, culminating in the attainment of Absolute Spirit.

The process whereby the concepts developed logically out of themselves and attained reality in successive syntheses was the rational self-differentiation of what Hegel called the Idea. This could equally well be named God or Universal Spirit. The Idea was the source of nature and, through nature, of mind; and this dialectical movement from one phase or 'moment' to another was an eternal one – it formed a coming-to-be and a passing-away which, in Hegel's phrase, neither came to be nor passed away. He thus claimed to have overcome the obsessive and apparently ineradicable duality which had characterized philosophy since Descartes, whereby an internal confronted an external (e.g., mind and nature). To Hegel, reality was one autonomous process, both real and – because logically concatenated – rational. Hence his famous statement that the real was the rational and the rational was the real.

III

What Marx did to Hegel was not so much to invert his thought as to bring it down to earth. According to Marx, who in this respect was much influenced by Feuerbach, it was not the Idea or God or Spirit which underwent dialectical development; it was matter. Matter was the basic reality, not thought. The concept of matter had a long history, dating at least from Aristotle's *Metaphysics*, but it had received its most complete elaboration and 'materialization' at the end of the 18th century, especially in the work of Holbach and Helvétius. Now the first law of matter, so conceived, was that it could not originate states in itself. But in applying the dialectic to matter, Marx caused this inert reality to burgeon and to originate different phases. It *underwent* such transformation, with no entelechy or psychoid to vitalize or dynamize it. Indeed, Marxians such as Engels grew as lyrical on the subject of matter as the idealists had done on the subject of spirit. As he wrote in the *Dialectics of Nature*,

Matter is an eternal development in which tthere arise, die and

> anew create themselves infinitely various fors of material movement.

Here the use of the concepts of 'eternity', 'infinity' and 'creativity' in so brief a space takes us a long way from the inert matter of classical materialism. The Marxist writer, Maurice Cornforth, argues that Marxism is itself critical of what is known as metaphysical materialism; but he does not explain, by what right Marxism arbitrarily adopts an entirely new view of matter. Indeed, this transformation of a mechanistic and deterministic process – for a materialistic process was precisely that – into a quasi-organic one, is nothing but philosophical sophistry; but the fact is obscured by lifting dialectical materialism out of the sphere of philosophy altogether and declaring it to be a sacrosanct metaphysic, and in due course an official state religion.

As a matter of interest, the term dialectical materialism was nowhere used by Marx. It was an invention of later Marxians, who employed the term so frequently and with such enthusiasm, as befitted a magic formula, that its primal orthodoxy was taken for granted.

A state religion needs periodical interpretation or adjustment by state philosophers and theologians. Consequently, it was appropriate that the leading scientist and theologican of the Soviet Union, Joseph Stalin, should issue, as Lenin had done before him with *Marxism and Empiro-Criticism*, his own exegesis. In an encyclical called *Dialectical Materialism and Historical Materialism*, Stalin wrote

> Our consciousness and thought, however independent and or self-determined they may seem, are simply the product of a material, bodily organ, the brain, which is a reflection of matter existing independently of consciousness.

This statement is open to many criticisms, some of them elementary; but I shall take one from the field of biology. If the brain is the 'reflection' of matter, and if matter is independent of consciousness, then the origin of consciousness at the cerebral level is inexplicable save by magic. For the brain and the nervous system, far from being ready made, arise structurally in the process of embryogenesis; and at what intermediate point in this process can consciousness be shown to arise? If it arises only with the development of the neurula or neural plate, how does a hitherto material process suddenly acquire a new capacity, that of psychogenesis? Or if, as in the micro-surgical grafting experiment of Hans Spemann, cells in the embryo normally destined to form the epidermis are induced, at an early stage of gastrulation, to develop instead into nervous tissue, how does a mere biologist manage thus to cross the frontier between the physico-chemical (i.e., material) realm and the realm of consciousness? (The answer is, of course, that there is no 'transition' from matter to life and mind, but a continuous developing vital/psychic process, since the birth of micro-physics has led to the abandonment of the idea of an inorganic world.) Still more mysterious is the notion that the fully-formed brain, being no more than a 'reflection' of matter, suddenly becomes invaded with consciousness, as if a light were automatically switched on.

It may seem that this was an extreme example of absurdity promulgated by a man who did not know what he was talking about, and who went on to commit further absurdities over the Lysenko affair. The degree to which the Soviet establishment, which included its chief and most distinguished scientists, truckled to Stalin's pronouncements may be observed from the verbatim report of the session of the Lenin Academy of Agricultural Sciences of the USSR, July 31st-August 7th, 1948, of which a full English version, punctuated with phrases such as 'long and stormy applause: all rise', was issued by the Foreign Language Publishing House in Moscow.

True, we have had our own Marxian scientists, e.g., J.D. Bernal and J.B.S. Haldane, and even such brilliant men as the Reith Lecturer for 1976, Dr Colin Blakemore, now professor of Natural Philosophy at Cambridge, who, whether strict Marxians or not, have committed themselves to statements which are equally open to question. Here is one:

> It seems to me inconceivable to-day that anyone could ever doubt that man's mind is his brain. For me, the 'me-ness of me' is undoubtedly situated about two inches behind my eyes, in the very middle of my head. But I am sure I feel this with such confidence because I accept the currently fashionable scientific evidence that it is.[6]

In an article in the *New Universitiies Quarterly* (Winter 1977/78), I submitted this view to an analysis of which I should have welcomed critical comment; but the silence that ensued suggested that I had presumed to question a dogma of the materialistic religion, for which consignment to oblivion was the most appropriate fate.

IV

In the Hegelian system, the dialectical transition from Spirit to Nature involved arguments of a prolixity unique to German metaphysics. At least I do not know of any philosopher – least of all J.H. Stirling, author of *The Secret of Hegel* (a secret which, as a commentator said, was 'well kept') – who has satisfactorily rendered this transition intelligible. And when Hegel set out to demonstrate the application of the dialectic to the historical process, he fell victim to his own panlogism, and arrived at conclusions verging upon the grotesque. Although he was expounding a Universal History, he excluded certain regions of the world from the domain of the 'World Spirit' – Australia and the Pacific Islands, as well as the ancient civilizations of Mexico and Peru – because, as he said, somewhat cryptically, 'they were bound to perish at the approach of spirit'. Indeed the whole of pre-history was in Hegel's view unhistorical because it preceded the development of the state, that 'march of God in the world'.

Moreover, even what Hegel admits to be true history is organized in the familiar triadic form: the oriental world (thesis), the classical world (antithesis), and, as one might expect, the Germanic world (synthesis). At the same time, all history exemplified the development of the consciousness of freedom. In the Orient only one was free (the despot); in the Classical World, some were free; in the Germanic world, all were free (sic). He even implied that the Prussian state, which admittedly was his paymaster at the time, represented the highest achievement of Spirit. These are only a few examples of the mode of operation of a dialectic which had got out of hand.

Although Marx did not resort to panlogism of this variety, his reverence for the dialectic caused him to interpret history with a rigid determinism. It is a commonplace of the textbooks that he reserved his most powerful invective for the Utopian socialists – Saint-Simon, Proudhon, etc. – but in fact he exceeded most of the Utopians in his messianic fervours. He grafted on to history a primitive communism at one end, and at the other a sophisticated classless and stateless communism in which the state should have withered away. History proper was wedged in between two ideal extra-historical epochs, because 'primitive communism' (as he defined it) was a myth, and, as a later Marxian, Georges Sorel, saw perfectly well, the communist dénouement was a myth too – even though its prelude in the form of a paralysing general strike was a necessary myth. In Hegelian terms, Marx's 'withering away of the state' was the withering away of history, since history was the history of the state. And if, as a result, God had ceased to 'march' in the world, this was because He had returned to heaven and taken the 'divine humanity' (to use Solovyev's term) with Him. What was that but the ultimate Utopianism? Not for nothing has Marx been called the last of the Hebrew Prophets, though he was in fact the son of a Jew converted to Protestant Christianity. As Christopher Davison said:

> He was one of those exiles of Israel like Spinoza, whose isolation from the religious community of their fathers only serves to intensify their proud consciousness of a prophetic mission.[7]

V

Nevertheless, in all Utopian thought there is to be found a concession to realism. In Marxism this takes the form of the idea of 'the dictatorship of the proletariat'. Marx himself said of his own achievement: 'The new thing I did consisted in demonstrating . . . that the class-struggle inevitably leads to the dictatorship of the proletariat'. That is to say, before a distintegrating capitalism can give way to communism, there must necessarily be an interim period during which the workers consolidate their gains and liquidate elements hostile to the 'inevitable' transition to the classless society. Many Marxians, including Marx, have been invited to say how long this transition period would last, and they have taken good care not to commit themselves too explicitly, except to imply that it might be longer than anticipated, on the principle that '*il n'y a rien qui dure comme le provisoire*'. When Trootsky wrote his *revolution betrayed*)1936), the course of events in te Soviet Union had suggested not merely that the proletarian dictatorship promised to be very long, but that it was a cloak for dictatorship plain. This scandal proved in due course so embarrassing to theoretical Marxians as to cause them, after several more decades, to exclude the dictatorship of the proletariat from their conceptual armoury. In Soviet Russia the term was officially dropped after 1961, when Krushchev, promulgating his new Party programme, declared that the dictatorship had given place to what he called a 'state of the whole people'. Without the winding up of history altogether, which it did not rest with man to effect, the state, as Hegel had taught and as Marx seems to have forgotten, was in no danger of disappearing. On the contrary, in its Marxist version, it promised to become more powerful, more coercive, more secretive in its operations, and, becuase of this, more corrupt. Once a communist system was adopted, indeed, it forthwith assumed dictatorial form; and from such tyranny, to date, no country has ever emerged, or showed signs of emerging, save for periodical and momentary 'thaws', 'springs', and brief glimpses of a 'human face'. These were the consequence of the victim turning restively in his chains. In such a system it was precisely the workers – those whose liberation had been the first item on the revolutionary agenda – who suffered most acutely; whereas a new class of bureaucrats or *apparatchiks*, the emergence of which Marx did not anticipate, arrogated to themselves special privileges. This new bureaucracy promised to be self-perpetuating in a manner reminiscent of nothing so much as the capitalist oligarchic expropriators who, in Marxist mythology, were themselves to be expropriated.[8]

Another reason for the original adoption of the concept of proletarian dictatorship at least in theory, was in order to reconcile two conflicting strains in Marxist thought: the idea that capitalism would progressively pauperize the workers – the 'law of increasing misery', which has proved fallacious – and the idea, based on the dialectic, that before capitalism could give way to communism, it must have fulfilled its historical role. Historical roles were very much a Hegelian conception. While the first principle implied that the capitalist system was inherently evil, the second implied that it was evil only in so far as it clung to power. The function of bourgeois capitalism was plain, positive and to some extent salutary; and nowhere was the point made clearer than in the place where we would least expect to find it. The following brief, if highly relevant, passage is not by an apostle of free enterprise, but by Marx and Engels in *The Communist Manifesto* (1848). I took the opportunity of quoting it in a university lecture; and not one of the students – French, and almost all radical in outlook, like their compatriot teachers – came near to guessing its context.

> The bourgeoisie was the first to show what human activity is capable of achieving. It has erected works more marvellous than the building of the Egyptian pyramids, Roman aqueducts, and Gothic cathedrals; it has carried out expeditions surpassing by far the tribal migrations and the Crusades, etc.

The point has been echoed by many Marxians or proto-Marxians: e.g., 'We must build up capitalism before we can turn it into socialism', as Bernard Shaw said in his *Intelligent Woman's Guide to Socialism and Capitalism* (1928); and Marx, despite his denunciations of the system, had taken a similar line in conformity with the materialist conception of history.[9] It served to ease the conscience of many apostles of revolution, including such celebrated *rentiers* as Shaw's friends, Beatrice and Sidney Webb. Echoing St Augustine's plea about purity, they said in effect: 'Make me a good socialist, but not before the historical moment arrives'. It must not be forgotten that Marx himself, a man of expensive tastes, lived largely on bequests from his wife's family, together with subsidies from his affluent fellow-revolutionary, Engels.

The dictatorship of the proletariat was designed to take over not merely the achievements of capitalism but 'the reins of government' too. As Lenin observed:

> Marx's teaching about the class-struggle leads inevitably to a recognition . . . [that] the overthrow of the bourgeoisie is attainable only through the transformation of the proletariat into a ruling class.

Although Marx in his book *The Class Struggle in France, 1848–1850* (1895) maintained that the rule of the proletariat as a class would be the prelude to the abolition of all classes, he failed to grasp that the 'transformation of the proletariat into a ruling class 'would in fact take the form, as happened in the first country to undergo a wholesale revolution (which again would have surprised him, as it contradicted his own prophecy), of the reign of a ruling-class of a special kind, namely a ruthless dictatorial one. Such a class was less rather than more likely to relinquish its power, least of all in favour of a regime supposedly classless and stateless. Finally, the references, particularly those in *The Communist Manifesto*, to certain members of the bourgeoisie 'going over' to the proletariat, above all those who had 'achieved a theoretical understanding of the historical movement as a whole' (a convenient description of Marx and Engels themselves, as well as privileged upper-class figures such as V.M. Molotov), served to disguise the fact that none of these men ever 'went over' to the proletariat or assumed any kind of classlessness (whatever that might have implied). On the contrary, they seized hold of the reins of the Czarist autocracy and, forming a new ruling class, strengthened that autocracy to a point where the liberties of the

Czarist regime – which had permitted enough freedom of expression to create a world literature with Dostoevsky and Tolstoy and in which there was enough practical initiative even as early as 1861 for landowners to address the Czar with a request to pay taxes[10] – were summarily suppressed. Moreover, the new ruling class produced an art and literature inferior to anything created under 'bourgeois tyranny', except in cases of genuine talent, which were prohibited altogether, or circulated clandestinely in *samizdat*, or, most ironical of all, smuggled to the capitalist West and there made available to become, in the case of a Solzhenitsyn, a world literature once more.

In other words, the 'dictatorship of the proletariat' had a convenient fiction, and 'the notion that the affluent party potentates belong to the same class (namely the proletariat) as the under-nourished drudges in the factories and on the farms' was demonstrably false.[11]

VI

The final fallacy of Marx to be examined here is concerned with his claim to have elaborated a socialism which was for the first time *scientific*. Hegel too had called his Logic a science. And for a materialist, scientific must imply empirical. Whereas Hegel's Logic of the Dialectic was a deductive exercise, covering the whole of cosmic reality, Marx concentrated upon the historical process and the supposed immanent dialectical laws of the historical process, which he held to be empirically verifiable. But the only *instance* of the operation of the dialectic triad in history was the process whereby feudalism (thesis) was contradicted by capitalism (antithesis), to result in the higher unity of the classless society (synthesis). But only two stages had taken place, and it was clear that the third stage was by its nature outside history altogether. Therefore it could not act as the receiver, so to speak, of the historical process. The deduction was from a single instance – if instance it could be called – and was therefore not an empirical pronouncement at all.

This is why so much Marxist exegetic, not least that of Neo-Marxism, and especially that issuing from our universities, possesses so dogmatic a character. Many examples could be cited: I will content myself with one, namely the academic Marxist symposium, *Philosophy and its Past*, by Jonathan Rée, Michael Ayers and Adam Westoby, published in 1979, and I will leave to another the necessary comment. Referring in particular to the contribution by Jonathan Rée, Roger Scruton, in a review of the book in *Encounter* (December 1979) observed:

> The Marxist 'dialectic' (which one senses in the background when one does not see it in the foreground of the author's thought) is a theory that tells us how ideas develop, but seems to leave unanswered the question how to determine whether they are true – a failing which immediately negates its philosophical pretensions.

Commenting on the contribution of Adam Westoby, the same writer remarks:

> His synopsis of Hegel's history of philosophy contains no argument, and rapidly sinks into dogma, invoking that future in which all mysteries will be dissolved, and in which all obfuscation will be succeeded by the world-view of 'the modern proletariat'. . .

Here we observe how the apocalyptic strain has invaded even the thought of young academic practitioners, who would no doubt be horrified to learn that their outlook derives from the messianic rather than the 'scientific' side of Marx. But anyone who can talk of the 'world-view" of the modern proletariat, which will resolve all social contradictions, is indulging in mysticism, not rationality.

That Marxism resembles some of the eschatological gospels which flourished, however fitfully, in the Middle Ages, has several times been pointed out, not least by Norman Cohn in his book *The Pursuit of the Millennium* (1972). Professor Cohn takes the view that among the prophetic systems known to Europe before Marxism, the most influential was that of Joachim of Fiore (1145–1202), a Calabrian abbot and hermit. His system envisaged three successive ages through which history was to pass, each being associated with a Person of the Trinity. The final age, the reign of the Holy Spirit, was to persist until the Last Judgment; but it postulated a Kingdom of the Saints which would be *transitional* to the winding up of history. (This transitional period was often envisaged as lasting for a thousand years: hence the use of the terms millennial and chiliastic.) It is easy to see that the Marxist 'dictatorship of the proletariat', a provisional exercise of power, forms a secular version of this persistent notion. Marx himself, when he began to form his view of the role of the proletariat, conceived of it in 'redemptive' terms.[12] As we study the development of Marx's thought and observe the great influence upon him not merely of Feuerbach but of Bauer, both of whom wrote prolifically on religion before renouncing it, we arrive at the conclusion that such secular mysticism, though in his case surrounded by a conglomerate of empirical fact, became more important for him than the Hegelian dialectic. 'Broadly speaking', Bertrand Russell wrote, 'all the elements in Marx's philosophy which are derived from Hegel are unscientific in the sense that there is no reason whatever to suppose them true'. Thus, 'the Hegelian trappings might be dropped with advantage'.[13]

What is clear is that Marx made the realization of his whole system conditional upon a change in human nature. He was not merely convinced that the overthrow of capitalism would make this possible, but he believed, though upon what evidence it is difficult to say, that such changes had taken place in the past. 'The whole of history', he wrote in *The Poverty of Philosophy* (1845), 'is nothing but a continual transformation of human nature'. But the transformation reserved for the future was of a kind never before contemplated at least at the secular level; for such perfectability outdid anything considered remotely feasible even by the most sanguine of the utopian socialists, and even by the most lofty religious seers.

The last word can be left to one of the most brilliant critics of Marx, the American Max Eastman (1883–1969), himself a lifelong radical:

> Unless you know through some avenue that is above the empirical determination of facts, that all contradictions are bound to resolve themselves in a higher unity, there is no proof in these facts that 'capitalist production creates with the necessity of a natural process the negation of itself' . . . Contrary to common belief, there is no proof anywhere in Marx's *Capital*. It is by . . . inferring the victory of the proletariat as a logical conclusion according to the Hegelian system, that Marx arrives at that 'iron necessity' of socialism, which is supposed to rest upon the overwhelming assemblage and analysis of facts in *Das Kapital*. It rests upon the relics of religious metaphysics; it has no other foundation.[14]

NOTES

1. Ernest Gellner, reviewing *Hegel*, by Charles Taylor, *Encounter*, April 1976.
2. David McLellan, *The Young Hegelians and Karl Marx* (1969), p. 140.
3. Benedetto Croce, *What is Living and What is Dead in the Philosophy of Hegel* (1907).
4. Jean Lacroix, 'La Philosophie Soviétique', *Le Monde*, 11. ii. 70.
5. *The Open Philosophy and the Open Society* (1968), p. 69.
6. *Mechanism of the Mind* (1977), p. 9.
7. *Religion and the Modern State* (1935), p. 86.
8. This famous phrase occurs in *Das Kapital*, chapter 32.
9. Cf. Peter Singer, *Karl Marx* (1980), p. 60.
10. Edward Crankshaw, *The Shadow of the Winter Palace* (1976), p. 180.
11. Stanislas Andrevski, *Social Science as Sorcery* (1972) points this out, p. 160.
12. The point is made in his essay 'Towards a Critique of Hegel's Philosophy of Right'. Cf also Peter Singer, *op. cit.*, p. 20–22.
13. *History of Western Philosophy* (1946), p. 816–817.
14. *Marx, Lenin, and the Science of Revolution* (1926), p. 103.

PROPHECY OR PHILOSOPHY? HISTORICISM OR HISTORY?

A world-outlook claiming to be scientific guarantees the Kingdom of Heaven

ANTONY FLEW

Fredrick Engels asserted, in a funeral tribute to his lifelong friend, 'As Darwin discovered the law of evolution in organic nature, so Marx discovered the law of evolution in human history. . .' But on that occasion the claim to the discovery of a law of historical development was not illustrated. Instead Engels proceeded at once to a statement of what they both liked to call (not *a* but) *the* materialist conception of history. He concluded the first part of his short address: '*So war dieser Mann der Wissenschaft*' (Such was this man of science).

In the second part Engels insisted, also or notwithstanding:

> Marx was above all a revolutionary, and his great aim was to cooperate in this or that fashion in the overthrow of capitalist society and the state institutions which it has created, to cooperate in the emancipation of the modern proletariat, to whom he was the first to give a consciousness of its class position and class needs, a knowledge of the conditions necessary for its emancipation.

Both the failure to specify the actual law of historical development supposedly discovered, and the references at the end to 'the conditions necessary' for proletarian emancipation, rather than to the conditions sufficient, may perhaps suggest a desire to maintain only some thesis other and substantially weaker than that of the first bold boast. There are, however, many workaday texts in both Marx and Engels quite unequivocal in their insistence upon an inexorable law of development, or inexorable laws. These, it seems, guarantee the ultimate blissful and none too distant consummation of the entire historical process. Nor is there any doubt at all but that a very large part of the appeal of Marxism always has been, and still remains, that it is believed to provide scientific proof that – as crude comrade Khrushchev used to say – 'Communism is at the end of all the roads in the world. We shall bury you!'[1]

(i) In the *Economic and Philosophical Manuscripts of 1844* Marx complains that the classical economists fail to bring out how 'apparently accidental circumstances' are nothing but 'the expression of a necessary development' (p. 323). The climactic end of that 'necessary development' is then proclaimed in the final sentences of the first section of the *Communist Manifesto*: 'What the bourgeoisie, therefore, produces, above all, is its own gravediggers. Its fall and the victory of the proletariat are equally inevitable' (p. 94).[2] Six years later, in an article on 'The English Middle Class' for the *New York Daily Tribune*, Marx allowed that 'though temporary defeat may await the working classes, great social and economical laws are in operation which must eventually ensure their triumph' (1/VIII/54). Then in 1867, in the original German Preface to the first volume of *Capital*, the book so long awaited as the prophet's promised proof, Marx explains 'why England is used as the chief illustration in the development of my theoretical ideas'. Everything discovered here will eventually be just as applicable elsewhere:

> Intrinsically, it is not a question of the higher or lower degree of development of the social antagonisms that result from the natural laws of capitalist production. It is a question of these laws themselves, of these tendencies working with iron necessity towards inevitable results. The country that is more developed industrially only shows, to the less developed, the image of its own future (p. xvii).

(ii) There is, therefore, no question but that Marx did claim to have discovered a law or laws of progressive development; laws which would have to be accounted as, in Sir Karl Popper's sense, historicist. It is equally certain that Engels fully endorsed this claim. But at least in publications after the death of Marx, Engels was prepared to recognize that all the rises must one day be followed by decline. Thus in 1892, in Section I of *Socialism: Utopian and Scientific*, Engels even goes out of his way to commend the usually despised utopian Fourier for recognizing that all human life on this planet must eventually end (pp. 18–9).

Historicist claims to be seized of inexorable laws of evolution will, however, possess no appeal stronger than that of the evidence and argument deployed in their support, unless they are reinforced by the further claim that 'the future walking to meet us all' must always be not merely better but even the best possible.[3]

Although Marx was, for reasons of Hegelian principle, reluctant to speak in any but the vaguest and most general terms about the world after the world revolution, he did say enough to make quite clear his own utterly confident expectations of a secular humanist version of the Kingdom of Heaven upon Earth.[4] The Hegelian principles come out about as sharply as Hegelian principles ever do in the last Marx letter to Ruge, published in the *Franco-German Year Books* of 1843:

> For even though the question 'Where from?' presents no problems, the question 'Where to?' is a rich source of confusion. Not only has universal anarchy broken out among the reformers but also every individual must admit to himself that he has no precise idea of what ought to happen. However, this very defect turns out to the advantage of the new movement, for it means that we do not anticipate the world with our dogmas but instead attempt to discover the new world through the critique of the old. . . . We have no business with the construction of the future . . . [nevertheless] there can be no doubt about the task confronting us at present: *the ruthless criticism of the existing order* . . . (p. 207: italics original).[5]

So no one, it seems, has any 'precise idea of what ought to happen'. Section II of the *Communist Manifesto* nevertheless concludes with total and categorical conviction. After the inevitable fall of the bourgeoisie and the equally inevitable victory of the proletariat, this proletariat – which will have been 'compelled, by the force of circumstances, to organize itself as a class' – cannot but 'make itself the ruling class, and, as such, sweep away by force the old conditions of production'. In so doing 'it will, along with these conditions, have swept away the conditions for the existence of class antagonisms and of classes generally, and will thereby have abolished its own supremacy as a class'. Finally – Presto! – the classless and conflict-free utopia: 'In place of the old bourgeois society, with its classes and class antagonisms, we shall have an association, in which the free development of each is the conditions of the free development of all' (p. 105).

Later than any Marx source employed so far is a passage cited in Melvin Lasky's *Utopia and Revolution*. This was found among the Marx papers only after his death. It was originally intended to go into the 1871 *Civil War in France*. That, as published, includes the notiorious, hard saying: '*Die Arbeiterklasse hat keine Ideale zu erfullen*' (The working class has no ideals to realize). But crossed out among the surviving papers is a revealingly different treatment of Fourier, Cabet, and other utopians:

> They attempted to compensate for the missing historical preconditions of the movement with fantastic pictures and plans of a new society, in the propaganda for which they saw the true means of salvation. From that moment on, when the working-class movement became a reality, the fantastic utopias disappeared: not because the working class abandoned the objective for which these utopians had reached, but because the true means had been found for its realization. . . Still, both the ultimate aims . . . announced by the utopians (i.e., the end of the system of wage-labour and class domination) are also the ultimate aims of the Paris Revolution and of the International. Only the means are different (quoted pp. 38–9).

No wonder that so many have been, and that so many still are, eager to accept this Marxist revelation of inevitable utopia; the more especially since they are assured that, appropriately to the self-images both of its own century and ours, this is no old-fashioned religious prophecy but a fresh finding of the new, unutopian and, of course, scientific socialism. One former Populist described his own feelings on reading the first Russian translation of *Capital*, and the feelings of many others too:

> The knowledge that we feeble individuals were backed by a mighty historical process filled one with ecstasy, and established such a firm foundation for the individual's activities that, it seemed all the hardships of the struggle could be overcome.[6]

2

The incredibility of any such secular revelation

The only accounts of the Last Days which Marx himself was prepared to provide were, as we have seen, studiously sketchy and abstract. Yet, surely, they should still be sufficient to make his prophecies altogether incredible? It was in their day all very well for the Saints and for the Fathers to develop a Christian historicism:

beginning with the creation of the Universe itself and of Adam, the man made in God's image; continuing to the predestined and foreseen Fall; on to the Incarnation; and culminating in the final establishment of God's Kingdom upon Earth. For in that scheme the particular species of our species-being was from the beginning created by the Almighty, having an all-seeing eye to its eventual and truly human destiny. We were created, in the splended words of the old Scottish *Prayer Book*, 'to glorify God and to enjoy him forever'. In that scheme the inexpungable guarantee that the Kingdom will indeed come, never thereafter to be undermined or overthrown, lay in the absolute power and promise of Omnipotence.

How different it is with the secular substitute, the true People's Democratic Republic of Marx. Here the existence of God and his Providence have been contemptuously denied. Supposedly we are all atheists now, altogether rejecting religion as an obsolete illusion – 'the cry of the hard-pressed creature, the heart of the heartless world, the soul of souless circumstance, the laudanum of the masses.'

How then can we fail to see the massive implausibility of this Marxist eschatology, indeed its internal incoherence? The whole continuing human life-process has perhaps never before been presented in so harsh a light. For instance, the *Communist Manifesto* proper begins: 'The history of all hitherto existing society is the history of class struggles'. And 'law, morality, religion', along with everything else once thought to stand between humanity and the abyss, are nothing but feeble figleaves miserably failing to conceal unlovely class interests (pp. 79 and 92). Yet this long succession of savage struggles is, we are assured, bound to end – and to end pretty soon too – in the annihilating victory of a class to end all classes: a victory to be followed, without fail, again in pretty short order, by the establishment of a conflict-free utopia.

Furthermore, the class cast to play the part of Redeemer in this secular salvation drama is supposed to be going to become, right up until the final revolution, progessively more impoverished, exploited, and degraded. So true is this that *all* its members will, we are told, continue to drop in these respects below the *average* of the class in question: 'The modern labourer . . . instead of rising with the progress of industry, sinks deeper and deeper below the conditions of existence of his own class' (p. 93)[7]

Even given the invaluable and indispensable deus ex machina assistance of Dr Marx and that 'small section of the ruling class' which 'cuts itself adrift, and joins the revolutionary class, the class that holds the future in its hands' (p. 91), however could such a battered, harried, exploited, ignorant, undernourished, and diseased proletariat produce a paradise of perfect harmony, populated by a race of superpersons so preveniently adjusted to their life together that 'the free development of each is the condition for the free development of all' (p. 105)? Whatever there may be to be said about the rest of his work, how can anyone refuse to concede that, whenever Marx speaks of the aftermath of the promised proletarian revolution, he becomes airborne above all the pedestrian sobrieties of history and sociology? At those times we have the infatuated Hegelian Rabbi, the species–intoxicated Hebrew prophet. With apologies to Engels, 'That is *not* the man of science!'

(i) So far in the present Section 2, I have been pointing out the incongruity between, on the one hand, the brightly shining, albeit excruciatingly vague and abstract, eschatological promise of Marxism: and on the other hand, the hard-bitten historical materialism which is supposed to provide its foundation. Yet that promise is, if anything, even more incongruous with an evolutionary, this-worldly account not of human history but of human origins. Suppose for a moment that you could swallow basic theism, and that you were innocent of all knowledge of the work of Darwin and his successors. Then it might perhaps be quite reasonable for you to expect the Kingdom of God on Earth as the promised consummation of the history of creatures God-designed for that end. You would not pretend to base your confidence in the future on that history, in your eyes almost uniformly deplorable. For you would believe that God created men specially to be fit subjects in his peaceable kingdom, and that that deplorable history was all, as it were, an aberration – the result of an unfortunate lapse from our original condition.

Then you read the *Origin of Species* (Penguin Books 1968, Harmondsworth), alertly appreciating the particular implications which Darwin himself was going later to spell out in *The Descent of Man* (John Murray: London, 1871). Should you not see his work as the most serious threat to your previous assumptions about our human nature, and in particular about our putative prior and perfect adaptation to life in the ultimate ideal society?

Suppose instead now that, like Marx, you are a militant atheist. Suppose too that like him – despite your vehement repudiation of everything you recognize as part of the heritage of either Judaism or Christianity – you have continued to harbour the same or at least similarly optimistic assumptions. Then you too, like the believer in our first supposition, surely should be disturbed over the implications of *The Origin of Species*? Yet Marx in fact was not: on the contrary. In 1861 he wrote in a letter to Lassalle:

> Darwin's book is very important and fits in with me as the basis in natural science of the class struggle. The crude English method of exposition must naturally be put up with. In spite of every defect not only has 'teleology' in natural science here received its death blow, but its rational meaning has been empirically demonstrated.

There is also another passage in which Marx smiles at Darwin for rediscovering among the plants and the brutes 'his own English society with its division of labour, competition, opening up of new markets, inventions, and Malthusian "struggle for existence" '.

Both passages present some difficulties of interpretation. But neither so much as hints that Marx discerned in Darwin's naturalism any threat either to his own apocalyptic eschatology or to the assumptions about human nature implicit in that eschatology. The second is frequently quoted nowadays by historians of science inclined to believe that to show that ideas were drawn from external and contemporary sources is to show that the account incorporating those ideas cannot either constitute or contain objective knowledge.[8] Happily it is by no means sufficient to reveal Marx as himself a client of this popular misconception. It would be better employed as an occasion for pointing out that, just as natural selection is precisely not a kind of selection, but an essentially non-teleological mechanism which accounts for what appears to be but really is not selection, so all the other normally intentional and anthropomorphic terms which occur in Darwin's theory have to be construed in a a similarly deteleologized way.

The second two sentences of the first passage, however, are evidence that Marx could not in the end be content with a Darwinian presentation of evolutionary biology. Certainly he was delighted to have ' "teleology" in natural science' receive 'its death blow': just so long as this was a matter of seeing off any idea of (special) creation by a transcendent Designer. But both the complaint about poor Darwin's 'English method of exposition', characteristically put down here as 'crude' or 'vulgar', and the talk about demonstrating the 'rational meaning' of the whole process, should suggest, what the only recently published *Grundrisse* so very clearly shows, that Marx remained always, as he had begun, a German philosopher.[9] Both the general historicist approach and the particular historicist beliefs derived originally from this sort of philosophizing rather than from all those later years of studying actual social and economic institutions – ploughing through bluebooks in the British Museum Reading Room, and so on. What, as an only very partially reconstructed Hegelian, Marx always wanted was to discover some sort of rational necessity in all actual development: even though the rationality was to be that of a wretched Hegelian dialectic logic, while the directedness was now to be immanent in the ordinary material Universe rather than attached to a possibly transcendent Mind or Spirit. The vulgarity and crudity of which Darwin is accused would, therefore, appear to have consisted in his failure to meet this rather special requirement.

One merit of his work in the eyes of Marx is, as we have already emphasized, that it disposes of all suggestions of '(special) creation by a transcendent Designer.' Yet its prime attraction for him seems to have lain in what, as we have also argued already, he ought to have recognized as a threat. For the first sentence of the first passage quoted read: 'Darwin's book is very important and fits in with me as the basis in natural science of the class struggle.' Certainly a struggle for existence between species of subhuman plants and animals must be allowed to probabilify the contention that all human history has been the history of class struggles. But that contention itself is well nigh impossible to reconcile with the desired conclusion that these class struggles are due very shortly to culminate in the overwhelming victory of the class to end all classes; a victory swiftly followed by the establishment of the conflict-free utopia to which we are all perfectly preadjusted. An evolutionary theory having struggled for existence as a central theme should, therefore, be judged to weigh the scales even more heavily against that cherished conclusion.

(ii) Perhaps we have no means of telling exactly what and how much Marx meant by saying that in Darwin the 'rational meaning' of teleology had been 'empirically demonstrated.' But in *Socialism: Utopian and Scientific* Engels came much nearer to asserting outright both that Darwin proved the reality of an overall continuing progress in the biological world, and that this demonstration provides strong support for Marxist historical materialism. Certainly these two conclusions were accepted as integral by Kautsky and by other leading defenders of the faith in what in his

Main Currents of Marxism (Clarendon, 1978: Oxford) Kolakowski calls *The Golden Age* (Vol. II, passim).

In this for many years most influential of all Marxist books, Engels himself begins: 'Nature is the proof of dialectics . . .' He proceeds then to argue that the daily advance of science shows that 'Nature works dialectically and not metaphysically: that she does not move in the eternal oneness of a perpetually recurring circle, but goes through a real historical evolution.' In particular and above all there is Darwin's 'proof that all organic beings, plants, animals, and man himself, are the products of a process of evolution going on through millions of years' (pp. 34 and 35). That the word 'evolution' has here to be construed as implying progress is made clear by the subsequent treatment of classical German philosophy:

> This . . . culminated in the Hegelian system . . . the history of mankind . . . appeared . . . as the process of evolution of man himself. It was now the task of the intellect to follow the gradual march of this process through all its devious ways, and to trace out the inner law running through all its apparently accidental phenomena (pp. 36–7).

In the remainder of the present Section 2 I attack this supporting suggestion that Darwin demonstrated that the biological world is governed by some sort of natural law of progress, and I insist that the whole future of life upon the planet Earth is now largely and increasingly dependent upon human action and inaction. Finally in Section 3 I argue that there neither are nor could be any kind of natural laws of human action; and that the entire Marxist project on its distinctive scientific side was from the beginning, therefore, utterly misconceived.

(a) The first suggestion that Darwin's theory promises progress lies in his employment of the catch phrase 'the survival of the fittest'. Yet, as has by now so frequently been pointed out, the survival of the fittest is here guaranteed only and precisely in so far as actual survival is the criterion of fitness to survive. In effect in this context 'fitness' is defined as 'having whatever it may as a matter of fact take to survive'. It is notorious that such biological fitness may be by other and independent standards most unadmirable. An individual or a species can have many splendid physical or mental endowments without these being or ensuring what is in fact needed for survival. Men who are in every way wretched creatures may, and all too often do, kill superb animals; while genius has frequently been laid low by the activities of unicellular beings having absolutely no wits at all.

It is in this light that we have to discount one or two over-optimistic mis-statements of the implications of the theory made by Darwin himself. The chapter on 'Instincts', for instance, in *The Origin of Species* ends with the sentence:

> finally . . . it is far more satisfactory to look at such instincts as the young cuckoo ejecting its foster-brothers – ants making slaves – the larvae of ichneumonidae feeding within the live bodies of caterpillars – not as specially endowed or created instincts, but as a small consequence of one general *law leading to the advancement of all organic beings – namely, multiply, vary, let the strongest live and the weakest die* (p. 263: italics supplied).

(b) Again, traditional contrasts between higher and lower animals, combined with the more recent recognition that the former are all among the later products of the evolutionary process, may raise hopes of finding in living Nature a passable substitute for Matthew Arnold's God: 'something, not ourselves, which makes for righteousness'. Julian Huxley, launching what became a lifelong quest for such a substitute, took as one of the mottos of a famous early essay on 'Progress, Biological and Other' in his *Essays of a Biologist* (Penguin Books: Harmondsworth, 1939) the final sentence in the penultimate paragraph of *The Origin of Species*:

> As all the living forms of life are the lineal descendants of those which lived long before the Cambrian epoch, we may feel certain that . . . no cataclysm has desolated the whole world. Hence we may look with some confidence to a secure future of great length. *And as natural selection works solely by and for the good of each being, all corporeal and mental endowments will tend to progress towards perfection.* (p. 459: italics supplied).

The conclusion italicized simply does not follow: '. . . endowments will tend to progress towards perfection' only when they are found in organisms not lacking something else needed to stay in the race; and, unless it is good for an individual or a species to die if it has just not got what it takes to survive, 'natural selection' does not work 'solely by and for the good of each being'.

Notwithstanding that he had once pinned into his copy of the *Vestiges of the Natural History of Creation* a memorandum slip to warn himself 'Never use the words *higher* and *lower*', Darwin still writes in the final peroratory paragraph at the very end of *The Origin of Species*:

> . . . from the war of nature, from famine and death, the most exalted object which we are capable of conceiving, namely the production of the higher animals, directly follows. There is a grandeur in this view of life. . . (p. 459).

(c) There is indeed 'a grandeur in this view of life', and it is something which should be part of the world-outlook of every modern person. But what is not to be found in evolutionary biology, Darwin's own occasional hints to the contrary notwithstanding, is any kind of guarantee of progress. The decisive, fundamental reason why we must not hope to find anything of the sort, either here or in any possible rival theory of subhuman ongoings, will emerge in the most illuminating way if we ponder the significance of two things. The first is Darwin's distinction between his own theory and that of Malthus. The second is that Darwin is specifically concerned not with selection but with natural selection. On the second, it has already been urged that, since it does not involve choice, natural selection is precisely not selection. The first distinction is made in the chapter '*Struggle for Existence*'. Darwin writes:

> A struggle for existence inevitably follows from the high rate at which all organic beings tend to increase. . . It is the doctrine of Malthus applied with manifold force to the whole animal and vegetable kingdom: *for in this case there can be no artificial increase of food and no prudential restraint from marriage* (pp. 116–7: italics supplied).

The cruces are: first, that, for the best of reasons, Darwin's theory leaves out man: second, that man is the creature which can, and cannot but, make choices: and, third, that it is upon the senses of these choices that the future not only of mankind but also of almost all other species now largely depends. So, if there is any legitimate satisfaction anywhere for the secular religious cravings of Julian Huxley, and of so many others before and since, then it can only be found, where Marx is thought to have found it, in the peculiarly human sciences.

The truth of the third of the cruces just listed comes out most harshly when we notice why we cannot echo Darwin's conclusion: 'Hence we may look with some confidence to a secure future of great length'. But, Armageddon apart, Quinton was stating nothing but a plain fact when, in an essay on *Ethics and the Theory of Evolution*, he said:

> [Man] has certainly won the contest between animal species in that it is only on his sufferance that any other species exist at all, amongst species large enough to be seen at any rate (p. 120 of IT Ramsey (Ed.) *Biology and Personality* Blackwell: Oxford, 1966).

The truth of our first and second cruces is underlined in the final clause of the quoted reference to Malthus. Their present significance will become clearer as I outline an interpretation of his work fully developed and defended elsewhere.[11] The theory of human population which Malthus published in the *First Essay* of 1798 was of a kind appropriate to a natural as opposed to a human science: indeed he seems to have held classical mechanics before his eyes as the ideal model. So his fundamental principle of population, 'a prodigious power of increase in plants and animals', the animal power to multiply 'in geometrical progression', is, therefore, construed as being, not only in plants and in the brutes but also in people, a power which must in fact inevitably be realized: save in so far as such realization is made physically impossible by the operation of countervailing physical forces. No wonder that the conclusions of this *First Essay* are harsh; describing always what supposedly has happened, happens, and will happen, necessarily, ineluctably, and unavoidably.

But in the *Second Essay* of 1803, which publishers and librarians misleadingly count as simply a second edition of the earlier work, Malthus introduced the notion of 'moral restraint', and so 'endeavoured to soften some of the harshest conclusions of the *First Essay*'. Although Malthus neither spelt out nor even saw the full consequences, this ostensibly modest amendment totally transformed his theory. For the amendment makes that theory recognize, what everything which is to constitute human science must recognize, the reality of choice. The fundamental power to multiply thus becomes a power in a quite different sense, the sense in which human beings are equipped with powers: powers to do so and so or not to do so and so, as they choose. The conclusions which follow from the theory become correspondingly, if not always much less harsh, at any rate more open. It is no longer a matter of inferring that this or that must happen, ineluctably and unavoidably, whatever anyone may do. Rather it is a matter of what must happen, unless of course some or all those concerned choose alternative courses; or of what does in fact tend to happen, although of course all the agents concerned could act differently, even if we can be pretty sure they will not.

It is altogether typical of the wayward and uneven course usually followed by the actual history of ideas: that Malthus first formulated 'the principle of population' as a statement of a physical power – misattributed to our peculiar species; that Malthus later, without really realizing what he was doing, reinterpreted it as the human power to choose between alternatives – which in that context it ought to have been in the first place; and that years later Darwin, reading the revised version 'for amusement', revised the principle back again to serve as the prime mover in a great scheme of subhuman biological theory.

3

The lawlessness of human action

Our own final task is to develop a refutation, not of historicist propositions in Marx only, but of every other contention of the same kind also. Here the first necessity is to indicate the inadequacies of what Popper himself gave us in *The Poverty of Historicism* (Routledge and Kegan Paul: London, 1957). These contributions begin with the official definition, which does not accord with his own usage. Popper asserts:

> It will be enough if I say here that I mean by 'historicism' an approach to the social sciences which assumes that *historical prediction* is their principal aim, and which assumes that this aim is attainable by discovering the 'rhythm' or the 'patterns', the 'laws' or the 'trends' that underlie the evolution of history (p. 3: italics original).

(i) This is in fact, at one and the same time, both not enough and too much. It is not enough, in that it fails to specify that for Popper the essence of historicism is belief in natural laws of historical development. Such natural laws assert: both that the occurrence of whatever they determine is as a matter of fact or, as some would prefer to say, contingently necessary: and that the occurrence of anything inconsistent with themselves is also correspondingly as a matter of fact, or contingently, impossible. That this is indeed the intended crux comes out most clearly in Popper's splendid Dedication:

> In memory of the countless men and women of all creeds or

> nations or races who fell victims to the fascist and communist belief in Inexorable Laws of Historical Destiny (p. v).

But, once we are seized of this insufficiency in the definition offered, we must also recognize that there is no call to reject – along with all talk of 'Inexorable Laws of Historical Destiny' – more modest suggestions that there are perhaps some rhythms, patterns or trends to be discerned in 'the evolution of history'. To reject all these too would surely be to repudiate the entire project of pointed, intelligible and illuminating historical writing? It is by the same token to give hostages to the historicist enemy. For it does provide such an enemy with good reason for contending that to jettison historicism is to abandon history as a serious form of inquiry.[12]

It is perhaps in the hope of forestalling such a charge that Popper proceeds to present what he holds to be 'a really fundamental similarity between the natural and the social. . .' This putative 'fundamental similarity' arises, he thinks, thanks to 'the existence of sociological laws or hypotheses which are analogous to the laws or hypotheses of the natural siciences' (p. 62). My own prime contrary contentions are: first, as everyone agrees, that history is the study of *res gestae*, or human actions, of things done; second, that there neither are nor could be any laws of human action as such; and, third, that precisely this constitutes the fundamental *dissimilarity* between the natural and the human sciences. The most elegant, direct, and decisive refutation of all historicist contentions follows immediately. For, if it truly is impossible to have any sociological or historical laws at all, then it must be still more impossible to have any historicist laws of historical development.

About regular, as opposed to historicist, laws of nature in the fields of sociology and historiography, I shall on this occasion make no more than two points. First, neither Popper nor Hempel – who have both laboured to establish that there are such regular laws by fielding collections of supposed specimens – actually succeeded in finding any. The candidates presented have all to be disqualified as either plain false, or merely tautological, or else as not carrying those implications of universal contingent necessity and contingent impossibility essential to your authentic law of nature.[13] Second, the suspicions of Hempel and Popper should have been aroused – at latest – as soon as they found that they were having to think up candidates out of their own heads, because none were pushing themselves forward ready named. For why is it that none of the works of history and sociology on our library shelves index references to Comte's Law or to Spencer's Law: parallelling those to Boyle's Law, to Ohm's Law, and all the rest of the apparatus in any textbook of physics?

The answer, in a word, is that there neither are nor could be laws of nature describing human action as such; laws, that is, implying that on some specified sort of occasion it is contingently necessary for agents to act in one particular way and contingently impossible for those same agents to act in any other way. There neither are nor could be any such laws, since the very notion of human agency is logically incompatible with these implications; and because we are all in a position to know that we very often are, in this crucial sense, agents. Or, to approach the heart of the matter from a different direction, human action constitutes one of the two contrasting kinds of paradigm case in terms of which either contingent necessity or the absence of contingent necessity are and have to be explained and understood.

The thesis of the impossibility of laws of nature describing human action as such is, no doubt, bold. So it is prudent to indicate right away two things which it does not imply. First, it is entirely compatible with some sorts of prediction. What it rules out as self-contradictory are all statements of the form. 'It is contingently necessary that they act thus and thus, and contingently impossible for them to act otherwise.' It leaves still wide open the frequently realized possibility of saying, and of knowing that we are perfectly right in saying, that they will as a matter of fact act thus and thus; although, of course, in as much as they are indeed human agents they always could – in the most fundamental sense, shortly to be elucidated – do otherwise.

Second, the same bold thesis is equally compatible with some sorts of explanation. We now need to introduce a distinction between two radically different senses of the word 'cause'. The nub of matter can be briefly put. When we are talking about the causes of some purely physical event – an eclipse of the Sun, say – we employ the word 'cause' in a sense implying both contingent necessity and contingent impossibility. The same is precisely not true with the other sense of 'cause', the sense in which we speak of the causes of human actions. If, for instance, I give you good cause to celebrate I do not thereby make it inevitable that you will celebrate. To adapt a famous phrase from Leibniz, causes of this second sort may incline but do not necessitate. So it remains entirely up to you whether or not you choose to make whoopee. What my thesis rules out, again as simply self-contradictory, is any complete explanation, in terms of physical causes as defined a moment ago, of behaviour admitted to constitute a piece of human conduct. That still leaves wide open the possibility of doing what historians and others so usually and so correctly do do. They explain why people did what they did in terms of the actual desires, plans and purposes of those agents themselves.

(ii) In the first part of this final Section 3 I began by setting out my own thesis in contrast with Popper's less drastic attempt at a refutation of historicism, and then tried to remove misunderstandings of that thesis. In the remaining two parts I shall: first, distinguish what I have called the most fundamental sense of 'could do otherwise' from its more frequent everyday derivative; and, second, simultaneously both elucidate the former expression and demonstrate how exceedingly common are the occasions for its true and correct application.

Consider for a start one everyday antithesis; between, on the one hand, someone in the ordinary and philosophically untechnical sense acting of their own free will; and, on the other hand, someone in the correspondingly ordinary and psychologically untechnical sense (not performing a compulsive action but) acting under compulsion. Both the persons who act of their own free will and the persons who act under compulsion act; their behaviour is not to be categorized with the spasmodic and involuntary tics, jerks, quivers, tremblings, flutters and twitches which are conventionally but misleadingly labelled 'reflex actions' or 'compulsive actions'.

Suppose we say of someone who did in this most ordinary sense act under compulsion that, as things were, they had no choice; or that, considering all the circumstances, they could not have acted otherwise than they did. Then these common and easily charitable expressions need to be construed with caution. If they really did act, albeit under compulsion, then it cannot be true: either that they literally had no choice at all: or that, in the most fundamental sense, they could not have done otherwise.

The point, rather, is not that they had no alternatives at all, but that they had no tolerable alternatives. It is not that, in that most fundamental sense still to be explained and justified, they could not have done otherwise; but that, although of course they could, it was in every way unreasonable to expect that they either would or should. The case, for instance, of the recalcitrant businessman, receiving from the Godfather 'an offer which he cannot refuse', is vitally different from that of the errant mafioso who is without warning gunned down from behind. The former is an agent, however reluctant. But the latter, in that very moment of sudden death, ceases to be.

This whole batch of idioms really is quite extraordinarily confusing. We have no business to be surprised that so many even of the wise and good have been, and are, confused. For the clear implication of the previous two paragraphs is that, when we say in the ordinary every day sense that someone had no choice at all, or that they could not have done other than they did, then we are not saying that in the most fundamental sense they did not have any choice, or that they could not have done other than they did. On the contrary: we are presupposing that they did, and that they could.

Confronting the Diet of Worms Luther said: 'Here I stand. I can no other. So help me God'. With apologies both to Freud himself and to his official biographer, to interpret this magnificent manifesto of the Protestant conscience as evidence for a necessitarian determinism is to require that we read Luther as at the same time both explaining and excusing what appeared to be, yet was not, an act of defiance upon the memorably implausible grounds that he had been suddenly afflicted with a paralysis rendering him literally incapable of retreat.[14]

The truth is, indeed, quite the reverse. To offer any explanation of behaviour as conduct, is to presuppose that the agent, in that most fundamental sense yet to be elucidated and justified, could have done otherwise. Certainly we may be able, in the light of the evidence available to us, to conclude that those people could not have done otherwise: where this means that it would not have been reasonable to have expected – in the purely descriptive sense of 'expect' – that they would in fact do otherwise. Again, we may be able, in the light of that same evidence, to conclude that they could not have done otherwise: where this means that it would not have been either right or proper to have expected – in the prescriptive sense of 'expect' – that they should do otherwise. But none of this counts in the slightest against – because, on the contrary, it logically presupposes – the proposition that, in the most fundamental sense, the sense essential to the very idea of human agency and conduct, they could have done otherwise.

(iii) So what is this most fundamental sense, and what warrant can be offered for insisting that we are all of us in a position to know that people often could do otherwise: with all the weighty consequences which, if this is indeed true, have already been shown to follow? The best account which I can give begins in one of the great chapters of Locke's *Essay concerning Human Understanding*: Book II, Chapter 21 'Of Power'.

There, in Section 5, Locke writes:

> This at least I think evident, that we find in ourselves a *Power* to begin or forbear, continue or end several actions of our minds, and motions of our Bodies . . . This *Power* . . . thus to order the consideration of any *Idea*, or the forbearing to consider it: or to prefer the motion of any part of the body to its rest, and *vice versa* in any particular instance, is that which we call the *Will* (p. 236: italics and punctuation original.)

The explanation continues in Section 7, marred only by the fact that he sees himself as spelling out what is meant by 'a free agent' rather than, more correctly and more fundamentally, by 'an agent'. The three Latin words in this next quotation refer to St Vitus's dance:

> . . . everyone, I think, finds . . . a power to begin or forbear, continue or put an end to several actions in himself. . . We have instances enough, and often more than enough, in our own bodies. A Man's Heart beats, and the Blood circulates, which 'tis not in his Power . . . to stop: and therefore in respect ot these motions, where rest depends not on his choice . . . he is not a *freeAgent*. Convulsive Motions agitate his legs, so that though he wills it never so much, he cannot . . . stop their motion (as in that odd disease called *chorea Sancti Viti*), but he is perpetually dancing: he is . . . under as much Necessity of moving, as a Stone that falls or a Tennis-ball struck with a Racket (p. 237: the unfamiliar typographical conventions are again those of Locke's century).

Now, let us call all those bodily movements which can be either initiated or quashed-at-will movings, and those which cannot, motions. Obviously there are plenty of marginal cases. But so long as these also are, as there are, plenty – indeed far, far more – which fall unequivocally on one side or the other, then we have stubbornly to refuse to be prevented from making a distinction of enormous practical importance by any such diversionary reference to marginal cases.

If, having thus seized the high ground, we remain resolute to hold it, then we are positioned to see off any and every necessitarian counterattack. For, once 'action' has been ostensively defined in terms of movings, there remains no possibility whatsoever of denying that all of us often are agents; and that, when we are, we must be able to do other than we do. The most infatuated thereoticians can scarcely hope to bring themselves to deny that in truth some of everyone's bodily movements are movings rather than motions. This once given, however, there is no room for doubt but that with respect to these movings, and in the most fundamental sense ostensively defined precisely and only by reference to such movings, they can do other than they do do.

Nevertheless, let us not in this moment of triumph claim too much. What has, surely, been proved is that there neither are nor could be any universal laws of nature describing human action as such; and that it is, therefore, still more impossible to discover inexorable laws of historical development. Yet this is not to deny, and it would be wrong to deny, that there are any humanly imposed and maintained impossibilities in history. For it is certain that there actually are innumerable contingent necessities and contingent impossibilities constricting the ranges of options open to particular individuals and to particular groups of individuals. The point is that these do not apply to all the various agents concerned; and that the propositions describing them, therefore, do not possess the kind of universality required of a law of nature. The impossibilities are for us, or for them, for everyone now, or for everyone then; they are not impossibilities for anyone and everyone, individually or collectively, always and everywhere.

We now have, for instance, formidably good experiential reason to believe that a Leninist regime once established cannot be overthrown by any efforts of those who might become persuaded that they stood to gain from pluralism and liberty. Yet even this irreversible could, of course, be reversed if the beneficiary power elite so chose. No one but a fool or a Marxist will suggest that in fact they ever would. Yet collectively they could, as agents, choose to abolish the socialist state; or even actually to allow it, as predicted, to wither away!

NOTES

1. Perhaps I may quote, in the comparative privacy of a footnote, where we may conceal our blushes, a verse written in 1935 by a future British Poet Laureate:-

   Revolution, revolution,
   Is the one correct solution–
   We've found it and we know it's bound to win.
   Whatever's biting you, here's something will put life in you. . .

2. It should not go either unremarked or undeplored that, presumably in order to maintain standing with a Radical constituency, A.J.P. Taylor mars his generally excellent work in the now widely used Penguin edition with a scattering of such irresponsible asides as: 'Even the countries liberated by the Soviet armies did not become Communist until later, when they were forced into Communist rule by the needs of the Cold War' (p. 44). Certainly it took time to make these countries what they are now. But the work was already proceeding from the beginning of the occupations, and there is pretty good reason to believe that there was no time when Stalin intended the willing surrender of any territory once conquered by his armies, or anything but Communist rule for those occupied territories.

3. It is the same poet again:-

   Yes, why do we all, seeing a Communist, feel small?
   There fall
   From him shadows of what he is building. . .
   It is the future walking to meet us all.

4. The most concrete statement, I think, anywhere in the *Collected Works* is in *The German Ideology*. In *Utopia and Revolution* Melvin Lasky, mischievously describes this as 'caricature of Leonardo da Vinci in a summer holiday camp' (p. 46). The oft-quoted passage runs: '. . . nobody has one exclusive sphere of activity but each can become accomplished in any branch he wishes . . . thus it is possible for me to do one thing today and another tomorrow, to hunt in the morning, fish in the afternoon, rear cattle in the evening, criticize after dinner, just as I have a mind to, without ever becoming a hunter, fisherman, shepherd, or critic' (quoted pp. 44–5).

5. Max Eastman in his illuminating *Marxism: Is it Science?* (Allen and Unwin: London, 1941) quotes the Father of Russian Marxism G.V. Plekhanov: 'A disciple of Hegel, remaining true to the method of his teacher, could become a socialist only in case a scientific investigation of the contemporary economic structure brought him to the conclusion that its inner lawful development leads to the birth of the socialist order' (p. 65: Eastman gives as the reference, '*From Idealism to Materialism II*)'.

6. I owe this quotation to Robert Wesson's valuable book *Why Marxism?* (Temple Smith: London, 1975). Wesson refers us only to 'Tibor

Szamuely 'The Birth of Russian Marxism', p. 69' with no further indication of where this work is to be found.

7. If, charitably, we construe this as an unhappy formulation of the immiseration thesis, then we must not neglect to notice, both that that thesis was shown to be quite untrue well within the lifetime of its authors, and that it was always and obviously inconsistent with the assertion – a scant four pages later – that 'The average price of wage labour is the minimum wage, i.e., that quantum of the means of subsistence which is absolutely requisite to keep the labourer in bare existence as a labourer' (p. 97).

Bertram Wolfe has pointed out that Marx was determined to find in capitalism a relentless tendency to impoverish the wage-labourer, and was not above suppressing recalcitrant falsifying facts. In the first edition of *Capital* various statistics are brought down to 1865 or 1866, but those for the movement of wages stop at 1850. In the second edition all the other statistics are brought right up to date, but those on wage movements still stop at 1850. See Wolfe's *Marxism: One Hundred Years in the Life of a Doctrine*. (Chapman and Hall: London, 1967), p. 323.

8. Compare and contrast Chapter 2 of my *Sociology, Equality and Education* (Macmillan, and Barnes and Noble: London, and New York, 1976).
9. Kolakowski's treatise begins perfectly: 'Karl Marx was a German philosopher' (Vol. I, p. 1).
10. See F. Darwin and A.C. Seward (eds.) *More Letters of Charles Darwin* (Murray: London, 1903), Vol, I, p. 114n.
11. See Chapters 1–3 of my *A Rational Animal* (Clarendon: Oxford, 1978), and compare my edition of *Malthus: An Essay on The Principle of Population* (Penguin Books: Harmondsworth and Baltimore, 1970).
12. See, for example, the semi-historicist E.H. Carr in his George Macaulay Trevelyan lectures upon the nature and implications of the historian's trade; a series first published, and later Pelicanned, as *What is History* (London: Macmillan, 1961). I have criticized this work, and in particular the present suggestion, in Chapter 3 of *A Rational Animal*.
13. I have in fact conducted more thorough examinations elsewhere: in *A Rational Animal*, Chapter 3, of the candidates sponsored by Hempel: and of Popper's in 'Human Choice and Historical Inevitability', to be published in the *Proceedings of the Russellian Society* (Sydney).
14. See, again, *A Rational Animal*, where the relevant references to the works of Freud and Ernest Jones are given in Chapters 8–9. A determinism defined in terms of physical causes will be, of course, necessitarian. But to say that someone's conduct is determined by their desires, plans, and so forth is not to say that any of these make it contingently necessary that they act in one particular way: I may want to eat the kipper, but it does not follow that I shall: nor even that I shall try.

THE PHILOSOPHY OF MARXISM

A Dialogue between
LESZEK KOLAKOWSKI & BRYAN MAGEE

MAGEE I think we ought to start by making it absolutely clear what the central doctrines of Marxist Philosophy are.

KOLAKOWSKI As you know, that is a controversial question. People differ very much about what the meaning of this philosophy is, and indeed whether we are dealing with one philosophy or two. With that caveat, I would say that Marxist philosophy is a universal philosophy of history which is supposed to embrace both past and future (this last point is very important). It does not embrace epistemology or metaphysics as separate realms, because Marx believed that the human mind and human thinking are entirely immanent to the historical process. According to him there are no universal, supra-historical criteria of validity for human knowledge.

MAGEE He believed that whatever our knowledge of the world may be at any given time, the way we acquire it and the way we validate it are historically conditioned?

KOLAKOWSKI Yes. Nevertheless, his approach was eschatological, in that it was about the ultimate destiny of mankind. He was dealing with the question of how the human race can be reconciled with itself and with the world it lives in – why there are conflicts, why individual interests and social interests diverge so much, why people don't feel at home in the world they live in. This was a Hegelian question to be sure: but Marx did not try to answer it in a Hegelian fashion. By this I mean that he didn't try to write from the perspective of spirit reaching ultimate conciliation with itself, seeing the world as its own product. He tried instead to understand how human conflicts, sufferings, lack of understanding, are rooted in the material conditions of life, specifically in the way the human race has to struggle for survival. The whole history of human development, or rather of human conflict, is summed up in the word 'alienation'. This refers to the way people create, or at least set in motion, forces which then escape from human control and acquire the appearance of external powers ruling people from outside. According to Marx, the characters in religious mythologies, which appear to people as foreign powers, are not the source of this aberration but rather the secondary product. The real source is alienation of labour – the process whereby the products of human labour take on, so to say, a life of their own, and people are no longer able to control them. It began when the exchange of commodities began, and the market was formed. All political and state institutions are seen by Marx as secondary products of the same alienation, the same estrangement. He believed, however, that alienation is not some kind of mistake which could have been avoided. On the contrary, it resulted inevitably from the division of labour, which is responsible not only for our human sufferings, splits and struggles, but also for all the technological and intellectual achievements of mankind.

MAGEE – because it made specialization possible, not only in matters of material production, but also in the arts and sciences, philosophy, religion, government, the professions – everything.

KOLAKOWSKI Everything. Division of labour was, so to say, the *felix culpa* of mankind, the original sin which produced at one and the same time all the good and all the evil. Even so, he was concerned with the prospect of alienation being abolished. He was convinced that it cannot be abolished by thinking about it. On the contrary, human thought – as the doctrine now known as historical materialism has it – is overwhelmingly under the sway of the human relations imposed by the needs of production. He even put it this way: human thought, religion, philosophy, law and institutions have no history of their own. Their 'history' is only the history of the relations of production: which means the social relations within which people produce and exchange commodities – are largely dependent on the level of technology.

MAGEE How did Marx propose that this alienation should be ended?

KOLAKOWSKI He didn't see it as being a question of what he or anyone else *proposed*. He believed he had discovered historical laws which would lead inevitably to the abolition of alienation. He did not think the mere intellectual process of understanding our human enslavement by man-made yet quasi-independent forces would of itself abolish the source and results of this alienation. Nevertheless, he regarded our understanding as a necessary condition. He believed there is one social class which has a historical calling, a historical vocation, to abolish alienation. That is the working class, which is itself reduced in Capitalist society to the status of a commodity, being bought and sold on the market just like any other commodity. Once this class realises its own condition, its own enslavement within society, it starts revolting against it. This class alone is able to start a revolutionary movement which will result in the abolition of private property – and consequently the abolition of alienation.

MAGEE Why did Marx want to see the abolition of alienation, if he regarded it as being as much a necessary accompaniment of all the good things in human development as of the bad?

KOLAKOWSKI He believed that human history has now reached the fortunate point at which progress does not need to be bought any more at the price which used to be paid for it. From the moment when the working class – which is a concentration of de-humanization, as he put it –

appeared on the historical stage, a society was achievable which is basically harmonious.

MAGEE But as you said a moment ago, he sees this development as not just attainable but inevitable.

KOLAKOWSKI It is inevitable, but in Marx's eyes that doesn't mean it's an anonymous process which can go on without human consciousness. He believed, on the contrary, that even if there are some historical laws which guarantee the success of Communism, these laws – by contrast to natural laws – operate only on condition that they are known.

MAGEE In short, conscious human beings are necessary agents in the operation of such laws?

KOLAKOWSKI Certainly. And the abolition of alienation, to Marx, means the same as Communism. He believed that Communism is the calling of mankind, and therefore that the whole of past history becomes intelligible only in terms of this final act of liberation.

MAGEE Didn't either he or Engels say that when Communism was achieved, the whole of human history up to that time would look like a kind of pre-history – that real human history would begin only with the dawn of Communism?

KOLAKOWSKI Yes, that's what he said: Communism will be not the end of history but the beginning of true history. What he meant, exactly, is difficult to say. But never mind. He believed that Communism, by abolishing alienation, would abolish the antagonism between individual and social interests, so that each individual would spontaneously and naturally identify himself with the community as a whole. Consequently – and this is an extremely important part of his Utopia – no mediating devices would be needed between the individual and mankind, which means no state, no laws, and so on. What will be left is only the individual, and mankind as a whole. In particular, we won't need such a thing as negative freedom any more. By negative freedom he meant freedom as defined by laws, because this implies that people should be free within the limitation of not doing harm to others – and that, of course, implies a conflict of interests. Once conflicts of interest are abolished, there is no need for what Marx called negative freedom.

MAGEE So he envisaged Communism as a state of total harmony, or at least conflictlessness?

KOLAKOWSKI Yes, but he believed that this was not something that could be established by peaceful propaganda, because obviously, in existing societies, class societies, there are very real conflicts of interest. As against the proletariat, which is in revolt against its situation, you have the bourgeoisie, determined to perpetuate that situation. Consequently, Communism can be established only by a violent proletarian revolution.

MAGEE You said earlier that Marx derived his philosophy in some degree from Hegel. What was the connection?

KOLAKOWSKI This again is a controversial question. There are various views, even extreme differences, on this problem. There are those who deny Hegelianism any importance in Marx, at least in the mature Marx. And there are those who assert the crucial importance of Hegelianism in the mature as well as the young Marx. I'm rather inclined to take the latter view. I think Hegelianism was of paramount importance in Marx's intellectual development – first of all in the eschatological orientation of Marxism. Marx believed in a sort of ultimate and final reconciliation of the subject and object of history, as Hegel had put it. In Marx's case he believed that human history would come to a stage at which the actual historical process and human thinking about the process would not be separate any more. This will be the final stage, the final reconciliation. Perhaps even more important is the idea that only the actual historical process itself is meaning-giving and value-producing, so that the historical process cannot be judged by universal or absolute moral criteria external to itself. There simply are no such criteria which could apply to history from outside. *Everything* is immanent to history. This too is a Hegelian idea.

MAGEE One striking feature of Marx's attitude to his own philosophy is his re-iterated insistence that it was scientific by contrast with other people's, which he usually describes as Utopian. What distinction is he making?

KOLAKOWSKI The expression 'scientific socialism' was taken by Marx from Proudhon, and its meaning was mostly polemical. Roughly, the idea was that socialist thinkers before him had mostly busied themselves with producing arbitrary notions of the perfect society. He abandoned this approach, and tried instead to see which of the real, actual trends in existing society could lead to the Communist transformation. Of course, his use of the word 'scientific' was not as we normally understand it today.

MAGEE The success of Marx's theories in capturing men's minds seems to me without parallel in the whole of history.

KOLAKOWSKI Except for religious movements.

MAGEE But the spread even of Christianity and Islam were nothing like as fast or as wide as the spread of Marxism. It took Christianity 400 years to spread over an area smaller than Europe – of course in different conditions, but nevertheless the appeal of Marxism has been itself a phenomenon. Why has it exerted this spell-binding attraction throughout the world?

KOLAKOWSKI I'm not sure if it is proper to speak in this context about the spread of Marxist *philosophy*. All over the world there are many conflicting variants of Marxism; many political movements incorporate a few shreds of Marxist ideology but have very often little to do with Marxism as it originally was. In fact – especially in the Third World – you find movements calling themselves Marxist, and being called so by the Press, for no other reason than that they get their weapons from the Soviet Union. That's what their Marxism consists in. Then we have peasant quasi-Marxism in China, for instance; or Marxism as an ideology of modernization for backward countries; or Marxism as a romantic vision of a society which would return to an Arcadia, which embodied a distrust or even thoroughgoing hatred of modern technology and science – an attitude completely alien, incidentally, to Marxism in its original version.

MAGEE Marxism has affected the thinking of all intelligent or educated people, has it not, at least in the West? We *all* look at the world differently because of Marx. What would you say are the respects in which he's influenced us?

KOLAKOWSKI I believe Marx has become an integral part of our intellectual culture less as a Utopian visionary than as the originator of what has come to be called 'historical materialism'. But we must be careful to make a distinction. If you think of historical materialism in a strict sense that implies that every detail of the historical process, including the whole cultural history of mankind, is entirely determined by the history of the relations of production, and that the relations of production are entirely determined by the technological level of development at any given moment – in such a rigorous sense, the theory is absurd. On the other hand, in a loose sense, it is trivial. The idea that you cannot understand the history of human institutions, and of political struggle, without taking into account the role of class conflicts, and of the technological level of society – is something which almost anybody is ready to accept. But it has become trivial only thanks to Marx.

MAGEE It is doing Marx a serious injustice to say that this contribution is trivial. To us now it seems incredible how everyone before him looked at history in a way which almost left economic factors out of account; but it is precisely because of Marx that their importance seems obvious to us now.

KOLAKOWSKI I would say that if it has become commonly accepted it was partly because Marx expressed his ideas in an absurdly extreme way. In this respect I would compare him to Freud, for instance. They were both people who expressed every idea in an extreme form, which is how they succeeded in calling our attention to important problems which otherwise would not have been noticed.

MAGEE They were great communicators as well as great thinkers.

KOLAKOWSKI Certainly. And that is why everybody is to a certain extent Marxist today.

MAGEE You, for much of your life, were a Marxist in the full-blooded sense, the totally committed sense, and now you're not. Why did you cease to be a Marxist? What do you think is wrong, basically, with Marxism?

KOLAKOWSKI There are many things which I have come to believe are wrong with Marxism. First of all, its claims to be a scientific theory are not valid at all – *it's not an empirical theory, not a theory which can be verified or falsified*. It is basically an ideology, including lesser ideologies within itself: for instance the theory of value, which is an ideological device without any empirical justification whatsoever. I believe also that Marx's and Marxists' pretentions to have knowledge of the entire scheme of things are completely unjustified. Lukacs in particular stressed how, according to the approach of Marx himself, we cannot understand the facts unless we can relate them to the entire scheme of things and this means we have to have knowledge of the entire scheme of things before we know the facts. And this, unfortunately, is exactly what Marxists think they do – and they act accordingly. I believe not only that Marxism is an ideology with unjustified claims to be scientific, but moreover, that it is both self-contradictory and dangerous to the values we ought most of all to uphold.

MAGEE What are your chief observations, then, on the relationship between this ideology and its practical application? There are, after all, two main schools of thought here. There are some who say that the reality of communism bears little or no relation to Marxist theory. And there are others who say, on the contrary, that communism as we have seen it in practice is what the theory was more or less bound to result in. Where do you stand on this question?

KOLAKOWSKI Well, it would be obviously absurd to think that there is a direct causal connection between Marxism and Gulag, or between Marxism and the totalitarianism of the Soviet system. However, I wouldn't at all say that the communist political system represents a degeneration of Marxism. Communism as we know it, both as a political reality and as an ideology, resulted from various historical circumstances, including special Russian conditions; but one of these circumstances was Marxist theory, which undoubtedly contributed to its establishment. Communist ideology – which means Leninism and Stalinism, roughly – is one of the legitimate interpretations of Marxist doctrine; crude and simplified but, even so, legitimate: not a travesty, but rather a simplified interpretation. Marx's vision of the perfect unity of mankind, and his mythology of the proletariat as the historically privileged class, were in part responsible for this development. He believed that people could not achieve freedom without achieving unity, and he believed that there was a technique for achieving the unity of mankind. He believed that with the expropriation of the bourgeoisie, conflicts of material interests would cease. *Why* they should cease he didn't explain. It's not at all obvious why, once we nationalize property, the same struggle for the distribution of surplus product should not continue.

MAGEE So long as there is a limitation on resources there is going, *in any kind of society*, to be conflict over how these resources are to be used.

KOLAKOWSKI As long as there is scarcity. And *scarcity is not an absolute concept*. Scarcity is related to needs. And needs expand. There is no limit to needs. Consequently, there is no imaginable society which could abolish scarcity, and therefore no imaginable society which could abolish the struggle over distribution. But I mean more than this. Marx really believed that once private property had been done away with, communism would have been basically established. That's what he said in the Communist Manifesto – that the whole theory of communism may be summed up in one single phrase: 'the abolition of private property'. If so, there is no reason why the Soviet Gulag should not be the model of a good communist society. Again, it was included in the Marxian concept of communism that the state would take over and centralize the entire economic machinery: if so, the communist police state is indeed the carrier of the greatest liberation in history. If you define the social class in such a way that to belong to a class depends on whether or not one has a legally established and legally inheritable right of ownership of some means of production, the Soviet state is a classless society, since all people are formally wage-earners, all the enormous privileges of the rulers and the glaring inequalities notwithstanding. Indeed, a concentration camp can be a good example of a classless society in Marxist terms so conceived. Marx believed that communist society would not need the concept of negative freedom because there would be no basis any more for conflicts of interest. Anything that appeared to be such a conflict would be just some remnant of the old society which could easily be suppressed. But negative freedom is just *freedom* – freedom in the sense of room which society, the social organization, the State, leaves at the disposal of individuals. Now if communist society does not need this freedom, the establishment of communism is compatible with its abolition. Briefly, Marxism is a fantastic belief that it is possible to institutionalize fraternity, to make it compulsory so that the sheer force of bureaucracy and police will make people brothers.

PART TWO

In Practice

FAILURE IN PRACTICE

Ronald Duncan

I did not contribute to *The God that Failed*. I should have done. In 1930 there were 3 million unemployed. Though never a Party member, I went to Brussels as one of the two communist delegates from the Cambridge University Fine Arts Society. A Bulgarian, Dimitrov, addressed the delegates; a week of meaningless babble. We lugged heavy packets of dialectical platitudes back to our hotel. There a fellow comrade, probably to indicate that all goods should be held in common, stole my emerald links: the only heirloom I had received from my father. The gesture affected me. Experience is more persuasive than argument.

Nevertheless, on my return to England I wrote the words for the Welsh miners to sing on their march to London. This was set to music by Alan Bush, a Party member. After that abortive jog to the metropolis there was a 'stay-in' strike in a coal mine in the Rhondda Valley. I went there with the intention of trying to persuade the miners at the bottom of the pit to be non-violent, perhaps facetiously believing that this would gain the sympathy of the owners of the mine and make a settlement more possible. I sent letters to them to this effect, and also had chewing tobacco and food lowered down.

That first night, I tried to lodge in a hotel in the Valley: it was full. I went to another; I went to six. They were all unable to take me in. I tried bed-and-breakfast establishments only to meet with closed doors. Consequently, I had no alternative but to sleep on the pavement in my clothes, beside a nightwatchman's brazier. Here I was woken by a policeman who accused me of vagrancy. He told me he would have to arrest me. I informed him that I had tried to get accommodation. He smiled knowingly and told me that the Communist Party had resented my intrusion and gone along to all hotels to make certain that I was not taken in. My present position on the pavement was the consequence. The policeman was not unsympathetic and advised me to catch the first train to London. He actually saw me on to it.

Not wholly disillusioned by these experiences, I wrote a pamphlet on non-violence in industrial disputes, a copy of which I sent to

Mahatma Gandhi. He asked me to live with him at his Ashram in Wardha; this experience I have described elsewhere.

But, on my return from India, I took the line that there were only two ways of looking at Marxism. One was to babble about it, as most of my colleagues were doing; the other was to see if it worked in practice. This I did by founding a Marxist community. I gave the land, the machinery and the stock, invited a dozen members to work the place on a communal basis, sharing equitably all profit over and above their subsistance. Various people chose to look after cows, some pigs, others machinery, etc. The experiment, which lasted several years, and which I have described in *The Journal of a Husbandman*, was a complete failure. It refuted *Das Kapital* empirically: cows' udders, half-milked; pigs, not fed; furrows, not sown; some members in bed when the revolution arrived, still in bed when the counter-revolution occurred. I observed that the only cultivation that came near peasant standards was on the small allotments allocated to married couples. They, too, were the only people who had sawn any firewood. After several years of enduring this squalor, the comrades sought social security in less arduous fashions. I was dumped with their refuse.

Even so, I again tried to read *Das Kapital*: I failed for the third time.

A few years later I decided to visit Russia and applied to the Soviet Embassy for a visa. They asked me which hotel I had booked in Moscow and demanded to see the receipt. I replied that I had been invited to stay at the British Embassy and it was not their custom to issue receipts. My visa was refused.

Nevertheless, I began to read Lenin. It occurred to me that there were many fundamental fallacies in dialectical materialism. For instance: if equality was a natural condition, then evolution itself could not have selected from that which was equal, either in seeds, monkeys or men. Secondly, I became conscious that if Lenin's thesis was that capitalism contained within it the germs of its own inevitable destruction it was, to say the least, a little unnecessary to take violent steps to destroy it. I decided to write a play on Lenin and became interested in his relationship with his mistress, Inessa, with whom he had lived *à trois* with his wife in Switzerland. I asked the cultural attaché of the Soviet Embassy for any information concerning this lady whose death had brought tears to Lenin's eyes. They refused to acknowledge that she had ever existed. This perversion of history did not please me, nor were my leftish views enhanced when I discovered that Lenin had been allowed by the

Germans to take a train across Germany during 1917 because he was, at that time, a full agent of the Wilhelmstrasse and was also in the pay of the Japanese General Staff.

I was not surprised to learn that Lenin's first act on becoming dictator was to hire the Tsar's chef, and later order a Rolls Royce from Hoopers. But I felt considerable sympathy for him when I learned that he had risen from his sick bed to write his final Testament in a vain attempt to prevent Stalin inheriting his position. Little wonder that my draft synopsis for this play was turned down by the National Theatre when the late Kenneth Tynan was dramaturge. The play was never written. That is to say not on paper, though the events in Prague and Afghanistan were curtains of their own. It was a pity that I was unable to quote Lenin's remark: 'democracy is a sledge to shove under the arse of the people. . .'

There is of course no necessity for me to look at the philosophical background to Marxism. Popper has torpedoed Hegel for all time. We are left with mere jelly-fish like Foot and Benn.

Popper rightly maintains that a hypothesis is not science unless it can be disproved; I believe that he might approve of my attempt to make an empirical response to communism when I started the community.

Nine years ago I did visit Moscow in transit to Delhi. Enough time to see that even the buffet had only three bars of chocolate in it, and they cost £1 each. This in a country that used to export food to Europe before the revolution. Only last year, I decided to visit Dr Armand Hammer, who has more than philosophic knowledge: he has experience. Let his statement speak for itself. As to the future, I believe Hegel was right only in one thing and that is: the state's first necessity is an enemy. The Soviets are proving that. It is my suspicion that our enemy is not wholly without, but that is something for Security, and not for me, to comment upon. But I am capable of looking at what I consider to be the most important aspect of dialectic materialism, that is *its complete misuse of language*. There can be no thought without words, no correct thought without the exact word. It is not necessary to wade through the whole of *Das Kapital*; all one needs to do, in my opinion, is to take any one paragraph:

> On the other hand a product, due to its use-form, may be wholly incapable of forming any element of productive capital, either as material of labour or as an instrument of labour. For instance any

> means of subsistence. Nevertheless, it is commodity-capital for its producer, is the carrier of the value of his fixed as well as circulating capital; and of the one or the other according to whether the capital employed in its production has to be replaced in whole or in part, has transferred its value to the product in whole or in part.

Here you will see the terms used are not defined, it is no more than an intellectual three-card trick. Shoddy verbosity: purpose, to cheat.

It is clear that we need a new dialectic, but that can only be found by artists of the calibre of Shostakovitch, or saints like Mahatma Gandhi, or Sakharov or Solzhenitsyn. Few; one cannot believe there are so few.

People tell me my apprehensions are misplaced and there will be no nuclear war. Their optimism makes me pessimistic. Has there been a case in history where a nation has been fully armed and not used its potential either for imperialistic motives, as we did ourselves, or because the nation thought it was encircled, as Germany did? The only hope is that the disillusion that Bukovsky, for one, describes in Russia, may come to the surface and disintegrate the system from within. Perhaps via Poland. After all, tyrannies have always been overthrown, though often by those that are worse. You cannot, surely, impose the kind of socialist serfdom that now obtains in Russia without there being a sudden and overwhelming resistance to it. The Marxists yatter and misuse the word freedom. What is freedom? Surely it is the choice to do that which may even be to one's own detriment. What is law? It is to prevent you from harming others. What is the state? It does not exist apart from the individuals that compose it. Individuality is all, conformity is rule by the lowest common denominator.

There is now little effective trace of Hitler or memory of Nazism. It is my hunch that fifty years from now there will be no remains of Marxism but a hideous grave of a poet manqué in Highgate.

A STUDY IN TRADE RELATIONS

ARMAND HAMMER

Interviewed by
RONALD DUNCAN

DR HAMMER: Mr Litvinov, Deputy Foreign Minister of the Soviet Union, in 1921 granted me a visa although they were not allowing any foreigners to go into Russia at that time, particularly Americans.

I had already been in business while I was a medical student at Columbia University. My father, who was a physician and had previously been a pharmacist, had met with some financial reversals. He had invested all his savings and earnings in a small pharmaceutical laboratory where he produced various preparations which he prescribed and marketed through drug-stores. However, the business was in bad shape as he had a dishonest partner. While I was studying medicine, my father came to see me. He said he had to buy out the partner and wanted me to take over the business as he was not well. So, I conducted the business activities during the day and studied at night. By the time I graduated from Columbia Medical School, the business was worth several million dollars! I guess I had a natural flair for business.

But, I still wanted to be a doctor, to follow in my father's footsteps. Consequently, I decided to sell the business to my employees and pursue my career in medicine, particularly research. I graduated from Columbia in June and, as my internship at Bellevue did not start until the following January, I used those six months to go to Russia to help them combat the typhus epidemic. I took a World War I surplus hospital field car with me.

When I arrived in Russia, my hospital was assigned to the Urals where I saw terrible scenes of hunger. The great famine of 1921 was in full swing and the refugees were fleeing from the Volga region. There was appalling suffering everywhere. People were dying and children were crying all night for a crust of bread. Unable to bear the devastating sights, I finally asked the local soviets, 'Why don't you buy grain from America?'

They replied, 'Because we are not recognised. We have a little gold but we are afraid it's going to be confiscated, and we have no way of organizing an agreement.'

I asked them how much grain they needed to feed the people until the next harvest. They said, 'A million bushels.'

Grain was then selling for $1.00 a bushel in the United States. At this price the farmers preferred to burn it rather than bring it to market. So, I agreed to buy a million bushels and ship it to the Russians on credit, and for every shipment of grain, the Russians would reload with products I could sell in America to repay the credit. The first contract was made in the Urals in the city of Ekaterinburg, which had been renamed Sverdlovsk. The wheat brought great rejoicing to the people of the Urals and the news came to the attention of Lenin, who sent for me to come to Moscow. That's how I met Lenin.

When I saw him, he said, 'We appreciate what you're doing. However, we don't need doctors. We need businessmen.' He continued, 'Communism isn't working. We have to change our economic policy. We are going to encourage foreigners to come here and take concessions. We are going to restore private trade.' The great New Economic Policy had just been introduced. Lenin suggested I be the first foreign concessionaire. I was captivated by his sincerity and his personality. He was the kind of leader in whom you could believe. I just felt I would be glad to throw in my lot with him and help. So I agreed.

He gave me two concessions: one for mining asbestos in the Urals, where I had seen a very rich asbestos mine, and the other for sharing in the monopoly of foreign trade – which was an outgrowth of my grain contract. I then returned to the United States to see Henry Ford senior. I convinced him to appoint me his agent in Russia for Ford cars, and Fordson tractors. I also became the representative in Russia for 37 other American companies. I exported from Russia in order to create funds for my imports – and for several years all the trade between Russia and the United States went through my hands.

Then, the Soviets wanted to set up their own trading company, Amtorg. They said if I would step aside and let them deal with Mr Ford directly, I could have any other manufacturing concession. I replied that I would like the concession to make lead pencils. They wondered why I chose pencils. I said, 'How are you going to teach people to read and write if you have no pencils?' They agreed and I went to Germany and learned how to make pencils. Then I brought a whole staff of German engineers to Russia with me. So, my pencil factory became the most profitable of all the businesses in which I had engaged in Russia. I had a virtual monopoly!

Finally, my friend Lenin died and I could not do business with Stalin. In 1930 I sold out all my interests in Russia and left.

I didn't return to Russia until 1961 – thirty-one years later – when President Kennedy asked me to visit Khrushchev to see if I could improve our trade relations with Russia. I was able to bring about a satisfactory relationship and Krushchev asked me to help them with their agriculture.

By that time, back home I was head of Occidental Petroleum Corporation, a big company with divisions in oil and gas, agrochemicals and fertilizers. So I organized a group to build ten huge fertilizer complexes in Russia. But then Krushchev lost his job!

Again, nothing happened to my relations with

Russia until Nixon went there in 1972 to a summit meeting with Brezhnev, and the Russians invited me to return and renew the project. I did so and signed an agreement forming an organization to import ammonia from Russia (ammonia is made from natural gas) and in exchange we would ship them phosphoric acid – a highly concentrated form called superphosphoric acid. This was a 20 billion dollar contract. For twenty years, there would be a billion dollars a year exchange – 500 million dollars on each side. We had just started this operation last year, when President Carter put an embargo on the shipment of phosphates. However, I went to see Brezhnev in February of this year and the Russians have not retaliated; they were still shipping their ammonia. So the contract is still in force and I hope that when the Russians get out of Afghanistan, the project will continue. And that, in a few words, is the story.

DUNCAN I understand that before the revolution in 1917, Russia was able to export wheat. Now that it is in desperate need to import wheat, would you say that indicates any kind of fallacy in the Marxist philosophy?

DR HAMMER No. The only fallacy I see in the whole Russian experiment is that I just think it doesn't work! They can do great things – and they have achieved a tremendous amount of these – if they put all their resources into one particular project, like building up a huge military power which they have done successfully. They are certainly a super-power in that sense. But when it comes to an even economy of growth, it just doesn't work because their weakness is that the people are not so altruistic that they're ready to sacrifice themselves for their neighbours.

I think the thing that is wrong with Marxism/socialism is not communism, because I don't believe there is any communism in Russia. You might call it Marxism, or socialism. But with the State controlling everything, there is a lack of incentive among the people. Perhaps a small number of Communist Party members or leaders retain a sense of purpose, but when you get down to the workers that make up the bulk of the population, they want to earn money to give them a good standard of living.

They want to have things to buy. When they go to the stores to buy things, there are lines waiting. Long lines. And when they get through the line, a sign goes up – sold out – nothing more. So, they are not very happy with that. There is no competition – as we have here.

In spite of all the faults of the capitalist system (and there are plenty), we have nevertheless built up a standard of living that's higher than any other. I think we have been able to give our people a lot of liberty – freedom of speech and freedom of religion – and freedom is very important. Establishing a police state to compel people to be good just does not work. You can't do it by outright force.

I have sympathy for the Russians and for what they are trying to do. I believe they are truly idealistic in the sense that they are trying to make a better world, but I don't think they will accomplish it the way they are going. Until recently, I felt they were going to try to do it by proving their ideology was better for the world. But, in using military force across the border of an unaligned country like Afghanistan, they made a great mistake. It has weakened Russia considerably in world opinion. I am hopeful that they will pull their troops out of Afghanistan. I further hope that we will be patient with them and not create a situation which could be very dangerous, because a cold war can easily become a hot war. We have to find a way to cool the situation. We don't buy their ideology and they don't buy ours; but I see no reason why we can't trade with Russia and have cultural exchanges with them so that the Russian people can see the way we live – see the freedom we enjoy and see our standard of living. I am optimistic that the situation is not such that it is impossible to improve it.

THE DARWIN OF SOCIOLOGY

COLIN WILSON

When Karl Marx left Trier at the age of seventeen, on his way to the University of Bonn, his notions about the future were hazy but delightful. His ambitions were enormous, although their direction was still undefined. On the whole, he was inclined to believe that he would become a poet – a great one, naturally – in the tradition of Goethe, Schiller and Heine.

Marx had every reason to be optimistic. His home background was comfortable and secure; his father was a successful lawyer, and they lived in one of the best houses in town. Karl, the eldest son, was expected to become a lawyer – a hurdle he intended to take when he came to it. He was secretly engaged to his next-door neighbour Jenny, daughter of Baron von Westphalen; and there is nothing like the love of a beautiful and aristocratic girl to engender self-confidence. He had a strong personality, a powerful intellect, and a natural gift for self-expression. Few men have started out in life with a better chance of success.

The success never came; on the personal level, Marx's life was a disaster. The disaster somehow transformed the poet of freedom, the successor of Goethe and Heine, into the creator of the surplus value theory, the man who claimed to have turned revolution into an exact science. The story of how this came about tells us more about the mind of Karl Marx than we can learn from the pages of *Das Kapital* and *Grundrisse*.

That year at the University of Bonn was untroubled by portents. Marx attended lectures on Greek and Roman mythology, on Homer, on law and on the history of art. He joined a poet's club, became president of a tavern club, and spent a day in gaol for being drunk and disorderly. (He was allowed visitors who brought bottles of wine and beer.) At the Poet's Club, there was more discussion about liberalism and socialism than about poetry. But this was part of his family tradition; his father was one of the leading liberals in Trier. And then – rather to his own surprise – Marx discovered that he enjoyed studying law. As a consequence, there now seemed to be no reason why he should not combine the careers of lawyer and poet, and settle down with Jenny in Trier. . .

At the University of Berlin – where he went next to study law – life suddenly became more strained and complex. Bonn, like Trier, had been an old-fashioned backwater; Berlin was an urban metropolis. The Rhinelander, with his provincial accent, felt like a nonentity. His reaction was to stop trifling and hurl himself into work. He not only worked; he composed three volumes of poetry and a fragment of a tragic drama modelled on *Faust*. These reveal that he was going through a period of spiritual turmoil and intellectual indigestion. He came close to nervous breakdown, moved out to the village of Stralau, and tried to think himself out of the morass of pessimism.

The crisis was due, oddly enough, to the philosophy of a man who had been dead half a dozen years – Georg Wilhelm Friedrich Hegel.

English readers – for many of whom Hegel is merely a name – find it difficult to grasp how this highly abstract and conservative thinker – the man who glorified the Prussian State – could have exercised such a powerful influence on the revolutionary and pragmatic Karl Marx. The answer is simple: that for anyone living in Berlin in the 1830s, Hegel was the most important and exciting thinker of the age. Like a mountain, his philosophy seemed to extend from the foothills of history and science to the misty heights of the Absolute Idea. He seemed, quite simply, the most comprehensive thinker who had ever lived. His most famous pronouncement is that the real is the rational and the rational the real. He believed that the spirit of man strives continually for freedom, and that human history is a record of this painful struggle. He was also regarded by most conservatives as revolutionary and highly dangerous. For as a rationalist he had scathing things to say about religion in general and Christianity in particular.

When Marx arrived at the Universtiy of Berlin – where Hegel had been a professor – the controversy was as bitter as ever. In 1835, one of Hegel's students, David Strauss, had published a life of Jesus in which some parts of the Gospels were treated as mythological – or as downright lies. This scandalised the Church; but it also enraged more extreme Hegelians, who felt that it paid far too much lip-service to the crude superstitions of Christianity. Bruno Bauer, a lecturer in theology, published a book denying that Jesus ever existed. The Gospels, he said, should be regarded as novels embodying the loftiest ideas of the age. . . The Prussian authorities were alarmed; ideas like this had precipitated the French Revolution. The Young Hegelians – the name given to Bauer's supporters – regarded themselves as philosophers rather than revolutionaries; but censorship and repression inflamed their sense of justice.

Marx was a down-to-earth young man who found Hegel's 'system' woolly and abstract. Like William Blake, he felt that 'I must create my own system or be enslaved by another man's', and set out to create his own form of pragmatic anti-Hegelianism. Inevitably, he went to the opposite extreme. Hegel was basically an optimist who believed that history revealed the expression of the spirit of freedom. Marx was inclined to pessimistic materialism; the soul, he declared in an epigram, is pure fantasy. There was an element of scepticism in him that drove him to despise human nature. Giving free rein to this savage pessimism, Marx found himself caught in his own net, dragged from literary despair into real nervous depression. He began a tragedy, modelled on *Faust*; but Goethe's Faust is an idealist, a seeker after truth who feels that human knowledge is a mockery; Marx's hero – Oulanem – expresses a despairing vision of human futility that comes closer to nihilism. Men are 'blind clockwork, made to be fools' calendars of time and space, having no purpose save to exist and be ruined. . .' Oulanem will 'smash the world to pieces with his curses' and then sink down to nothingness. Marx's biographer Robert Payne has pointed out that *Oulanem* is a *Faust* without a Faust; it only has a Mephistopheles, a man who feels that 'Everything that exists deserves to perish.'

Oulanem marked a genuine crisis in Marx's life; it was at this point that he came close to nervous breakdown and moved to Stralau, where he took long walks, wrote essays on philosophy, and immersed himself once more in Hegel. This time he emerged a convert. He had discovered that the Hegelian philosophy was less abstract than it looked. More than that: that it was a kind of blueprint for revolution. For Hegel believed that history is the story of man's slow march towards freedom. In the Orient, only one man was free: the king. In ancient Greece and Rome, the citizens were free but slavery was taken for granted. In modern times we have arrived at the notion of freedom for all, but it is still not a reality. But one day it will become so. . .

What enthralled Marx about Hegel was the rigid and scientific nature of the demonstration. Marx was an illiberal liberal, a humanist who disliked human beings. He believed firmly in freedom, not because he thought Man ought to be free, but because he felt *he* ought to be free. And he was not. His father had landed himself in trouble by making a harmless speech containing a few liberal platitudes. All around him in Berlin, Marx could see the attempts of the authorities to hold back the rising tide of freedom of thought. Marx, like Hegel, believed passionately in freedom of thought. Unlike Hegel, his thought tended to be negative and destructive. Neither was he willing, like Hegel, to concede that this Prussian State was the best possible compromise between individual freedom and the chaos of anarchy. Hegel had seen the Prussian State from above, as one of its favoured employees; Marx was seeing it from below.

So at the end of three weeks, during which he read Hegel day and night, Marx was drunk on the wine of freedom and reason. He found it all so intoxicating that he decided to abandon the study of law, and pin his hopes on becoming a lecturer in philosophy. Now his doubts were gone, the future once more looked rosy. He would continue the work begun by Voltaire and Hegel, and continue the struggle for the emergence of human freedom. And this was largely a matter of using his powerful intellect to pour good-natured scorn on the church, the king and the bourgeoisie. No occupation can be more delightful for a man with a gift for sarcasm.

This revolutionary optimism led him to take the first disastrous step towards exile and poverty. He and Bruno Bauer – now a close friend and admirer – wrote a pamphlet together which appeared to be an attack on the infidel Hegel by a pious Lutheran; in the tradition of Defoe's *Short Way with Dissenters*, the aim was to exaggerate the reactionary case until it looked ridiculous. Some reviewers were taken in by it. But, as usual, the authorities over-reacted. Bauer lost his job and had to move to Bonn; Marx's hopes of obtaining a lectureship in philosophy melted away. It was clear that the University of Berlin would not even grant him his doctorate.

Still, life remained pleasant. Marx was an immensely dominant man who needed to shine in a circle of admirers. In Berlin he had many; one idealistic revolutionary, Moses Hess, declared him to be already – in his early twenties – the greatest philosopher alive. Other members of the revolutionary Doctorclub – of which Marx was unofficial secretary – were men of influence and wealth. Together they launched a newspaper, the *Rheinische Zeitung*, published in Cologne. At the age of twenty four, Marx became a leading contributor, then – for five months – the editor. It published attacks on censorship, the government, and various political abuses – such as an edict forbidding peasants to gather dead wood in the forest. After a year, it was suppressed. But Marx had had a taste of personal authority, and he loved it.

Marx's father had died of tuberculosis in 1838, and the family in Trier were now living in straitened means. Marx received only a small legacy and, when that was gone, continued to write home demanding more money from his mother and sisters; this was usually forthcoming. In June 1843, Marx married the faithful Jenny. Jenny's mother gave them the cash for their honeymoon; otherwise, they were penniless. Back in Jenny's home – in Kreuznach – after the honeymoon, Marx devoted himself to a long and violent essay on 'the Jewish question' in which the Jews – with their religious bigotry and materialistic outlook – are condemned as enemies of the human race.

He also wrote an essay in which he concluded that the vehicle of the future revolution would be 'the proletariat.' And after almost six months in this peaceful backwater, he decided it was time to move to the centre of revolutionary politics – Paris. For Jenny, at least, the road was now to be mostly downhill.

By now – when Marx was twenty five – the leading tenets of his 'philosophy' had emerged; they would remain basically unchanged for the rest of his life. It was based on a crude and violent atheism. (He had already coined the epigram 'Religion is the opium of the people'.) From Hegel he had taken the premise that the real is the rational and vice versa, and that reason is the ultimate expression of the spirit of history. Hegel had started with a scathing contempt for Christianity and religion in general; this had gradually given way to a recognition of the role of Christianity as a stage on the way to spiritual freedom; and in the last sections of the *Phenomenology of the Spirit*, where he speaks of religion as consciousness of Absolute Being, Hegel has moved close to a mystical evolutionism. Marx might have done so if his life had been more peaceful (although this is difficult to imagine); at all events, he never moved beyond this simplistic, negative atheism, in which religion is simply the expression of human delusions about the 'transcendental'.

His social philosophy is equally simplistic; its fundamental tenets are taken from his friend Moses Hess. Society is unjust because the capitalists and the bourgeoisie have cornered all the wealth. Not only that: they *exploit* the proletariat, forcing them to give their labour for mere subsistence wages. The 'ideal' answer would be for each worker to be given the full value of his labour, but this is not practical because all workers are, in effect, linked together. (Marx had no use for individuals; he loved to lump people together into abstractions like the State, capitalists, the proletariat – habits of thought derived from Hegel.) So the workers must revolt and take back their 'stolen' wealth. They have nothing to lose and everything to gain. All that 'extra' wealth that at present is syphoned off by the capitalists will now be given to the State and used for the good of the majority. It all looks and sounds marvellously simple.

The most noteworthy thing about the expression of these ideas, even in the early essays, is the attempt to make them sound *inevitable* and impersonal, as if he is writing mathematical formulae. Clearly, this is the major legacy from Hegel. Hegel 'demonstrated' that human history could be understood by Reason, and seen to be a mighty progress towards spiritual freedom. *This* is obviously the aspect of Hegel that converted Marx. He was overwhelmed by the scientific rigor of the demonstration, and dreamed of doing the same thing for the coming social revolution. He declared patronisingly that his aim was to 'stand Hegel back on his feet'.

Now in Denmark at about this time, Søren Kierkegaard was launching a bitter – if unnoticed – attack on Hegel, which concentrated on that same tendency to make vast generalisations, and to ignore the individual. But Kierkegaard was less than fair to Hegel. For Hegel himself was aware of how easy it is to talk nonsense by talking in terms of abstractions. And he had invented his own attempt to insure against this form of falsification; he called it the 'dialectical method'. Hegel agrees that philosophy needs to use abstractions like Man, History, space and time; he also agrees that anyone who thinks in terms of such abstractions will end by contradicting himself. For abstractions ignore delicate shades of meaning, and in the long run, the 'shades' may make all the difference to an argument. You could say – by way of a crude parallel – that geometry tells us how to work out the volume of a cube or a sphere, but it cannot tell us how to work out the precise volume of – say – a fat lady. You have to adopt the purely practical method of immersing her in water. And Hegel insists on continually checking all his useful abstractions against reality, and allowing them to develop and grow. It gives his philosophy a reassuring air of common sense. It also means that apparent contradictions keep getting resolved when seen from above, so to speak. This is the famous progression from thesis and antithesis to synthesis, which Marx turned into the cornerstone of his method. (In fact, Hegel uses the expression only once.)

Why was Marx so concerned to make his doctrine of revolution look scientific? It was a matter of temperament. He was a man who lacked patience with his fellow human beings. He also had little patience with fellow revolutionaries like Lasalle and Proudhon, who based their arguments on love of humanity; this struck Marx as sentimental trifling. In fact, Marx's revolutionism was based on rage and disgust, and he never ceased to talk with satisfaction about the day when blood would flow in the gutters and the bourgeoisie dangle from lamp posts. The more eggs that got broken, the better the omelette would be.

The rage and disgust were the outcome of frustration. Marx was a very highly dominant individual – one of the most dominant men of his century. Modern zoology had shown that all animal groups contain a 'dominant five per cent', the natural leaders; but among that dominant five per cent, there is a tiny percentage of *very* dominant individuals, the leaders of the leaders. Marx was one of these. He moved to Berlin at the age of eighteen as an unknown young man; within a couple of years he had become the natural leader of the Hegelian revolutionaries, including Bruno Bauer. Marx was the kind of man who needed power – and to say this is no criticism of such a dominant individual. Fate handed him lifelong obscurity. In the few small realms in which he could exercise power – the liberal Cologne newspaper, his revolutionary circle, his own family – he exercised it like Jupiter throwing thunderbolts. But as far as the world was concerned, he remained a nonentity. Even when he later became a correspondent for an American newspaper, he was just another European revolutionary, not *the* revolutionary he felt himself to be. Unlike Hegel, Marx was never sweetened by success. Because he was a frustrated man, Marx had no gentleness in him. A fellow revolutionary, Carl Schurz, wrote of him: 'I have never seen a man whose bearing was so provoking and intolerant. To no opinion which differed from his own did he accord the honour of even a condescending consideration. Everyone who contradicted him he treated with abject contempt; every argument that he did not like he treated with biting scorn. . .'

It is also important to realise that Marx spent most of his life convinced that the Revolution would happen tomorrow – or at least, the day after tomorrow. It took a very long time for him to become convinced that the workers were not at this moment on the point of rising up and slaughtering their exploiters. The French had overthrown their masters in 1789; now it was merely a matter of time before it happened again. And when that day came, Marx wanted to be sure that he would be the Robespierre or Marat. It was not that Marx consciously thirsted after power. He simply felt that he was the most dominant and intelligent individual he had ever encountered; that being so, he must inevitably become the leader of the Revolution. In Berlin, he was still uncertain about his future destiny; it might lie in literature. After all, Goethe achieved European fame at twenty five with *Young Werther*; Marx might do it with *Oulanem* or his poems. . . By the time Marx moved to Paris, he had abandoned the dream of being a poet. Now he placed all his hopes of fame on being the prophet of the coming Revolution.

For Jenny, Paris was the first taste of the insecurity to which she had committed herself. Marx talked to Heine and Bakunin – both, as usual, granted him instant equality – and attended the *salon* of the Countess Marie d'Agoult, Liszt's mistress; he edited a yearbook of revolutionary essays and poems and contributed to a German newspaper called *Forward*. He renewed acquaintance with Friedrich Engels, the son of a German manufacturer, and they planned a book denouncing Bruno Bauer – Marx now felt the young Hegelians were sentimentalists. He spent his days making contacts with exiled revolutionaries and his nights sitting in cafés. Jenny had her first baby, went to Germany to see her mother, and gave way to fits of depression about the uncertain future.

In due course, the king of Prussia protested to the king of France about suggestions in *Forward* that he ought to be assassinated. The king of France told the exiles that they either had to promise to give up political activity, or get out of France. Jenny sold her furniture to provide Marx with the coach fare to Belgium, and Marx left for Brussels, leaving Jenny behind with friends in Paris. She rejoined him a few weeks later, after a miserable and freezing journey; soon afterwards, she became pregnant again. When the summer came, Marx went off to Manchester with Engels, whose father owned textile mills there; then they went to London, where he encountered more exiled German revolutionaries – they called themselves the League of the Just. Marx was struck by the fact that the British seemed to have no objection to revolutionaries – at least, they were allowed to operate freely and openly, instead of being constantly shadowed by police and *agents provocateurs*, as in France and Belgium.

The more Marx saw of revolutionaries, the more he became convinced that he was the only man who knew anything about the subject. Most of them struck him as vague incompetents. They spent their days trying to rouse the working classes to a sense of injustice, all in the name of humanitarianism and freedom. This was pure waste of time. Marx had convinced himself that the Revolution was inevitable. He remained obsessed by the Hegelian vision of history as a gradual unfolding of human freedom. But Hegel believed this would come about through Reason, through ideas. Marx was convinced that ideas are merely the outcome of economic conditions. Mankind had progressed through the Asiatic, ancient, feudal and bourgeois ages, each dominated by its own modes of production. Now the industrial revolution had brought the age of revolution. Humanitarianism was irrelevant. This would happen anyway. . .

Which explains what seems otherwise self-destructive, almost suicidal, in Marx's conduct: his lifelong tendency to quarrel violently with other revolutionaries. Marx invented the Political Purge. The first happened in Brussels in 1846, when Marx's group invited a revolutionary named Wilhelm Weitling to a meeting, and Marx denounced him as a dangerous trifler. 'Nothing can be achieved without doctrine', Marx roared, and when Weitling accused him of being an armchair revolutionary, Marx lost his temper and stormed out. Weitling's friend Kriege was the next. Even the celebrated Proudhon, the man who had declared that property is theft, was denounced and consigned to perdition. Over the years, Marx quarrelled with just about every famous revolutionary of his time. (The only man he approved of was Blanqui, who was also in favour of making the gutters run with blood.) Marx was completely obsessed by his own dream: the dream of violence, of bloody revenge on the oppressors. It was necessary to his sanity. His 'Hegelian' demonstration of the inevitableness of revolution was his justification. The 'bleeding hearts' were nuisances. What the masses needed was not sympathy, but more oppression, to drive them to revolution. Oddly enough, Marx had less in common with Proudhon, Fourier, Saint-Simon, John Stuart Mill and the rest than with Napoleon and Bismarck. 'The philosophers have only interpreted the world', he declares in the *Theses on Feuerbach*, 'the point is to *change* it.' Marx never seems to have suspected that his 'Hegelian' demonstrations of the inevitableness of Revolution were unconscious justifications of his own obsessive need to be the Leader, the Moses armed with the Tables of the Law.

In 1846, Marx and Engels formed the Communist League in Brussels. In 1847, the League of the Just in London asked them to cooperate, and invited them to a conference. Marx quickly managed to persuade them to change their name to the Communist League. He expressed dislike of their motto: 'All men are brothers', declaring that he felt no brotherhood for most people; he suggested the alternative: 'Proletarians of the world, unite!' Asked to draw up a programme for the new League, Marx went back to Brussels and wrote the *Communist Manifesto*.

It was in this work that Marx first clearly formulated his new philosophy of history. The feudalism of the Middle Ages collapsed, and a new power arose – the bourgeoisie. Feudalism had been oppressive; but it had embodied religious and human virtues. The bourgeoisie were ruthless egoists whose only aim was money and power. So the feudal serfs became the exploited proletariat (a word coined by the Italian revolutionary Sismondi). But the exploiters had created their own executioners, since the workers were one day bound to recognise that they could destroy the exploiters . . . and after the Revolution, the bourgeoisie would simply be replaced by the State. The State would abolish private property, rights of inheritance, and the family. All men would be obliged to work for a living. And since an industrial society can create far more wealth than it needs, the surplus would go to the State, to be used for the benefit of all. This was the Marxian Utopia, designed to replace the wicked, selfish world of the bourgeoisie. To anyone who might feel doubts about all this obligatory 'freedom', Marx might have replied with a passage from an earlier manifesto, written for the London conference. 'Communists are not out to destroy personal liberty. They do not intend to turn the world into one huge barrack or gigantic workhouse. . . In no social order will personal freedom be so assured as in a society based on communal ownership.'* But Marx was not really interested in what happened after the Revolution; his dreams were of burning palaces and vengeful proletarians steeping their hands in the blood of the oppressors.

The cause of the revolution, Marx predicted, would be economic:

* These words were probably written by Engels.

a slump that would cause the workers to rebel. In 1846, it began to look as if his dream was about to be realised. There was famine all over Europe, and a consequent depression in trade, with widespread unemployment. But Marx might have drawn a lesson from what happened during the Irish potato famine of 1845–46; the peasants died by their thousands; a few grain shipments were robbed and a few workhouses stormed, but there was no revolution. By the summer of 1847, the slump was causing starvation all over Europe. Everyone agreed that the basic trouble lay in the greed of the bourgeoisie. (For example, French wine was usually so adulterated that it was practically impossible to export it.) A quarrel between Catholics and Protestants in Switzerland sent the wind of revolution across Europe. In 1848, the Italians revolted against their various princes, kings and grand dukes. In France, the king was forced to abdicate and flee to London. Vienna revolted against Metternich. In Dresden, Wagner fought on the barricades. And in Belgium, the government decided that it had tolerated Karl Marx for long enough. He had to go. Jenny was arrested and spent a night in jail with prostitutes. Marx fled to Paris, then to Germany. He had just received a legacy of six thousand francs from his father's estate; convinced that the Revolution had at last arrived, he gave most of it to the Belgian workers to buy arms. In Cologne, he used the remainder of his legacy to launch another revolutionary newspaper, and made it an effective instrument of propaganda. But the revolutionaries quarrelled amongst themselves, and a new Assembly debated philosophical issues instead of seizing its chances. The king of Prussia sent in troops and refused to become a constitutional monarch. Slowly, the tide of revolution subsided. Marx was put on trial for treason, but argued that he had only been supporting the rights of the National Assembly against the monarch; the jury was convinced and acquitted him. But he was ordered out of Germany. He returned to Paris, was ordered to go and live on the coast of Brittany, and decided to move to London. And there, suddenly, he found himself in a country where Revolution was only a distant dream.

Marx arrived in London in the summer of 1849. He died there thirty four years later, still poor and unknown. During those early years, he and his family came close to starvation – largely because Marx had no intention of looking for employment. They were evicted on to the street from their lodging in Chelsea, and the youngest of their children collapsed and died as he was playing in front of them. Two more would die later. They moved into small, cheap rooms in Soho, and lived there for six years. Jenny's darkest hour came when she discovered that her husband was the father of the baby about to be born by their maidservant, Helene Demuth. But Jenny was as impractical as her husband, and Helene Demuth kept the household together; so there was no question of dismissing her. Marx was terrified that the news of the illegitimate birth would reach the comrades in Europe and undermine his authority; he wrote indignantly to one friend about 'the unspeakable infamies which my enemies are spreading about me' and flatly denied them. Later, he fostered the rumour that Engels was the father of the child. This was plausible: Engels was having a liaison with a working class girl – typically, Marx and Jenny declined to know her – and was far less concerned about his personal image than Marx.

The remainder of Marx's life need not concern us in detail. During his first fifteen years in London he remained in relative isolation, working in the British Museum, contributing articles to Horace Greeley's *New York Tribune*, quarreling with other revolutionaries. In 1864 he became active in the first International Working Men's Association, and, with his usual manic diligence, set about trying to take it over and get rid of 'enemies'. He laboured at *Das Kapital*, convinced it would finally make him rich. (Engels was getting tired of paying Marx's debts.) Volume One appeared in 1867, and was ignored. The Paris Commune of 1870 aroused his hopes that the Revolution had at last arrived. Marx wrote a pamphlet about it that brought him some measure of fame. But there were more bitter disagreements within the International, with a violent left – under Bakunin – preaching bloody revolution while a working class right preferred trade union activity and 'gradualism'. As usual, Marx won in the end – at the cost of destroying the International. It was a small price to pay for someone determined to crush all opposition. But Marx again went into isolation; during the last decade of his life, he suffered a great deal from depression. It had finally dawned on him that the Revolution would not arrive in his own lifetime. He was shattered by the death of Jenny in 1881, and by that of his eldest daughter in 1883; he died of an abscess of the lung in March, 1883. *Das Kapital* was still uncompleted; the remaining two volumes, edited by Engels, appeared after his death.

Perhaps the oddest thing about this immense 'bible of economics' is that even its admirers are willing to admit that its central arguments are probably fallacious. Bernard Shaw – who read it in

French in the British Museum Reading Room – said that he was excited by it because it was a 'Jeremiad against the bourgeoisie', but as a socialist, he was fundamentally opposed to Marxian doctrines, and preferred the economist Jevons. Edmund Wilson, another socialist, whose *To the Finland Station* might be subtitled 'In Praise of Marx', talks quite cheerfully about 'a central fallacy of Marxism. . .'

The central fallacy, quite simply, is the concept of 'surplus value', upon which Marx bases his whole demonstration of the downfall of capitalism. The value of a 'good' (economists insist on using this grotesque word as the singular of 'goods') is dependent on the labour that has gone into it. This labour is measured in hours. A capitalist gets his profit by forcing the labourer to work more hours than he pays him for. The labourer needs, let us say, the 'value' of six hours of labour to keep himself and his family alive for one day. The capitalist makes him work ten hours, and pockets the 'value' of the extra four hours. This is 'surplus value'.

However, says Marx, a modern factory needs something else beside labour to operate. It needs raw materials and machines. And these, according to Marx, cannot produce a profit – or surplus value. If, let us say, a capitalist buys sheets of leather to turn into shoes, it is the labourer's effort that turns the leather into shoes, and which constitute its surplus value.

At which point, of course, anyone with an atom of common sense is going to ask: 'Why?' If I happen to be a shoemaker, and I buy sheets of leather, there is nothing to prevent me, let us say, from expending a very small amount of labour in slicing it into leather bootlaces, and making a 500% profit.

The same applies to machinery. According to Marx, you cannot get 'surplus value' out of a machine because you cannot exploit it as you can a man. And if an employer can get a thousand pounds worth of use out of a machine, then the manufacturer will do his best to charge a thousand pounds for it. . .

Again, this is clearly nonsense. A machine *is* a device for producing surplus value, by exploiting the laws of nature. The 'value' of most machines is far greater than that of the material and labour that has gone into them. Anyone who remembers the scene in *Three Men in a Boat* in which they try to open a tin of pineapple without a tin opener will grasp the enormous value of a simple machine. If a shopkeeper tried to exploit this value by charging ten pounds for a tin opener, his customers would tell him what he could do with it.

Marx's 'demonstration' of the downfall of capitalism depends on this assertion that only human beings can produce surplus value (or profit.) As machines replace human beings, employers will find their profits dwindling. One capitalist will gobble up another, but the profits will go on dwindling until the whole system collapses. . . 'The expropriators will be expropriated'. But if the notion that a machine cannot produce surplus value is false, then the whole argument collapses.

What it means, quite simply, is that *Das Kapital* cannot be regarded as a useful contribution to the literature of socialism or communism. Its justification – Marx's personal justification – is that it supplants all the old humanitarian works about social justice, sweeping aside their emotional appeal as irrelevant, and replaces them with a scientific demonstration of the 'inevitability of communism'. Why is it inevitable? Because the capitalists are their own enemies as well as those of the working class. And the bloody struggle for profit is bound to end in the destruction of the profiteers by those they have made miserable. . .

Expressed in this way, the demonstration looks convincing. That is, provided we accept a number of assumptions that Marx regards as fundamental. The first is that in a 'fair' society, the worker would receive the full value of his labour. Engels – left with the task of defending Marx – even went so far as to argue that in simple, primitive societies, profiteering is unknown. 'The people of that time were certainly clever enough – both the cattle breeders and their customers – not to give away the labour-time expended by them without an equivalent in barter.' Second, we must accept that history passes through a number of inevitable periods, and that the epoch of the Worker's State is the only possible successor to the age of bourgeois capitalism. History since Marx has shown that this is quite simply untrue. In most industrial societies, the spread of technology has not led to bloody Revolution and the expropriation of the expropriators, but to the gradual transformation of the workers into members of the bourgeoisie. Russia was not a highly industrialised nation at the time of the Revolution; neither was China or Cuba, nor any of the other countries in which a revolution has occurred spontaneously. (It is necessary to distinguish such countries from nations like Hungary, Czechoslovakia or Poland, where communism has been imposed by Russian domination.)

Once this has been said, it can be seen that the fundamental objection to Marx is to his completely unreal view of human history and human nature. There never *was* a period when 'simple people' were uninterested in making a profit. This is not because human beings are wicked, but because they are driven by an urge to solve problems and to improve their condition. It is, in short, an evolutionary urge.

Marx omits this urge from his picture of society and labour. According to Marx, this is basically a mechanical affair. A man puts so much labour and skill into a product – say, making a table – and the product acquires a certain value. Take *all* the products of everybody in society, and we have the total labour-value, which ought to be ploughed back into that society. Instead, says Marx, wicked parasites called capitalists have managed to insert themselves into the process, and steal a large proportion of this value. They play no more real part in the process than a thief who picks your pocket or a sex maniac who commits rape. Such a view amounts simply to a lie. Once again, it ignores the essentially *creative* aspect of human activity. A painter who paints a great picture, a musician who writes a great symphony, has not expended more *labour* than any builder who puts up a bungalow; the symphony or picture is worth more than a bungalow because the creator has added an imponderable element that Hegel might have called 'spirit', but which a modern psychologist would probably describe as the urge to self-fulfillment or self-actualisation. A good businessman brings this same element of creative originality to his dealings, and in doing so, produces more 'surplus value' than any number of conscientious carpenters making tables and chairs. Such 'creative' labour makes a society prosperous in the same way that worms add to the fertility of a field. A purely 'Marxian' society would be an inert mass in which nothing would grow.

The point is easy to grasp if we imagine two neighbouring societies, one of which contains only good communists, perhaps because the 'entrepreneurs' have all deserted, and one of which has the benefit of a double-portion of these 'exploiters.' The Marxist society would continue to produce surplus value through the manufacture of various products. But there can be no doubt that its neighbour would get the best of the bargain, and that its economy would expand as a consequence, simply because a number of 'men of enterprise' are contributing that imponderable element of self-actualisation. In fact, we can see plenty of practical examples of this situation. In Russia, Stalin firmly suppressed all writers with a tendency to think for themselves; the result is that modern Soviet literature still has a dull and homogenised quality. It is the countries who have accepted exiles like Solzhenytsyn and Anatoly who have received the benefit. The State-regulated economies of most Soviet bloc countries remains oddly sluggish, in spite of 'five year plans'. A novel like Dudintsev's *Not by Bread Alone* shows why: in a State-regulated economy, there are no natural channels for the expression of originality – even for the assimilation of a new idea for casting iron drainpipes. Significantly, Dudintsev himself has written no more major works; his development as a writer would depend upon further exploration of this notion of freedom of creativity, and this runs counter to the Soviet philosophy.

In his funeral oration for Marx, Engels called him 'the Darwin of sociology'. The comparison is more accurate than Engels realised. Darwin had apparently demonstrated that nature is a machine, and that evolution can be explained mechanically. In fact, Darwin never set out to demonstrate anything of the sort; he was concerned only to show that, where science was concerned, a full understanding of evolution could be achieved without the *need* for 'free will'. George Eliot's husband, G.H. Lewes, used the interesting phrase: 'the inevitable tendency of analysis to disregard whatever elements it provisionally sets aside'. Darwin *provisionally* set aside the notion of free will (or creativity). His disciple T.H. Huxley firmly discarded it and produced an 'automaton theory' of living beings. In the second half of the 20th century, biologists are beginning to discover that the automaton theory is inadequate, and are struggling to recover some of those elements that Darwin 'provisionally set aside' and Huxley threw into the waste paper basket.

Marx went further than Darwin: where revolutionary theory was concerned, he was prepared to scrap free will from the beginning. In fact, it was essential for him to scrap it to make his 'demonstration' of the collapse of capitalism come out right. He insisted, unconvincingly, that there would be plenty of room for freedom and creativity after the Revolution. In fact, the State would finally wither away, and a kindly anarchism would prevail, in which transformed human beings would live in permanent peace with their neighbours. Until 1870, Marx continued to believe that this revolution would occur within his own lifetime. He died exhausted and disappointed; but Engels carried on his work, and *Capital* became – as Marx had hoped – the 'bible of the working class'. In due course it inspired Lenin to seize control of the Russian revolution (which had been caused by the incompetence of the old aristocracy rather than by the wickedness of the exploiters). The Marxian principle of a State-regulated economy was immediately put into effect – and within a decade, it was clear that all Marx's predictions were wrong. It was *not* a formula for freedom and prosperity and happiness. The oppressors were as oppressive as before, but they now claimed to exercise control in the name of the People. And the economy slumped.

Where had Marx gone wrong? Simply in leaving out of account that 'creative element', the 'dominant five per cent'. He claimed to be a realist, and poured contempt on the moralists; yet he made the mistake of passing an essentially moral judgement on history, and condemning the wicked oppressors as if they were a special criminal class. Engels inadvertently revealed the fallacy when he talked about the 'simple' stage of society when people had no desire for profit; he was exposing the utopian dream that lay at the root of Marxist philosophy. What happened, in fact, was that as soon as the oppressors were exiled and their lands appropriated, a new dominant five per cent, cruder and crueller than the old landowners, seized the power, and things remained much as they were before.

Arguments *ad hominem* are always dubious; yet in the case of Marx, they are almost unavoidable. Edmund Wilson admits:

> It is impossible to read *Das Kapital* in the light of Marx's life . . . without concluding that the emotional motivation . . . behind Marx's excoriation of the capitalists and his grim parading of the afflictions of the poor is at once his outraged conviction of the indignity and injustice of his own fate and his bad conscience at having inflicted that fate on others (i.e. his family.)

Marx was himself one of the most dominant members of the dominant five per cent. Associate after associate noted the demonic craving for power. When a naturally dominant man is continually frustrated, his natural flexibility vanishes in the face of his frustration; he is likely to become what Van Vogt calls a 'Right Man', a paranoid individual who will under no circumstances ever admit that he might be in the wrong. All the evidence indicates that Marx was a highly developed case of this obsession.

Under different circumstances, this dominant personality might have come to acknowledge that his real problem was to achieve the position that he felt appropriate to his dignity and brilliance – like Shaw's Undershaft, who declared: 'I was a dangerous man until I had my will: now I am a useful, beneficent, kindly person'. Since this particular kind of self-knowledge was denied to him, he remained a dangerous man, who transformed his 'outraged conviction of the indignity and injustice of his own fate' into a 'Jeremiad against the bourgeoisie'. But since he declined to recognise the importance of his own frustrated dominance in his sense of outrage, he also omitted it from his picture of society. This is why his social theory has proved unrealistic in practice, and why the communist countries are the worst possible advertisement for the Marxian philosophy of freedom.

The final paradox of Marxism can be seen if we consider the lesson of his life rather than the confused message of *Das Kapital*. For it is this: that when a highly dominant individual finds himself trapped in a repressive system he will devote all his energies to the overthrow of that system. In practice, communism has proved even more repressive and authoritarian than the democratic capitalism Marx hated so much. The conclusion is unavoidable. If his work predicts the downfall of capitalism, his life predicts the downfall of communism.

THE SOCIAL STATUS OF MARXISM

ALEXANDRE ZINOVIEV

In order to examine this question, it is first necessary to make the following distinctions:

(1) between science, religion and ideology;
(2) between the pretensions of Marxism and its actual achievements;
(3) between the role of Marxism as a possible solution to the problems of a bourgeois or other non-socialist society and Marxism as the ruling ideology of an existing socialist or communist society.

Furthermore, it is necessary to distinguish between the fundamental essence of Marxism and its subsequent adaptations.

For the purposes of this essay, I define a communist society as a socialist society of the type which arose in the Soviet Union, and which constitutes the classic model for all other countries following the same path.

Science, religion and ideology do not exist in isolation one from another, without reciprocal influence. Religious learning lays claim to the creation of a world picture and to the explanation of different natural and social phenomena. Both religion and science contain elements of ideology. But more recently anti-religious ideologies have come into existence; science has achieved extraordinary progress, providing increased knowledge of the world and of man himself; much religious learning has lost its former ideological role and has been pushed into the background of history. So it is now possible to distinguish fairly clearly between the social functions of these three phenomena.

The aim of science is to supply knowledge to society, to order its comprehension and use. Scientific concepts tend towards lucidity, certainty, simplicity. Scientific theories require verification; i.e. corroboration, or refutation. Religion deals with the phenomena of the soul, with the religious feelings of people, with belief. Ideology, as distinct from science, is constructed from indefinite, ambiguous expressions, open to varying interpretations. It is impossible to prove experimentally the assertions of an ideology and it is impossible to refute them – they are meaningless. Unlike religion, ideology demands no belief in its postulates, but merely formal recognition or acceptance of them. Religion is impossible without belief in that which it proclaims. Ideology can flourish amid complete lack of belief in its slogans and programmes. It is very important to make this distinction. This often seems bewildering; in the Soviet Union for example, nobody believes in the official ideology, and yet it prospers. How can this be? It is because people do not believe in the ideology, that they accept it. Belief is a condition of human psychology, of the soul. Whereas acceptance is only a particular form of social behaviour. When there is belief in an ideology, then historical confusion occurs, causing the ideology to assume the uncharacteristic functions of religion. When the attempt is made to prove or disprove the principles of an ideology by intellectual arguments, then it is confused with science. The aim of ideology is not the discovery of new truths about nature, society and man, but the organisation of social consciousness according to some predetermined social pattern.

Of course, ideological texts and speeches do have an effect on individuals. However, their main function is to influence the masses. Ideology is not intended to be understood – an impossible exercise, or simply not worth the trouble – but it must be accepted. And to achieve this a system of compulsion and punishment is set up. Some people choose to conform and thereby gain successful careers and have some happiness. For many, existence without the guidance of an ideology is generally impossible. At one time, for example, the Christian Church operated in such a manner. It combined within itself not only religious, but also ideological functions, and on occasions made use of the former in the interest of the latter.

Let us now turn to Marxism. Historically it emerged as a claim to the scientific understanding of everything in the world. It is generally known that Marx applied himself even to mathematics. Although he never managed to understand some of the questions, now grasped even by muddle-headed schoolchildren, nevertheless he left appropriately wise instructions for his descendants. It is now necessary to talk about Engels. He comprehended all forms of the movement of matter, from mechanical motion to thought. He explained the origin of the family, of private property, of government. Indeed, his pronouncements covered such a wide area that now it would be necessary for all the Academies of Science in the world to devote themselves to the correction of his mistakes and absurdities. Lenin also contrived to develop logic, not having the slightest idea about the contemporary state of logic, but finding out about it from a school textbook and from the wild ideas of Hegel.

Marxism now proclaims itself as a science, a higher science, a most scientific science. Specialists in Marxism study in the universities just like specialists in physics, chemistry, biology, mathematics. . . Often they study alongside science specialists, their difference only becoming apparent when, for example, one physicist begins to do research in the field of microphysics, and another writes books about the implications of the utterances of Lenin and Engels for the progress of physics; when one mathematician proves theorems, while another examines the pair plus and minus by analogy with the pair bourgeoisie and proletariat. Specialists in Marxism obtain learned degrees and titles; they are elected to Academies of Science, etc. And it is necessary to recognise that there are facets of Marxism which may be examined from a scientific point of view. However, in the main, Marxism – at least in the Soviet Union – long ago lost the characteristics of a science and turned into an ideology in the strictest possible meaning of the word. Perhaps, it now shows the very classic pattern of an ideology. Such is the irony of history. Until now Marxists have insisted on the fact that, thanks to Marxism, philosophy has for the first time become a science. On the contrary, Marxist philosophy has in fact moved away from science to the furthest possible distance, and become the nucleus of an ideology.

The striving of Marxism to look like a science is accounted for by a complex of causes both historical and sociological. Science had acquired such importance in society that to advance other than in the name of science was simply outmoded. It was even believed that paradise on earth could be brought about scientifically. Marxism came into existence through a struggle against religion and other forms of ideology by opposing them with its scientific view of everything taking place in the world.

But the main thing that determines the pseudo-scientific appearance of Marxist ideology in a developing communist society is its actual role in the functioning of this society: a role involving the means of government of the masses, the standardisation of their behaviour, the exploitation of the lowest strata of the population by the highest, etc. Marxism disguises itself as a science, making it easier to represent the established society and its leadership as superior and natural products of the objective laws of history, to explain any mercenary interest and misgovernment as brilliant scientific foresight, etc. During the first years of Soviet society, Marxism played a role similar to religion for the largest and most active sector of the population. There was belief in its postulates and slogans. It possessed the souls of those people. But gradually this belief disappeared, especially after the Second World War. So Marxist ideology had to make even greater efforts to be attractive, by pretending to be another sponsor of science. For in our time of scientific insanity it would be an inexcusable folly for a ruling state not to keep up with the times.

But apart from its scientific claims, Marxism also professes to represent the interest and aspirations of the oppressed and aggrieved classes of society – an expression of the age-old hopes of earthly paradise. But dreams and desires by their very nature have nothing in common with science. Social dreams are the essence of Utopia. The transformation then of Utopia into science is ruled out – contemporary science and the practical experience of mankind testify to this.

It is possible, by means of analysis, to show that Marxism, is not a science. Not one Marxist concept – literally not one! – follows the logical rules of scientific construction. Not one assertion of Marxism – setting aside empty platitudes – can be scientifically verified. For example, Lenin gives 'his own' illustrious 'definition' of matter as 'objective reality, given to us in sensations'. By this, he naively supposes that matter is a most general concept. But by the rules of the definition of concepts the expression 'objective reality' will be more general than matter; and the expressions 'objective reality' and 'given to us in sensations' from the point of view of the construction of concepts are more 'primary' than 'matter'. I have not yet mentioned the fact that the expression 'objective reality' is no clearer in meaning than 'matter'. But expressions of such a kind, profound in appearance and hollow in essence, give the impression of high science. Devising their own communist paradise on earth – and naturally calling their inventions scientific communism – the founders of Marxism and their followers disregard the most elementary demands of experimental science; the latter does not exist if its object does not exist. But if their 'scientific communism' is considered even as a scheme for a future society, then it is possible to detect ignorance of the very rudiments of a truly scientific approach. For example, they absolutely disregard the inevitable division of society into social groups with different living conditions, and a natural hierarchy. In consequence of which the well-known slogans 'to each according to his labour' and 'to each according to his needs' either become empty propaganda, if they are taken literally, or they are realised in a form diverging from their textual appearance: namely, the labour of the superior is evaluated higher than the labour of subordinates, and needs are determined subject to the social position of the individual.

The strongest evidence of the fact that Marxism is an ideology and not a science, is the contradiction between theoretical Marxism and its practical application. More than sixty years experience in the Soviet Union and the experience of many other communist countries has given absolutely undeniable evidence concerning the nature of these supposedly Marxist societies: a low living standard for the greater part of the population, enforced attachment to the place of residence and work, enormous differences in the standard of living between the higher and lower levels of the population, the repression of any different trends of thought, the absence of civic freedoms, the self-seeking, the bribery, the system of privilege, the mismanagement, the spectacular extravagance of the leadership, the militarization, etc., etc. And how does Marxism react to these facts? Soviet Marxism and Marxism in other communist countries simply do not acknowledge them, considering any mention of them as a slander. Western communists try to convince us they are building a communist society without these deficiencies, and are preserving the best features of democratic societies. It is hard to devise anything more absurd, especially from a scientific point of view. Scientific research of real – not fabricated or ideological – communism couuld with no special difficulty reveal that all these facts are not accidental. they are essentiall the inevitable results of the precise realisation of the positive ideals of Marxism. Although Marxism began its historical career with the intention of explaining scientifically the path of social progresss, it has in fact completely renounced the very scientific understanding of society, by which it assumed the role of the ruling state ideology.

I think that there is no need to discuss the conduct of Marxism in the capacity of ideological dictator in the past history of the Soviet Union. It is well known to everyone: the base actions, the forgeries, the crimes. . . If everything were described in detail, stripping away the ideological machinery of Marxism through the years of Soviet history, even the enemies of Marxism would not believe the truth of this picture. It is said that Marxists followed good intentions. As is well known, the road to hell is paved with good intentions. But in reality the members of this Marxist army of ideologists aimed only to satisfy their own egoistical needs. And this is not possible, according to the social laws of history. I mean normal social laws, and not that senseless Marxist twaddle about the laws of society, with which the leaders make fools of themselves to millions of ordinary people.

Marxism turned out to be a highly convenient form of ideology because it gave rise to a vast torrent of ideological texts, demagogic promises and slogans, resembling science, but not requiring any scentific training to produce. Anyone can soon learn to manufacture perfectly Marxist texts and speeches for any situation. It is precisely the ambiguity and formlessness of Marxist concepts that make them ideal for the ruling sections of society, for the interpretation of Marxism becomes the prerogative of the higher party leadership. And in this way the system is perpetuated.

WHAT IS LEFT OF MARXISM? OR THE BABY AND THE BATH WATER

A.L. ROWSE

The influence that Karl Marx has had on the twentieth century is simply astounding, or even fantastic when you consider that there were other thinkers who were as penetrating and as prescient as he was, or even more so, who have had not one tithe of his influence or none at all. De Tocqueville, who was at least as penetrating about society, has had very little; John Stuart Mill offers immeasurably more hope with his emphasis on freedom and the value of the individual, his hatred of the subjection of women and insistence on their equality with men – very relevant to the world of Islam today. Yet where is Mill's influence compared with Marx's? The world would be a much better place if it listened to John Stuart Mill instead of Marx.

Marx dismissed him contemptuously with the remark that his eminence was due to the flatness of the surrounding country. It is like his dismissal of 'Liberty, Equality, Fraternity', with 'Why don't they say what they really mean, "Infantry, Cavalry, Artillery"?' Or again his dismissal of the peasantry with 'the idiocy of rural life.' I prefer rural to urban life today, and I fear it must be admitted that, though Marx had genius, he was rather a nasty, envious German.

There remains the problem: why has he had such a prodigious influence? The answer is largely that – like Marks and Spencer, Ford or Morris – he was on an upward-moving escalator. The people at large, the working classes, were everywhere coming to the forefront of society, and their affairs, well-being, interests, claims, demands, etc. have become the main concern of politics all over the world. He made himself the most insistent and consistent, the most systematic and tireless, voice of all that, intellectually as analyst, dogmatically as prophet. I am not saying that he was right – we can all point to where he was wrong; but he was more relevant to what was coming about than anybody else. I think that that partly explains the extraordinary phenomenon.

There is a very useful vulgar cliché we must be careful not to empty out the baby with the bath-water. There may still be something in Marx's analysis of society that remains relevant to us, when much of the prophetic element has drained away, been falsified by events. As a historian I have found Marx's way of looking at history illuminating and fruitful – as Tawney (though a religious idealist) did; other people have had penetrating insights into the determining influence of economic factors, the distribution of property, the structure of classes and the conflicts of interest between them, the formative effect of those forces upon men's thinking, the forming of ideologies in accordance with them, etc. Some of this appears in the work of Harington, which attacted Tawney to write about him. We might say that much of it is already there, or implied, in Aristotle's *Politics*.

So I begin by making a distinction between the analytical side of Marx and the dogmatic, between the intellectual contribution Marx had to make and that of the prophet, the practical politician (though not very successful in his time), the prophet of social revolution. Actually, it is difficult to disentangle the two, they are so intertwined and dependent on each other in his case. Of course, he can be criticised and faulted on both sides, like any other thinker – Burke, for instance, whom I find much more congenial. Still, the social revolution has taken place, or is visibly taking place, all round us: Marx wasn't so far out there. Again that helps to explain the phenomenon.

We can all too easily be aware of the faults in his prognosis, the ways in which his forecasts and expectations have turned out to be wrong in detail. No social thinker should be so certain and dogmatic as to what is going to happen; a historian realises that things often turn out differently from what we expect. That is to say, especially the surface events of history; but it does not mean that one may not be able to tell the way the stream is going, the general direction. Here Marx was right enough, but he would have done well to be more sceptical, like Burke or de Tocqueville, Mill or Matthew Arnold, who also saw very well how things were going in their time.

Marx had the insight to see the dominating importance the working classes would come to have – so, as a matter of fact, more agreeably had Matthew Arnold.[1] But the two sides of Marx's mind were in conflict. The active revolutionary who had taken part in the movements of 1848 made him simplify the issue into a struggle between Bourgeoisie and Proletariat, meaning industrial workers.

This position, taken up for practical purposes, made him oversimplify the complexity of class relations and conflicts, and deformed his intellectual statement of the matter. In fact, he never completed his intended analysis of class; his dogmatism led him astray and all those of us who were influenced by Marxism intellectually.

As I very much was, in common with my generation. Perhaps a personal confession will make the point clear. When I wrote my *Politics and the Younger Generation* I expected, as a good Marxist, that – since the working classes were the majority of the nation – the day would come when they would realise their own interest and form the basis of a permanent Labour majority in Britain. So far my expectation has not been fulfilled: large sections of the working class vote Tory, and not a few middle class people vote Labour. But what about the future? I may merely have been premature.

Marx thought that capitalism – like other forms of social and economic organisation in history – would come to an end. He was ambiguous about whether it would end by revolution or evolution. Lenin was altogether more dogmatic a Marxist, and yet he ended his life very near to despair at the way things were going. 'Workers' Control' proved a complete failure, of course, like running an army from the ranks, an ideological illusion. 'War-time Communism' was strangling and starving the USSR. Lenin was forced to introduce the New Economic Policy with its gradualism – he contemplated ten years of it and called for piece-work wages and Taylorism, i.e. payment in accord with productivity. Communism has never been able to solve its economic problem: look at the USSR or Poland today. Or Czechoslovakia, which under capitalist democracy, was the most efficient and prosperous country in Central Europe; and now. . .! If this is what Lenin, the most dogmatic of Marxists, was forced to recognise, what had been so wrong with Fabian gradualism after all?

Trotsky too was reduced to something near despair. He wrote,

> It is absolutely self-evident that, if the international proletariat – as the result of the experience of our entire epoch and the current new war [1939–1945] – proves incapable of mastering society, this would signify the foundering of all hope for a socialist revolution, for it is impossible to expect any other more favourable conditions for it.

Of course they are incapable of mastering society, or even running anything constructively, as Trotsky knew in his heart of hearts, when he let fall the phrase, the 'congenital incapacity of the proletariat to become a ruling class.' QED. The revolutionary proletariat has been everywhere led by lower middle-class types, when it has not been led by an upper class one like Lenin. (Ernest Bevin was very exceptional: he was capable of leadership, a great man, but not a Marxist and certainly not a revolutionary.)

Trotsky, like Lenin, arrived at some very tentative conclusions at the end of his life – then to what point the certainty earlier, with all the concomittant suffering inflicted? He committed himself to the 'theory' of world revolution, and they all expected the Marxist revolution, following Marx, to take place in the most highly industrialised country, favourably Germany. The *real* revolution that took place there was Hitler's, who had a far better grasp of the psychology of the German masses than ever the respectable (in spite of an illegitimate child by a servant in the house) upper middle-class Marx. Hitler certainly knew what was what about the German people – as Mussolini knew about the Italians, and Stalin the Russians.

Marx's outlook, like Trotsky's, as a Jew's, was perhaps naturally cosmopolitan, internationalist, and omitted what has been and is the strongest political force in the world – nationalism, and one might add religious communalism, rather than communism. Look at India, Iran, the Middle East, North Africa, or even Northern Ireland. No wonder the hopes placed upon Marx's International vanished like smoke in 1914; or consider the cynical game Stalin played with the Third Communist International, subjugating it simply to Russian national interests. Not many ideological illusions in that quarter! Stalinism, with its murders of millions, including hundreds of thousands of believing Communists, of most of Lenin's colleagues, must have made Marx turn in his grave in Highgate cemetery. He can never have expected such barbarism, what Shostakovich calls 'the extermination machine.'

Marx put forward the blissful theory of – after the proletarian revolution – 'the withering away of the state.' Not much evidence of the withering away of the state in USSR or any country under the heel of communism; but instead a society hamstrung by bureaucratisation, retarded of free movement, piling up armaments and nuclear power. Power, the exertion of force – that is what is basic in history, and the post-Revolution history of Russia is continuous with its 19th century history and its interventions in Poland,

Hungary etc: 'the jack-boot of Europe.'

Except that Tsarism was more civilised. Exile to Siberia? When one reads the correspondence of Lenin, one sees that he was quite well-placed in exile there for getting on with his work, books, company, discussion, as if one might be rusticated for the winter in Maine or Alaska. The Tsar Nicholas I interposed personally to withdraw Tolstoy from front-line fighting, to safeguard the life of a promising writer. What a contrast with Stalin and the Marxist treatment of the arts and sciences – the deformation of science with the official patronage of the nonsense of Lysenko about genetics, Stalin's personal stopping of Shostakovich from creating any more operas after his 'Lady Macbeth of Mschensk' – we might have had a dozen. In music it is more possible to cover one's tracks than in literature or the other arts, but Shostakovich has told us that every one of his symphonies is a tombstone.

And communist architecture and painting, all under the blight of 'social realism', the constant criticism according to Party orthodoxy by third-rate bureaucrats – it all means the brutalisation of the arts. Imagine being told how to write one's books by the bus-conductor! Such lowering of standards is to be expected when the people come into their own – as one sees it everywhere in the history of the 20th century compared with the 19th, the appalling record of civilised Germany, for instance, the contrast of even the Kaiser's Germany with Hitler's. One observes the same brutalisation everywhere, with the decline of the upper classes and their more civilised standards, and with the people in power.

Marx can hardly not have seen that, with the spectacle of what happens when the people get on top, as in the course of the Revolutions of 1848 and the Paris Commune. With his revolutionary fixation he heartily approved; he cannot have cared much about the humane side of things, any more than Lenin did. I do not find much humanity in either: conservative sceptics – witness Burke or Shakespeare – are much more sensitive about cruelty in human affairs, and realise how thin the crust of civilisation is and, when it is broken through, what cruel dark waters are beneath. Letting loose the flood waters of revolution produces only far more suffering than what went before.

When people argue that communism in Russia has slightly advanced the standard of living of the masses in general, the answer is plain. With the development of modern technology standards of living are, and can be, improved immensely; they would have been much more so in Russia but for the dead weight of communism upon their economy: it doesn't work, and they cannot get it right without throwing communism over. (Oddly enough, it was Bukharin who held that decline in productivity always accompanied revolution. QED. The reason is obvious.)

Witness Poland, witness China. It is probable that the Chinese experience is more important in the long run than what happens anywhere else. The Chinese form almost a quarter of the human race, occupying the largest area of the earth under a stable civilisation for the longest stretch of time. It is of world importance that they seem to be turning their back on communism with the realisation that – after some achievements which could have been arrived at anyway, as in Russia – it does not work.

Enough of the actual situation and of current affairs: any journalist can see what is what about them.

What is left of Marxism intellectually? Nothing is left of all the philosophising, the inverted Hegelian dialectic with its

> principal laws of the transformation of quantity into quality and vice versa; the law of the interpenetration of opposites; the law of the negation of the negation.[2]

Thus Engels: what chaff all this is, Marx's *Kritik der Kritischen Kritik*, Engels' *Die Heilige Familie*, Lenin's *Dialectical Materialism and Empirio-Criticism*. It is all a game, like Lenin's favourite chess, useful only as mental exercise. There is no point in any of it, valueless like most philosophising, as even the philosophers themselves realise today, in the wake of the sainted Wittgenstein.

The most obvious lacuna in the Marxist *Weltanschauung* is in regard to psychology, and that renders its view of historical processes far too simple and rigid. Basically, Marx's is a rationalist psychology, the assumption being that people are rational and follow their interests when they recognise them. Historians and practical politicians know that that is not at all true. All through history we recognise people who act against their interests though they know quite clearly what they are. Often they do not know. Historians realise that men are capable of rationality, but for much of the time are quite irrational, act from all kind of emotional motives or none, from prejudice, vanity, stupidity, envy (odd that academics, so full of it, should not recognise its importance as a force in history!), psychotic motives, etc. Burke realised all this very well;

Marx, hag-ridden by Hegel and German philosophical idealism, hardly at all.

I have always named this defect in idealist thinkers 'the Rationalist fallacy.' It is possible to detect a certain *rationale* in history – the determining factors of geography offer a case in point; one does not need to be completely sceptical and see no patterns at all – as the disillusioned Liberal, H.A.L. Fisher, confesses in his *History of Europe* – but the processes of history are subtle, complex and winding, with many reactions and returns, differing rhythms and *tempi*. It falsifies history to impose a sociological strait-jacket upon it, contrary to its nature.

There goes along with this a middle-class idealisation of the masses, as with Rosa Luxemburg (she was right to condemn Lenin's terrorism), Lukácz, Gramsci, Nitwitz, and all. None of that idealistic nonsense with a real proletarian like Ernest Bevin, or – for that matter – with D.H. Lawrence or me: we *know*.

Interestingly enough, Marxism has a point in observing that ethical standards and moral conduct do vary to some extent from class to class. And some fruitful insights come from a Marxist approach to the arts, literature for example. We can all see that the literature of a given time is an expression of the society of that time, the character of its social order, with ideas, values, prejudices, limitations appropriate to it. This is reflected not only in the nature and content of the literature – dominant epic, drama or novel, chronicle or history – but also in the aesthetic form. Literary forms have their own internal evolution, but this again is influenced by, and even expresses or reflects, the external influences of society and social factors. These matters can be profitably followed up, as they were by that admirable historian of literature, Sir Leslie Stephen, in his *English Literature and Society in the Eighteenth Century*. On again with an encyclopaedic scholar in W.P. Ker, who well understood how indispensable it is to the understanding of literature to study it in terms of the society that produces it, cf. his *Form and Style in Poetry*.

So we see that something useful remains, provided that we use it empirically and undogmatically. We might conclude that there is often something in the analysis, which is then ruined by theorising and systematizing into dogma in the appalling manner of German philosophy (see Santayana's *Egotism and German Philosophy*, a most penetrating and salutary work, totally overlooked by the philosophers). Most economic historians, I fancy, would agree that much was valuable in Marx's description of the Industrial Revolution and his analysis of industrial processes and relations in the first volume of *Capital*. When he got on to theory, transcending the labour theory of value into his theory of surplus value – which involved assuming the whole character of a given society – he found it impossible to arrive at a satisfactory working theory, as conventional economists did within the assumptions and limitations they accepted. They accepted them as if true for all times and places, like the laws of mathematics. They are not, and orthodox economics seems to be in as much confusion as Marx left his economic theories in. He at least came to appreciate their historical relativism; that is why he could never clinch the theory, left it unfinished, and the last volume of *Capital* a history of what theories of value had been.

A historian would conclude then that to systematise what may be useful insights and erect them into philosophic structures is always mistaken, in the manner of German 19th century philosophy – a blind alley. I have always regarded its portentous influence as intellectually disastrous. For Germany it was an element in the actual disaster diagnosed by the historian, Friedrich Meinecke, in *Die Deutsche Katastrophe*. It is this German philosophising element that was the worst side of Marx intellectually and has led to such deformation in the Marxist tradition.

When I was young I used to subscribe to the periodical *Unter dem Banner des Marxismus*; beneath its stacks of paralytic abstractions one could recognise nothing of the real world at all. No wonder Hitler had little difficulty in putting his foot through such cardboard structures. A dose of Hume's scepticism, or of the English empiricism Marx so much despised, would have done him all the good in the world; but then he would not have been recognisably Marx, or done so much damage in it.

For myself, I have absorbed just so much of Marxism as was useful to the historian and, to a lesser extent, the understanding of class interests and their conflicts which occupy so much of the field of politics.

NOTES

[1] v. my *Matthew Arnold: Poet and Prophet*.

[2] q. David McLellan, *Marxism after Marx*, 12.

THE APPEAL OF MARXISM AND VILIFICATION OF THE BUSINESSMAN

A Psychological and Sociological Explanation

STANISLAV ANDRESKI

The supply of talent for business depends not only on the material rewards and opportunities but also on the esteem in which this field of activity is held. The obverse side of this esteem is the influence of the notions which cast the businessman into the role of an exploiter, who takes away the wealth from the real producers, rather than a benefactor who, by his initiative and ability, makes an indispensable contribution to the production of wealth. This view is the quintessence of Marxism. Therefore, if we can explain the roots of its appeal, we shall find a part of the answer to the question of why the spirit of enterprise has been flagging.

One does not need to be starry-eyed about businessmen to find their demonization puzzling at first sight. True, the profit motive lacks moral appeal, but one sees plenty of desire for money in other walks of life, including 'the caring professions'. Moreover, in contrast to many hypocritical politicians, academics or officials, the businessmen at least deserve the credit for not concealing their concern for material rewards. What is more important, despite its many serious shortcomings (which, in my opinion, call for very substantial reforms) the market economy with private enterprise is the only system which has supplied an abundance of goods and services to all sections of the populations in the countries where it has reached a high level of development. One only needs to look at the Berlin Wall to see how its benefits are appreciated by the subjects of Marxist governments. Since these facts are so obvious and can be verified at first hand by anyone who cares to take a trip to the borders of East Germany or Czechoslovakia, the influence of Marxism can only be explained along the lines which Marx and Engels have followed in their treatment of other ideologies: that is, by looking for the services which this doctrine renders to those who profess it.

Leaving aside the somewhat different situation in the poor undeveloped countries, we can take as our first cue the fact that in the industrialised countries there are very few blue collar workers who are interested in Marxism, while its devotees are found almost entirely in the class of diploma holders employed (or seeking to be employed) by the state or its subsidiaries: that is to say, people whose incomes come from the money, a large part of which is taken from the blue collar workers as tax.

It may appear very strange that anyone should seek a remedy for the ills of our civilisation in the books of an author who (though very talented, learned and creative) wrote them when railways were just being built, when there were no motor cars, let alone aeroplanes, no electric light, no telephones, no statistics; when trade unions and joint-stock companies, whose future importance he has not been able to guess, were just beginning to appear. To bring out how obscurantist is the parading of an antiquated doctrine as if it were the latest discovery, it is enough to ask: what did Marx say about the consequences of automation, television, medical prolongation of life, environmental pollution, the population explosion or atomic energy and weapons? We may be less surprised at this fixation if we bear in mind how difficult it is to eradicate superstition; that in this scientific age millions of people believe in fortune telling and in most ultramodern sky-scraper hotels there are neither floors nor rooms numbered 13. Nonetheless, a more specific explanation must be sought of why this doctrine rather than another is the object of veneration.

Most of the errors of Marx and Engels have been exposed long ago. Given the neglect of the economic factors in the historical literature of the early nineteenth century, the 'materialist' (that is, economic) interpretation of history had the great merit of a shock therapy which, by making exaggerated claims, helped to correct the equally one-sided preoccupation of the historians with ephemeral incidents and doings of the great. However, innumerable examples – a kamikaze pilot on a suicide mission, a martyr, or a Hindu dying of starvation yet refusing to kill a cow – show beyond any doubt that the material interests can be overridden by other motives. The conception of 'the material basis' as something separate from 'the superstructure' of ideas is nonsensical because 'the material basis' consists not only of the tools as physical objects but also of the ideas of how to make and employ them. The notion that 'the mode of production' determines the political 'superstructure' was contradicted by the founders themselves when they called for an uprising instead of waiting for a technical invention which might bring about socialism. A practical demonstration of the falsity of this notion was given by Lenin and his followers who seized the political 'superstructure' and then used it to smash the old mode of production and to create a new one. The latter was entirely their invention because (as Lenin himself complained) Marx left no instructions about what to do after the expropriation of 'the capitalists'. And, of course, the place and time of the revolution were at variance with the theory. When we see people sticking to a belief in the face of clear evidence of its falsity, we must enquire into the motives which may prompt self deception or dupery or (what is most common) an amalgam of both.

Many writers and orators before and after (but independently of) Marx deplored the condition of the poor, condemned the greed and selfishness of the rich, and protested against the institutions (often the market) which they blamed for these circumstances. The saying of Jesus about the camel and the eye of a needle was taken very seriously by the early Christians. Much earlier, similar sentiments were voiced repeatedly by the Hebrew prophets. Irreligious communism began during the French revolution with Gracchus Baboef. The famous phrase 'property is theft' was coined by Joseph Proudhon whom Marx vilified. No-one needs Marx to find a historical support for criticising the inequalities of wealth. Nonetheless, Robert Owen, Blanqui, Cabet, Fourier, Proudhon and all the other eloquent preachers of equality are seldom mentioned while Marx continues to receive totemistic genuflexions. Why? The answer is that Marx's doctrine has the unique advantage of being able to serve two purposes simultaneously: it can be used for attacking one form of inequality as well as for camouflaging another . . . it condemns the capitalist and exonerates the bureaucrat. Thus, it provides a convenient justification of the bureaucratic revolution whereby the élite, deriving its privileges from the ownership of wealth, is replaced by one whose privileges stem from administrative power.

If people were more rational, the absence of any blueprint of a new social order would have put off potential followers, because what is the good in pulling down the old order if you don't know what to put in its place? In fact, however, this omission has acted as a magnet rather than deterrent because it attracts to the doctrine people motivated by sheerly destructive impulses, who do not care what will happen afterwards so long as they can destroy what they hate or merely give vent to their destructive urges. Secondly, the lack of a blueprint permits an alliance for the purpose of destroying the old order between people with very different views on what kind of new order they want. Thirdly, it permits the use of Marx as a totem of an order of which he himself would in all likelihood disapprove. Had he been more specific about what he wanted to have after the revolution, he would not have sketched, we can feel confident, Stalin's prison state as the communist ideal; but, because he said next to nothing about it, even people in charge of gulags can claim to be implementing his ideas. Thus his position as a totem rests upon his negligence as a guide.

The great advantage of Marxism as an ideological weapon is that it fosters hatred against the rich rather than compassion for the poor; and that its dismissal of ethics liberates its followers from any constraint on the choice of strategy in struggle for power. Perusing the works of Robert Owen or Henri de Saint-Simon, we can see that they were moved by compassion for the poor and appealed to altruism in which they saw the foundation of a new and better order. In contrast, the writings of Marx abound in humourless expressions of coarse venom, and lack any signs of compassion for the suffering or concern for justice. The tone of his writings is in keeping with his conduct of which the most striking example was his treatment of his illegitimate son – the only proletarian to whom he was related. Abusing the power of a Victorian employer and having made his servant pregnant, Marx dismissed her and afterwards gave no support either to her or to his proletarian offspring who lived with his mother in a slum, while his father found new 'wage slaves' to serve him. It is not surprising that his message appeals to self-seeking pseudo-levellers.

When stripped of the pretentious mumbo-jumbo in which it is couched, Marx's theory of value and surplus value boils down to an assertion that all profit is illegitimate – indeed, stolen from the workers. Only those who work with their hands are deemed to have contributed to the production. The functions of innovation, enterprise, risk-taking, organising, management and technical expertise are disregarded; and no share in the proceeds can be legitimated within this scheme as the reward for performing them. The later Marxists have recognised the contribution of technicians and managers, but only in so far as they remain pure sellers of their labour. As soon as they acquire a share in the business, they become exploiters. The man who runs his business makes money solely because he owns it. His enterprise, commercial judgement or technical and managerial skills have nothing to do with it. He is not a businessman (etymologically – a busy man), not an enterpriser but a capitalist – a usurer. The word 'capitalism' (one of the many neologisms invented by Saint-Simon) was given currency by Marx who thereby put into the limelight the less appealing side of the market economies as we have known them – namely, the existence of large unearned incomes and possessions – and occulted the features which are more likely to elicit admiration, as they are widely regarded as contributing to progress: energy, initiative, pluck, skill, hard work and other traits associated with the word 'enterprise'. Indeed, if we disregard the fact that of all the economic systems which have come into existence up till now, competitive private industry working for the market has given the greatest scope to the aforementioned propensities and talents so necessary for progress, a condemnation of this system almost inevitably follows, because little could be said for a system the only result of which would be large unearned incomes for a small number. Here we have one more example of how attitudes can be surreptitiously manipulated by labelling.

The serviceability of Marxism in the political arena is not limited to its condemnation of profit because the open message that 'all profit is theft' is coupled with the blinkering unspoken assumption that 'there can be no theft other than profit'. This is done by defining class solely in terms of the relationship to the means of production, putting on one side those who own them and on the other, those who do not. The old conception of class – still common among ordinary people who have not been brainwashed by doctrinaires – is that it has to do not only with ownership but also with other forms of privilege and power: with how well you live, what you can afford or cannot afford to do; whether people bow down to you or treat you with contumely . . . in the final resort with the barriers between the rich and powerful on one side and the poor and powerless on the other. According to Marx, in contrast there is no power or privilege which is not rooted in ownership of the means of production. The society is divided into the exploiters who own the means of production and the exploited, who sell their labour. There is no room in this scheme for exploitation by other means such as pocketing money taken from the workers as tax. You can easily see why the party bosses in the communist countries cling to the doctrine which enables them to claim that they have abolished inequality and created a classless society because they have abolished private ownership of the means of production, and that all their perks do not add up to a class privilege because they do not own the means of production. As they are merely paid for their work, they are (according to the theory) proletarians like the drudges on the shop floor, and therefore their dictatorship is the dictatorship of the proletariat.

Unlike the writings of other prophets of socialism who spoke about the rich and the poor, Marx's obsession with the ownership of the means of production could also be relied on to justify the attack on poor and hard-working peasants, craftsmen and shopkeepers, and the grabbing of their modest means of production in order to deprive them of all independence and to make the power of the rulers total.

Although it cannot take such extreme forms in the countries which have not fallen under the sway of a totalitarian bureaucracy, the function of Marxism is basically analogous here: it also rules out by definition any accusations against those who live on money raised through taxation that they might be exploiting the workers. No matter how little they do, or how worthless or even harmful are their activities, they cannot be condemned as exploiters because they do not own the means of production. So the official who travels around the world on eye-washing 'development missions', staying in luxury hotels, the professor who spends his time on politicking, gets a second salary from a quango (and, if in Oxbridge, lives, dines and wines in splendour, served by a 'scout', without having to pay for it), the idle community relations officer, the student who gets an equivalent of a three years free stay in a holiday camp . . . they all can get an unconditional absolution from the Marxist theory and tut-tut with good conscience about the wicked capitalists sitting on the workers' backs. Public expenditure is hypocritically presented as a transfer of wealth from 'the capitalists' to the workers, whereas in fact it is mainly a transfer from the blue collar workers to the administrative class and its educational appendages.

To forestall misunderstandings, I must make clear that, although I view with grave misgivings the colossal waste of the taxpayers' money which is, in fact, going on in most countries, and regard it as one of the greatest dangers to this country's economic future, I am very far from believing that all public expenditure is *a priori* undesirable. It seems to me doctrinaire to regard public expenditure as either intrinsically good or bad. To my mind, its merits depend on how much is spent on what, with what results, and at what cost. Nor do I envisage a return to the nineteenth century 'night watchman state' as either desirable or feasible. Indeed, in some areas – especially in matters of damage to the environment and of unpriced external costs imposed on third parties – I would even favour stricter regulations. One of the most weighty arguments against nationalisations is to my mind the evidence that a government is less likely to regulate with wisdom and moderation the affairs of an industry which it owns: for instance, ecological protection in Sweden, West Germany or the U.S.A., is much more effective than in any country of the Soviet bloc. Obviously, no modern state could function without a large body of administrators and other public employees. As a matter of fact, in this and a number of other countries, many (perhaps most) of these are dedicated, punctiliously honest, hard working and capable people who are discharging indispensable tasks. It is just as silly to demonize the civil servants as to imagine that all businessmen are blood-sucking crooks. However, the health of a society, like that of an organism, is a matter of balance and proportion. No matter how useful, nay indispensable, is an organ, it can cause incapacity and death if it grows beyond its proper size. And one of the great dangers to the survival of our civilisation is the seemingly irresistable hypertrophy of bureaucratic bodies and their educational and other appendages.

A strangulation of the economy by red tape is not in the long term interest of the members of the administrative class. Many of them see it clearly and would like to put a stop to the blind Parkinsonian mechanisms of hypertrophy. But a reversal of the trends is made more difficult by an ideology which removes all moral restraints on bureaucratic parasitism. A vicious circle springs up, analogous to what happens when somebody takes to drink or drugs in consequence of an initial weakness of character which is then aggravated by the addiction, and he starts on a downward slope.

A key role in spreading the ideological miasma is played by people who claim to pursue a scientific study of society and politics, and who, therefore, should be the most immune to the allurements of a simplistic and obsolete doctrine. Though surprising at first sight, their predilection for Marxism can easily be explained along the lines of a Marxist interpretation – that is, in terms of economic interests – as dogmatism is the surest method of reducing work while drawing unreduced pay. Any society – but especially the modern industrial –

is such a complicated system that studying it in an open-minded and careful manner is arduous and frustrating, as after much work one arrives at conclusions which are often uncertain, usually tentative and sometimes completely inconclusive. As we cannot make experiments in the scientific sense, the only method of arriving at conclusions, which may have somewhat firmer foundations than opinions of intelligent laymen, is by comparative analysis of social structures and their past and present changes – which involves extensive reading of historical and contemporary materials. The inter-wovenness of all aspects of social life, moreover, creates the need to acquaint oneself with the neighbouring branches of learning. Avoidance of such laborious studies can be justified by adhering to a simplistic doctrine, and confining one's reading to the works of one man plus a few of his disciples who merely repeat the master's words.

Because the social sciences progress slowly, it is advisable to read the old classics where one can often find useful insights which have been unnoticed, forgotten or not fully incorporated into current thinking. The literature is vast, as there have been many great minds. By elevating one of them to a god-like status and disregarding all the others of equal originality, one can reduce one's reading list to a small fraction of what it ought to be. Furthermore, to understand and remember the various interpretations, assumptions and arguments – to go into the various shades of contradiction, agreement and complementarity, bearing in mind all the 'ifs', 'buts', 'partlys' and so on – calls for considerable intelligence as well as good memory. If such knowledge is not required, and replaced by a single and simple doctrine the door to academic appointments is opened to individuals of small brain power or allergic to swotting. Conversely, if such people are given jobs totally beyond their ability, or contrary to their predilections, they will naturally gravitate towards an ossified doctrine which will protect them from having to admit their incompetence and parasitism.

It is only fair to admit that not all the Marxists are unintelligent and averse to mental effort. As in other sects, there are among them a few individuals of outstanding knowledge and ability whose fanaticism stems from neurotic tendencies which only a psychoanalysis could unravel. However, they are acclaimed so widely and given a preferential access to the media because they help a crowd of individuals at best fitted for simple routine tasks to make an easy living at the workers' expense by regurgitating simple slogans, and to gratify their egos by posturing as scientists while rejecting the cornerstone of the scientific outlook, which is, of course, that no one is infallible and no theory is beyond refutation by new arguments or data.

They have been particularly successful in promoting their doctrine in the field of educational theory and sociology where they have arrived within a shot of their annihilation as serious subjects. Their advances have been helped by a kind of ratchet mechanism: the Marxists always have a good chance of obtaining appointments controlled by liberal minded scholars who (even when they are prominent members of the Conservative Party) usually lean over backwards to show their tolerance; whereas wherever the Marxists gain influence, they have no scruples about choosing the means to ensure that no one who does not share their creed will have a slightest chance of getting in.

The success of the Marxists in extending their influence in the educational institutions – which has been even greater on the Continent and is very marked in Canada and the United States – disproves their own theory according to which these parts of the world are ruled by the capitalists who always act to protect their interests for, in fact, considerable sums are now spent on maintaining people who incessantly denigrate the existing system and want to destroy it, and even greater sums on providing them with a paid, captive audience.

While the Party 'agitators' in Soviet factories, offices and farms preach about the duties of the citizen and exhort the workers to work harder, drink less, obey the chiefs and not complain, the efforts of their friends in the West are directed towards making people despise work. In contrast to the outlook of the pioneers of the labour movement, who regarded the willingness to work as a moral virtue, and believed that everybody ought to work, the chief message of today's Left is that nobody should have to work and that everybody should get everything for nothing.

One of the ways in which Marxism stimulates bureaucratic hypertrophy and parasitism presents an analogy to the old trick of pickpockets and bag snatchers: when they are being chased, they try to mislead the passers by who might stop them, by shouting 'catch the thief'. Likewise, Marxism gives the diploma-holding class a series of verbal tricks which help them to put out a smoke screen over the fact that they are the biggest takers of the blue collar workers' money by drumming it into the latter's heads that, regardless of the actual circumstances, they are always exploited by those who organise and direct their work.

THE FALLACIES OF COLLECTIVISM

H.D. PURCELL

It will do no harm to begin by defining our terms. Marx makes it very clear that communism is the millennial condition of man which will result from the withering away of the state. Anyone who has read *Capital* (as few Marxists have, in my experience) will know that countries like the Soviet Union and China are not, and do not claim to be, communist societies. Communism is their ostensible aspiration, but socialism is the fact. Marxist socialism is established by the 'dictatorship of the proletariat' which is seen as a necessary, if temporary, stage in the achievement of communism. *Rien ne dure comme le provisoire*.

Planned collectivist societies are of course possible and, if they have ideals which go beyond mere economic survival and welfare, may well outlast the alternatives. Plato's Republic was inspired by the Lycurgan institutions of Sparta, which lasted for centuries. But the Spartans were dedicated to preserving their ethnic identity, and their constitution lacked an essential ingredient of communism, namely, egalitarianism. Or one might consider the Rule of St Benedict, which lasted from the sixth century down to the Second Vatican Council, (and even now manages to stagger on, though deprived of the splendid Latin plain chant which gave its austerities meaning). But the Benedictine Order was strictly hierarchical, and theoretically regarded all earthly considerations as secondary. I have sometimes indicated monasteries to Marxists as examples of enduring collectivism, but somehow the notions of poverty, chastity, obedience, and prayer fail to arouse any particular enthusiasm.

There have been many examples of religious sectaries whose social systems did fulfil the necessary communist conditions of egalitarianism (for *hoi polloi*, at any rate) and theoretical ownership of goods in common. Either they were crushed because of the threat they posed to established order (Albigensians, Taborites), or they survived, no longer communist but transformed out of all recognition. (What person unaware of their origins would associate the modern Ismailis with the historical Assassins or the modern Memmonites and Hutterites with the frenzied Anabaptists of Münster? While religious zeal remains strong, it transcends mere personal survival, and therefore strengthens the chances of group survival: 'He that findeth his life shall lose it'. The sociobiological mechanism is now obvious, but even this cannot long maintain a system which conflicts with inherited behaviour patterns.)

Secular communism has a survival record vastly inferior to the religious variety, and the place to study it in microcosm is North America. As Rose Wilder Lane tells us in her *Discovery of Freedom*

> Hancock, Harvard, Shirley, Tyringham, and Massachusetts; Alfred and New Gloucester in Maine; Mount Lebanon, Watervliet, Groveland, Oneida (Community silver) in New York; South Union and Pleasant Hill in Kentucky; Bethlehem and Economy in Pennsylvania; Union Village, North Union, Whitewater, and Zoar in Ohio; Enfield and Wallingford, Connecticut; Bishop Hill, Illinois; Corning and Bethel, Missouri; Cedarvale, Kansas; Aurora, Oregon; and scores of other American towns and cities, were communist settlements.

Rose Wilder Lane missed the failure of communism in the first permanent British settlements in North America. She can hardly be blamed. This failure is not mentioned in any of the history textbooks. But George and Betty Stoll, who took to the sea in protest against the progressive collectivisation of the United States, and now run the extraordinary free-enterprise Flint School aboard two fully-rigged sailing ships, have not missed these examples. Drawing on material published by the American Foundation for Economic Education and other sources, they give detailed quotations from contemporary accounts which show how close those early settlements came to failure because of their attempts to establish a community of goods (*The Telltale*, the Flint School Journal for October-December, 1977). The Jamestown colony in Virginia was set up with the following rules:

1. That the colonists should own nothing.
2. That they were to receive only as much food and clothing as they needed.
3. That everything secured by trade or produced from the land should go into the common store.

As the Stolls remark:

> Of the 104 men that started the colony in 1607 only 53 survived the first year and even those had to be marched to the fields 'to the beat of a drum' simply to grow food to keep them alive in the next year.

We recognise the familiar pattern do we not? This might have been the Ukraine in the 1920s. Fortunately, Captain John Smith was very much more intelligent and humane than the Party members who presided over the murder of the kulaks and the forced collectivisation of the Russian farms. This is what Captain Smith has to say:

> When our people were fed out of the common store, and laboured together, glad was he who could slip from his labour, or slumber over his task he cared not how, nay, the most honest among them would hardly take so much true paines in a weeke, as now for themselves they will doe in a day; neither cared they for the increase presuming that howsoever the harvest prospered, the generall store must maintain them, so that we reaped not so much Corne from the labours of thirtie, as now three or foure doe provide for themselves.

Once the land was shared out, production rapidly increased. Such were the beginnings of civilisation in Virginia.

The case of the Plymouth colony was no better, and it is worth noting that, in spite of the usual emphasis on the religious nature of this colony, 67 of the original 102 colonists were not members of the extreme English Separatist Church, but were non-separatist Protestants hired to protect the interests of the joint stock company financing the venture. So we cannot class it as an example of purely religious communism. Governor Bradford, who was in charge, left a description of how within the first two or three months half the company died of exposure and disease. By the time the *Mayflower* departed, only 23 children and 27 adults were left. During 1621, they sowed and harvested together, and in October their first harvest went into the common store. (They gave thanks, entertaining the local Indian chief, Massasoit, and his braves, who responded by presenting them with five newly slain deer.) In November, the *Fortune* arrived with thirty more settlers, mostly young men. But they had not brought with them 'so much as a bisket-cake', and so were a drain on the common store. In 1622, they worked together again, but the harvest was poor, and they starved during the ensuing winter. Richard Grant, in *The Incredible Bread Machine*, dwells on the miseries of that time. Eventually, Governor Bradford had the good sense to confer with the notables amongst them, and they assigned to each family a parcel of land:

> This had very good success; for it made all hands very industrious, so as much more corne was planted than other waise would have bene by any means the Gov. or any other could use, and saved him a great deall of trouble, and gave farr better contente. The women now wente willingly into the feild, and tooke their little-ones with them to set corne; which before would aledge weakness, and inabilitie; whom to have compelled would have bene thought great tiranie and opression.

(There is no evidence that our forefathers in the seventeenth century were stupider than we are now. In fact, what evidence there is indicates the opposite. Sir Fred Hoyle has pointed to the much higher proportion of outstanding people in the much smaller population of Elizabeth I's reign, and Elizabethan plays (like those of the Greeks in the fifth century B.C.) were acted at a speed which is almost unbelievable today, when big cuts have to be made and stage business substituted.) Governor Bradford saw the implications of what had happened, and expressed his views in the sinewy prose of the period:

> The experience that was had in this common course and condition, tried sundrie years, and that amongst godly and sober men, may well evince the vanitie of that conceite of Platos and other ancients, applauded by some of later times; – that the taking away of propertie, and bringing in communitie into a comone wealth would make them happy and florishing, as if they were wiser than God. For this comunitie (so farr as it was) was found to breed much confusion and discontente, and retard much imployment that would have been to their benefite and comforte. For the yong-men that were most able and fitte for labour and service did repine that they should spend their time and streingth to worke for other mens wives and children, with out any recompense. The strong, or man of parts, had no more in divission of victails and cloaths, than he that was weake and not able to doe a quarter the other could; this was thought injuestice. . .

So much for the Communist maxim, 'From each according to his ability, to each according to his need'. As in the Jamestown colony and everywhere else that it has been permitted, the widespread distribution of private property had rapid and beneficial results. (This is what Belloc and Chesterton meant when they promoted 'Distributism', though they could make no headway against a hostile or indifferent press.) Bradford continues his account in a lyrical vein:

> By this time harvest was come, and instead of famine, now God gave them plentie, and the face of things was changed, to the rejoysing of the harts of many for which they blessed God. And the effect of their perticular [*viz* private] planting was well seene, for all had, one way and other, pretty well to bring the year aboute, and some of the abler sorte and more industrious had to spare, and sell to others, so as any generall wante or famine hath not been amongest them since to this day.

And so it goes, right down to the communist paradise created by Reverend Jim Jones, (I see him as a misguided but logical reformer) who came to realise that, in view of built-in differences, equality could be achieved only in death. Studying his colony in detail, one is astonished at the number of parallels with the Anabaptists – right down to the indiscriminate terror and sexual restrictions.

Egalitarian communism having proved unworkable so often on a small scale, we are now asked to consider whole societies which ostensibly 'aspire' to it. No wonder the anarchists have seen through the deception and denounced it. They really do want to create a condition (I cannot say a *state*) of affairs in which there is no more coercion of any kind, no more property and no more competition. They do at least have the merit of making straight for their throughly impractical goal, (and we ought to treat them with forbearance, unless big money moves in to support them for its own purposes).

The argument from scale is a false one. Authoritarian Marxist societies are kept going because they contain enormous black, and even bigger grey, sectors which to some extent redress the balance of their inefficient economies. The advantage of this, from the Party's point of view, is that anyone who does well out of illegal or semi-legal activities is automatically a criminal, or could swiftly be regarded as one. A society in which everyone has to break the rules in order to survive is one in which the state has complete power over the individual. This can be true in the West also. It is no accident that the Italian Communist Party, with its vast property holdings, has not made an issue of those four million or more Italians who are known to exist but have forgotten to have themselves enrolled by the bureaucrats. (Nor is this attitude of mind confined to outright Marxists. Social democrats can also sometimes be made to admit that the need to bend the rules a bit makes individualist nuisances nicely vulnerable.)

But though the effects of collectivism are not immediately apparent in large-scale economies, because of the survival of free-enterprise in its nooks and crannies, they are inexorable all the same. I liken money to the oil in a petrol engine. When the engine is running smoothly, the oil is evenly spread throughout the system, and particularly benefits the working parts. But when the engine begins to slow down, the oil collects in the sump. So the money gravitates towards the unproductive bureaucracies, or else towards the crooks – usually both. When normal services become illegal, or are penalised by excessive taxes, then the profits tend to be made in prostitution or gambling or drug-trafficking. 'Might as well be hung for a sheep as a lamb' is the nasty logic of this situation.

And what of those social democracies in which welfare services have been extended without restriction to all? Well, remember the case of Uruguay. Before the war, Uruguay was a model welfare state. Eventually, it lost sight of any sort of proportion. The result was economic breakdown, the Tupamaros, rule by junta, etc. Nor can it be said that the New Britain is doing particularly well. No nationalised industry is making a profit, and the drain from these and the grossly inflated bureaucracy now amounts to an intolerable burden. As for the NHS, can anyone still persuade himself that it is now the boast of Britain? Even in Sweden, the pleasant draught of fantasy is turning sour. A socialised state, in C.N. Parkinson's telling image, is like an army going nowhere in particular, the main concern of which is care for its own wounded.

This is the point where the woolly-minded (and perhaps some of the not-so-woolly-minded) protest their innocence. It was a wonderful dream, they say, but somehow or other it failed to become reality. Is it really anyone's fault? Yes, I think it is. I am contesting the notion that the trend towards collectivism has arisen as a natural response to the evils of capitalist monopoly. I think the two work hand in hand. To think otherwise is to argue that concentration of economic power in too few hands is to be cured by concentrating it in even fewer hands.

As Spengler (himself a socialist) once remarked, no form of socialism is ever established without support from the bankers. The lie that the Bolsheviks established socialism in Russia in response to popular demand is propagated in their very name, which falsely claims that they represented the majority. But the Russian workers and peasants never voted – in these professional agitators. In his *Eastern Front, 1914–1917*, Norman Stone demonstrates that, far from being a hopelessly backward society, Tsarist Russia had the fastest-growing economy in the world, and by 1914 had become the world's fifth industrial power. What brought her down was a combination of hideous inflation and price controls (Western politicians, please note). The first of course is always produced by mistaken (or criminal) monetary policies, and the second can always be relied upon to create dreadful shortages, even in the midst of plenty. Both are typically collectivist mechanisms: inflation because it robs the saver in order to transfer the value to others who have not contributed to the savings; and price controls because they are intended to supply the non-producer with goods subsidised at the producer's expense. No wonder the Russian masses looked on apathetically until it was too late. The French peasantry did the same at the time of the French Revolution.

My grandfather, Arthur Burbury, was manager of Grace's Bank in London for many years before the First World War, and told me of the consternation with which the Manchester cotton industry regarded the rapid rise of competition from Russian textiles. The Americans too were seriously disturbed by the rise of such a competitor in so many different fields. In fact, Wall Street had every motive to encourage changes which would have the effect of crippling this growing giant. Just as the destruction of the British Empire was the main result of the Second World War, so the destruction of the relatively free Tsarist economy resulted from the First. Is it wicked to wonder whether such results might have been intended? Of course it is true that the Russian Empire remained largely intact, but a systematic liquidation [*viz* murder] of the engineers and kulaks would go far to reinforce such a suspicion, even if there were no other evidence. The key role of engineers in industry need hardly be stressed, and Soviet agriculture has never recovered from collectivisation, because it is precisely substantial independent farmers upon whom any successful agricultural development must be based. Before 1914, Russian exports were growing year by year, and the country had a large surplus of wheat, even though distribution problems led to local scarcity. But since its beginnings, the Soviet state has had to import most of its technology and much of its food from the West. Its enormous armies and interlocking bureaucracies are directly dependent on American loans. And these loans are in effect created out of the air, in the form of high-interest-bearing debt, so that all the interest paid is pure profit to the creators of the credit. No wonder the American banking system finds it profitable to maintain the captive Russian market. What moneylender ever wants his victim to pay him back the principal? The almost incredible obstructiveness of a socialist bureaucracy becomes readily comprehensible when we realise that its purpose is to promote inefficiency and increase the need to borrow. A master gives (or lends) a slave his food and clothes, and the slave has to work to 'repay' him. But what if he refuses?

My grandfather was in St Petersburg at the time of the Bolshevik Revolution, and told me of the enormous sums which were made available to the self-designated champions of the poor and oppressed. In his monumental work, *Wall Street and the Bolshevik Revolution*, Anthony Sutton documents the way in which Trotsky and his fellow conspirators were funded by the New York finance houses. But even Mr Sutton leaves some of the more sordid evidence in the dark. What about the banker friends who funded and encouraged Rasputin? His activities discredited the royal family through the credulity of the Empress, just as Cagliostro's activities besmirched the reputation of the French royal family before 1789. It is time that someone republished the original French edition of *Les derniers jours des Romanofs* (1920), by Robert Wilton, the *Times* correspondent in St Petersburg. It contains information I have never seen anywhere else. But none of this calls in question any of the facts adduced by Mr Sutton, whose *Western Technology and Soviet Economic Development – 1917–1930* also deserves careful reading. And the story of cooperation between Wall Street and the Kremlin continues down to the present day.

Again I seem to hear those anguished objections. 'How can you claim that capitalists and communists would cooperate? Are they not at opposite ends of the political spectrum? The spectrum, may I remind you, repeats itself. Infra-red shades into ultra-violet, and so does socialism into capitalism. Only the mirage of communism covers this connexion. Both socialism and capitalism are interested in monopoly, and particularly monopoly of the money supply, as Bakunin saw long ago. They cooperate in so far as their interests coincide, however much they may squabble over the spoils. That is why tycoons prefer socialism. It means big government contracts and the elimination of any rising competition through a punitive tax system.

The cooperation of monopolists on the 'Left' and 'Right' is obfuscated by use of the term 'liberal', which used to mean believer in free-market theories, and now means a supporter of rampant collectivism and egalitarianism. Carroll Quigley's book, *Tragedy and Hope*, provides us with detailed information about the way in which the conspiracy works, from the standpoint of a sympathetic insider. Only when one understands the range and scope of what we are up against, can one see why the whole trend of legislation, backed by the opinion-forming media, is towards collectivism. Popular demand is manipulated wherever possible, and otherwise ignored and discounted.

Finally, we come to the claim that people are now better off than ever before. The advocate of collectivism uses the *post-hoc-propter-hoc* argument that since technological advance has continued after the introduction of socialist legislation, therefore the legislation is in some unspecified way responsible for it. This is nonsense. There is no positive correlation between the degree of collectivisation and the pace of economic advance. In fact, what evidence there is points in the opposite direction. Countries like South Korea, Taiwan, Hong Kong, and Singapore, which are developing rapidly, have free-market systems, whereas Britain and America, which are rejoining the Third World by leaps and bounds, are becoming more and more socialist.

It is the application of scientific inventions which has made possible the enormous increase in the production of manufactured goods which marks the modern age. An advanced society can carry an actual majority of providers of peripheral services, or even unproductive bureaucrats, provided they are not allowed to interfere with the actual producers. But any form of collectivism ensures such interference at all levels, and chokes the passage of economic life-blood.

In any case, there are signs that the momentum of technological advance is slowing down, and that this has a lot to do with the conformism induced by liberal-leftist thinking. A superstructure of technology can only be erected on a solid foundation of scientific discovery. But science can only be developed in freedom. That means the freedom to discuss and study the most sensitive issues, not just the currently fashionable fads. Take the case of William Shockley. When he played a key role in inventing and developing the transistor, he started something which profoundly affected the world in which we live, and was hailed as a pioneer. But when he turned his attention to the more important problem of eugenics, he rapidly became an un-person. Was not the same intelligence at work in both cases?

What is more, the whole economic system, based on cooperation (if that is the right word) between 'capitalist' and 'socialist' appears to be coming apart at the seams. The gross expansion of dollar credit internationally has created such a reservoir of Eurodollars (at least $1,000 billion, rising by twenty per cent per year) as can never be absorbed into the world economy. (As an interesting detail, it is worth remembering that the Moscow Narodny Bank was the first to start re-lending these dollars on a big scale.) As these enormous sums begin to flow back into the United States, the American people are beginning to suffer hyper-inflation – a trend which I do not think can be reversed. Meanwhile, there is a very dangerous community of interest making for war: the Soviet desire to repudiate enormous debts and the desire of Wall Street to find a way out of an impossible situation of its own making. No cooperation, however conspiratorial in its origins, is for ever.

Meanwhile, in the Third World, dependent populations are increasing as never before. Marxism distorts and frustrates the free market, leaving the people much worse off than before. It politicises life to the point where power becomes a matter of life and death, and it makes the governments utterly dependent on foreign aid. Yet it is this foreign aid (in the form mainly of loans) which has the function of maintaining the bureaucracies which would otherwise have broken down – to the inestimable benefit of the Third World economies. All this has been demonstrated beyond any shadow of doubt by Professor Bauer of the London School of Economics. But I would go beyond this and point to the fact that the loans were created out of the air in the first place, in the form of interest-bearing debt, so that country after country is paying out a large share of its export earnings in the noble cause of servicing its debts. Have you ever wondered why an 'emerging' nation is never considered to be truly independent until it has a Marxist government? I suggest it is because Marxism means inefficiency and dependence. In Southern Africa, for example, nations become 'independent', only to find that they are completely at the mercy of Anglo-America for their export earnings. When we talk about people being better off nowadays, which people do we mean? For most of the world, dependence leads to debt, and debt increases misery. The masses of India have less to eat now than they did in the nineteenth century.

Wherever we look, we see the evil effects of collectivism: debt, dependence, inefficiency, poverty, politicisation, and obscurantism. It is time we began to study the mechanisms whereby collectivism is imposed. And it is time we realised that the vision of an egalitarian utopia which lies behind all forms of collectivism is nothing less than the death wish in superficially attractive guise.

VLADIMIR BUKOVSKY

Interviewed by BERNARD LEVIN

'No matter how I looked at it, it was clear there could be no other university for me but Vladimir Prison. Even if they didn't stick a new stretch on me, I'd be in exile until 1983, when I would be forty-one and that was no age for studying. And there was nothing good to be expected when I was let out. Only green-horns . . . look forward to their release and count the days. Life outside appears to them as some bright, sunny, unattainable shore. But I was in for the fourth time. I knew that there is nothing more disillusioning in life than to be released from jail. I also knew that I had never managed to last longer than a single damned year outside – and never would. Because the reasons that had landed me in jail in the first place would land me there again and again. These reasons were immutable, just as Soviet life itself was immutable, just as you yourself could never change. You would never be allowed to be yourself, and you would never agree to lie and dissimulate. And there was no other way out.'

from
Vladimir Bukovsky
'To Build a Castle – My Life as a Dissenter'

LEVIN Vladimir, when and how did you first fall foul of the authorities in your country?

BUKOVSKY The first kind of trouble I had was when I was 17. We decided in school to make some kind of satirical magazine which as far as we were concerned, was totally non-political, just a joke about school life as we saw it, but it appeared that we had inadvertantly made a mockery of the party line. The whole adventure was defined by the authorities as ideological subversion and I was dismissed from school and my head master was dismissed from his job as well.

LEVIN How did that go down in your family? Normally, if a child comes home and says he's been thrown out of school the parents are in hysterics.

BUKOVSKY Well, it wasn't only hysterics, it was terrible fear, because my father was summoned to party headquarters and got his party reprimand.

LEVIN For bringing up such a disgraceful son?

BUKOVSKY Yes, because parents are held responsible in our country for the ideological upbringing of their children.

LEVIN What did your father do for a living?

BUKOVSKY He was an official Soviet writer and a member of the party of course. So he had some trouble with them as well at that time, and my mother also. As you can imagine, they weren't happy about what we had done, but at least, they understood, that I wasn't trying to subvert the Soviet society deliberately.

LEVIN Was there a feeling in your parents that they agreed with you – that you might get into trouble, you might get them into trouble, but at least you were right and they admired it?

BUKOVSKY No. They didn't tell me, but officially they said: look, these children – I wasn't the only one who had been involved and punished – really didn't understand what they were doing; they've tried to be funny, and they really had no political motive behind it. And I think they aggravated their case by saying it. To me they only said: you are stupid; you are grown up enough to understand that this kind of joke will land you in trouble.

LEVIN When was your first serious trouble, the real political stuff that you couldn't deny was political?

BUKOVSKY Oh, the first time I was arrested was in 1961. I was 19 and a student. We gathered together in one of the squares in Moscow to read Samizdat, or underground poetry. You wouldn't find it officially sold anywhere. It was poetry written by the poets executed during the Stalin era, or poetry that had been banned. . .

LEVIN But this was, presumably, during the Khrushchev era when a lot of rehabilitation was going on.

BUKOVSKY Yes, but they preferred to have their rehabilitation from above and they wouldn't permit us to do it ourselves. So it was a trouble for a year at least. The authorities had been embarrassed and had tried to silence us by stopping these readings, one way or another. Most of us had been expelled from the Universities and other institutions, of course, and eventually in 1961 they decided to stop it for ever. They arrested about a dozen of us and that was the first trouble. But this time I wasn't in prison for long; I was just interrogated and released, then interrogated over several months until I escaped from Moscow; I knew I was going to be imprisoned eventually, so I gave them the slip.

LEVIN When did you first go to prison then, and what for?

BUKOVSKY It was 1963, and I was arrested because, while searching my home the KGB discovered a forbidden book, written by a Yugoslavian author, Djilas, called *New Class*. It was published in Russian abroad and somehow smuggled into the country, and I borrowed it just for one night to make a copy, so when they came to my place I had the book in my possession, which is a criminal offence.

LEVIN And how long did you get?

BUKOVSKY I didn't get a prison sentence; I was declared insane, and I spent something like fifteen months in the so-called special psychiatric hospital.

LEVIN Now, in countries like ours, obviously, people in mad-houses are, usually, genuinely mad. The Soviet Union seems to have perfected an entirely new technique of putting the sane ones in mad-houses. You experienced that. What actually happened? They can't pretend you're *really* mad, or do they?

BUKOVSKY They do.

LEVIN The thing we hear, which is very interesting, is the argument which must present itself very strongly to the Soviet authorities: this man says our society is no good; we know that our society is paradise, therefore he must be mad. Now, that seems to me to be a very powerful argument, because if you believe in this society, this wonderful workers' state, and somebody says it's all rotten, the only explanation could be that he's mad. Is that actually what motivates them?

BUKOVSKY More or less; it's a bit more sophisticated, since they use Marxist ideology to prove it. According to Marxism, anybody's mind, or conscience, is shaped by the environment. We have had something like thirty years of socialism in our country, therefore people's minds, or thoughts, must be socialist. If they are not, there can be only two explanations: one, this chap is hired by the world imperialism; and the second is, he's mentally ill. . .

LEVIN Describe, if you will, if indeed you can bear to, the life of a sane man in a Soviet lunatic asylum.

BUKOVSKY It's a very lengthy subject. People who are committed to these places for political reasons, are kept in so-called special psychiatric hospitals. There are two types, there are ordinary psychiatric hospitals like you have here for those people who ask to be treated, and the special types, which are indeed a kind of prison, with the same security system, guards, and searchlights, and you are loocked up in the cell for twenty-four hours as in any other prison. ut in addition you have doctors, nurses and orderlies, together with the guards watching you, and checking up on you and running the whole place. So you have a double burden, one of the prison part and another of the psychiatric hospital. Those with whom you are locked up are usually crazy people, who being deranged, committeed, say murder, or rape, or something, and you are supposed to be kept together with them under the law, not like in the camps or in prison where they are supposed to be kept separately from the criminals. Of course, you have your share of trouble, sitting with these kind of people in the same cell. Then for disagreeing with the doctor or with the nurses, or infringing any kind of regulation, you are treated with drugs. You might be beaten, but you can't complain; you are abnormal, or mentally ill. The orderlies are usually criminals themselves, who are simply serving their term by working in these places. They are also locked up. Being a type of hooligan they usually beat up the really sick people, but it wouldn't make much difference whether you are ill or not; they would take your food from you, or your warm clothes – if you're lucky enough to have some – because the place is terribly cold. If you try to complain, they protest that you've been in an excited state of mind and you've tried to attack them and that's why they've been forced to use violence to restrain you. Then, the next day, the doctor would look through these entries in the watch book, and without even summoning you or chatting with you, would prescribe some kind of treatment for this excitement. Sometimes, you are treated for a very long time. If you've had some trouble with the nurses or orderlies, first they would beat you, second they would report you. Next day when giving you the injections, they would beat you up again and again report on you, and it would go on and on. I've known cases where people have been killed eventually.

LEVIN You came from a tyranny into a land of freedom; or did you? Have you been disappointed or disillusioned with what you actually found when you came to the west?

BUKOVSKY Well, somehow we believed, living in the Soviet Union, that we were a different type of people; we must be inferior because we have this bloody tyranny, and you have not. So you must be much better. After a couple of years living here, I discovered for myself that people are basically the same, so in one way it's good; it means that one day we will have freedom in our country; in another way it's very bad; it means that one day you might have some trouble. This worries me considerably, especially because people in this world don't care much about what they have.

LEVIN What do you think about our attitude to our freedom? Do you really think freedom is in danger in this country?

BUKOVSKY Well, it's in danger everywhere because freedom is a very fragile thing.

LEVIN But what could hurt it in Britain?

BUKOVSKY Many things – an imbalance of power one way or another, could endanger it very quickly; some kind of over-reaction to any kind of situation can undermine it or destabilize it. Disregard to freedom itself destroys it and democratic institutions.

LEVIN What about the world you move through now, did that surprise you? Your countryman, Solzhenitsyn, has had some very severe things to say about the quality of life in the west.

BUKOVSKY Life in the west very much differs from one country to another. I travel constantly, so I can compare one country's wealth with another, and see that one country has more freedom than the previous one. In general there is prosperity, but people really don't appreciate it. While it's only natural not to notice say, the air you breathe, until you're deprived of it, whenever you exercise your freedom, you must remember that those rights are given to you together with a responsibility for society. People forget this in many countries. They abuse their rights, without any kind of regard for other people.

LEVIN What can we do to help the people who are still there, battling as you did against this thing?

BUKOVSKY Before saying something about help, let's agree that the main thing for us is not to be hampered. We are constantly hampered by people who, mainly out of ignorance or fear of Soviet power and threats, inflict on us disasters such as those Olympic Games. The people who decided to stage the Games in Moscow were totally irresponsible, or totally ignorant. Hundreds of people were arrested, just because the authorities decided to rid the areas of the Olympic Games of any kind of trouble maker. The so-called dissidents themselves were only a minority, but tens of thousands of ordinary people were threatened with removal because they were seen drinking a bit more than is permitted, or grumbled about the shortage of food. And you can imagine the fear it produces. Because of this huge campaign of repressions, the atmosphere in Moscow has been very similar to 1953.

LEVIN Tell me something, if you would, about the life of the ordinary Soviet citizen, the day to day life of the man and woman who don't want to get mixed up in politics. Is their life so very different from what it is in a country like this?

BUKOVSKY It's more or less easier in Moscow or Leningrad, which are the show cities and where the shops are better supplied just in order to show it to the foreigners and tourists, but in all other places, you would be very lucky to find meat, and in some areas they haven't seen sausages for say ten years or more. I remember a friend of mine visited me in Moscow with his son who was nine years old. I decided to give them a treat, so I bought some sausages and started to slice them, and this small boy was frightened; he just pulled his father's sleeve and asked in a whisper 'what is it?' Throughout his nine years he had never seen sausages.

LEVIN But the rulers of the Soviet Union cannot *want* their people to be poor, and hungry, and not see meat from one year to the next, if only because it must in the end, produce discontent. Why can't they do something about it, in their own interest, not because they are noble altruistic people?

BUKOVSKY At some time in the 60s, shortly after Stalin's death, there was great discussion among the specialists and the party rulers, of what they should do about the repeated agricultural disasters. Some of them suggested a return to capitalism in agriculture, introduce some private enterprise, on a big scale, permit them to produce as much as they wish, and pay them real money, even on the collective farms; let them be, but let the people be paid real money. Some experiments were staged in agricultural areas like Altai, Kazakhstan, Ukraine, Kubain, etc. and produced surprisingly excellent results. The yield in very small experimental fields was ten times that of the usual farm, and the people earned, say, three or four times more; the whole thing worked efficiently and the supply was overwhelming. But after some time they closed it down. Their argument was quite clear: if we return to the capitalist system, it will mean unemployment, because you don't need so many people employed in agriculture if one can produce ten times. And because they would earn more, they would be more independent. Then, there would be inflation. So they decided to stop these new reforms. But, I would say, the major argument against these reforms was that the party apparatus would lose control of the economy; it would become a free market economy and they wouldn't tolerate it.

LEVIN Let me come on to something else now. The educational system in Russia seems to me to be a paradox, in that, on the one hand it is clearly locked into rigid Marxist teaching; on the other hand, to take the most obvious example, we're always hearing the numbers of scientists that Russian schools and universities turn out. Now you can't do that simply by ideology, as indeed the Chinese found, with the catastrophe they had in education. If you're being told that Marxism-Leninism is everything and teaches you everything, how can you be a scientist, of all people, who has to speculate, and think, and theorise, and look into things?

BUKOVSKY I think we never went as far as the Chinese did, and we never substituted Marxist doctrine for mathematics or physics. Perhaps they did in the thirties, I wouldn't know exactly, but certainly in my time and from the beginning of the fifties they were very keen on natural science, and I would say that the standard of education in natural science in the schools is much higher than in an average school in England. They are very serious about it, but at the same time, all the so-called humanities – or Humanitarian subjects as we would call them – they would be taught from the Marxist point of view. Only geography, for example, or literature; and history would cover only the history of revolutions and the uprisings of the proletariat. They would explain the whole of history in terms of class struggle and revolutions. Lenin once said that literature must be class oriented and couldn't be otherwise, so they would tell you plenty of rubbish about Tolstoy being the reflection of Russian revolution or something. And you're supposed to learn it as a normal subject and to pass your exams in it, so it's given in such a way you can't reject it; you can't argue with it, it's your subject, almost like mathematics.

LEVIN But that must, inevitably, have a deadening effect on the whole society, which cannot be to the interests of the rulers, after all, in any society, can it?

BUKOVSKY Well, it's true. This system of education can produce plenty of good scientists because, no matter how strong the party disciplines and indoctrination are, around the age of 14, 15, 16 and up, children understand what actually happens, and are simply taught to be hypocritical. They learn to live a double life, unless they study science, which is taught in a good way. I would say it's much more fashionable in our country to go into science, and very despicable to go in for the party subjects like history; so most of the young people choose to study physics, or chemistry, and so on.

LEVIN When you said that at 14, 15, 16 'they' already know, do you mean that the average Russian pupil in an ordinary school, from an ordinary family really understands the true nature of Soviet society?

BUKOVSKY With me it was very early simply because I had lived in a very troubled time, when Stalin had just died and been exposed as a criminal. But I am amazed to what extent the average child is cynical in our time. I think at the age of 15 or 16 they would understand a lot, almost everything.

LEVIN Is that something that is discussed in the home, between parents and children, or among parents, among children? I understand, of course, it is not something to shout aloud in the street, but in the privacy of the home?

BUKOVSKY A lot of things have changed since I was a young kid myself. In my childhood parents would be very reluctant to say anything; they knew what kind of reprisals could be expected. Nowadays, especially in the ordinary working families, people are much more outspoken. They curse and complain about the lousy life they have, and the children would understand it anyway from the standard of life they lead. In the intellectual families, the parents would be much more cautious, because they know how much trouble they can still get into. Reprisals in the country wouldn't be made so much against a working family saying something openly as against the intellectual family.

LEVIN There's something that fascinates me about resisters like you, which is that you grew up entirely within the Soviet system, you were not allowed to read anything that wasn't officially approved, nothing shown on television, your schooldays, the teaching, everything, was absolutely pre-arranged, censored, filleted in every way. Now, somewhere inside you, you found a standard by which you could judge the truth and falsehood of what you were being told and you came to the conclusion that this was evil and had to be resisted. So where did you find, not the strength to resist, but the feeling that you had to?

BUKOVSKY Well, actually to take the first part of your question, I think that most people understand it's evil and bad. During my life in the Soviet Union, and I lived there 35 years, I have met fewer communists than I've met in two and a half, three years, living here. Most people I've met, even those who officially are members of the party, are simply cynical people who have joined the party for better promotion, better wages, career and things like that and they do it quite openly and the authorities overlook it. They are quite happy; it is much better for them to have cynical but reliable working people, rather than some great believers, because you usually have trouble from the believers. One day they are believers, the next day they are disillusioned; and if they are in a high position it means trouble for the system. The only difference between me and my friends and some other people in our country is that the majority of people would accept this double standard, the kind of double life, double mentality, the cynicism and the hypocrisy . . . and they would really regard it as normal; whereas for me it was revolting right from a young age.

LEVIN To what extent are they conscious of the fact that there is such a thing as liberty somewhere outside, and that they don't have it?

BUKOVSKY Well, I'm pretty sure that in the life of any individual in the Soviet Union there comes a moment when he suddenly understands all these things. Some of the people may live for a long time in their environment without being aware of it, just following the usual routine; but as soon as they have the smallest problem – say, some trouble with their living conditions or the shortage of food in the local shop, or perhaps they are underpaid at work, and they try to complain and achieve justice – they encounter the bureaucratic wall of Soviet society. Actually you can't penetrate it. And the more people try, the more they are disillusioned. It happens very quickly. So, since everyone in the Soviet Union has some kind of trouble sooner or later, I presume none of them would still be ignorant of the kind of bureaucracy we have. It's a very revealing thing. Propaganda still influences people, especially when they are young and don't think independently. And because the propaganda suggests that everything is perfect in our society, as soon as you discover the smallest drawback, you are immediately in conflict with official propaganda: it must be a lie, and if the official propaganda is lying, why does it do so? Maybe they are lying 100 per cent?

LEVIN Do you think there is anything in the argument that Russia has always had a bureaucracy, it's always been a centralised autocratic state whether under the Tzars, Lenin, Stalin or Khrushchev; and that there's something in this huge land and its ungovernability, if you like, that makes these things happen whoever's in charge?

BUKOVSKY I've heard this argument many times, from quite different people, not necessarily from western communists only, but sometimes from very learned professors of history both here and in the United States. The trouble with this argument is that it's totally unscientific. There are many countries right now who have the same fate, take China, or Cuba, or Yugoslavia if you wish, none of which are directly under Soviet control. Nevertheless you would find basically the same traits in their societies, the same oppressiveness, the same centralisation and bureaucracy; so my natural conclusion is that it stems not from our nature as Russians but from the ideology and the systems imposed on the society, namely from Marxism.

LEVIN It seems that we're leading towards one remarkable question, which is this: you stress that the average man and woman in the street believe that the system under which they live is rotten; you state also that the people running it are themselves cynical. If the leaders don't believe it and the people don't believe it, why don't they do away with it? Who's gaining out of this?

BUKOVSKY I presume nobody. There is a very good Chinese proverb that says: if you are riding the tiger, you can't jump off it. The Soviet authorities are perfectly aware of some disastrous aspects of developments in the country and none of them are believers in what they are doing, but they can't change it, none of them.

LEVIN Why not?

BUKOVSKY Well, imagine any of them trying to do it. Supposing Brezhnev decided tomorrow: Let's change it, let's brush off all this Marxism nonsense. He would be immediately dismissed and the next chap would take the job.

LEVIN Yes, but we're talking about a system where none of them believe in it, according to you.

BUKOVSKY That's true, but they would take advantage of Brezhnev's mistake. Ideology is still used as a kind of railroad; your country may deviate from it, none of them would believe, but if you deviate, you're vulnerable, you can be pushed over; so I imagine the politburo would gather together and go on and on saying the same things in the same language, all of them knowing it's rubbish. Certainly our rulers believed it in the beginning, but after fifty years when everyone can see the results, who would be brave enough to stand up and to say something to be immediately executed? None of them.

LEVIN When the Czech spring happened in 1968, Dubcek and his colleagues threw off the whole apparatus of communist rule and paid for it with invasion and subugation as we know. However, Dubcek, Svoboda, Kriegel – they all came up through the party system. Nobody had ever heard of them as dissidents before they decided one morning that enough was enough. Are there not somewhere in the Soviet Union Russian Dubceks, working their way up, knowing what nonsense it is but going along with it until one day, they will be in a position to do what Dubcek and co did in Prague?

BUKOVSKY You can still have somebody like Dubcek say in the Baltic States, in Georgia or in the Caucasus, or even in the Kremlin – there have been one or two who've tried to revive the national culture and things like that – but you wouldn't find these people in the central apparatus. The selection procedure is too careful, and the situation itself would never permit them to do exactly the same job as they were doing in Czechoslovakia.

LEVIN But do you have any hope at all for the future of your country, that you were born in and presumably you would like to go back and live in as a free man in a free state, do you have any hope for it at all, and if so, where, what is the hope?

BUKOVSKY During the last twenty years the situation in the country has changed very noticeably, not because the authorities wished to liberalise us, but simply because they retreated under the pressure of a public movement inside the country. It's very slow, this growth of independent forces in the society, but eventually they will gain more and more momentum, and the authorities have already started to give way.

LEVIN Do you think this will continue?

BUKOVSKY Certainly it will; it may take something like fifteen or twenty years more, nobody can predict, but the result is inevitable and the society will change.

ANDREI SAKHAROV

Interviewed by OLLE STENHOLM

This interview first appeared in *Index on Censorship*, Volume 4, 1973

SAKHAROV The (Soviet) state represents an extreme concentration of economic, political and ideological power, that is, extreme monopolisation. It stares you in the face. You could say, as Lenin did at the start of our revolution, that it is simply state capitalism, that is, the state acting as sole proprietor of the entire economy. But in that case there's nothing new at all about this socialism. It's simply capitalism developed to its extremes, the sort of capitalism you have in the United States, for example, and other western countries, but with extreme monopolisation. We ought not to be surprised, then, that we have the same problems, qualitatively speaking, the same criminality, the same alienation of the individual, as the capitalist world. With the difference that our society is an extreme instance, as it were, extremely unfree, extremely constrained ideologically. And – what is probably the most characteristic feature – it's the most pretentious society; It's not the best society, but it claims to be far better than all the others.

STENHOLM What do you see, in concrete terms, as the greatest defects in Soviet society today?

SAKHAROV The absence of freedom, almost certainly. The absence of freedom, the bureaucratisation of the administration, the utter irrationality and the dreadful egoism of it, a class egoism, if you like, concerned in essence only with preserving the existing system and maintaining a facade of decency to cover up what is a very unpropitious internal state of affairs. A society very much on the decline. I've said all that in my writings. And that it must be widely known, common knowledge to all careful observers that all our social services are more for show than matters of fact. That applies to education, to the way it's organised, and to the health service. People in the West often say this: 'Yes, you do have many shortcomings, but on the other hand you have free medical assistance!' Well, it's no freer here than in most western countries, in fact it's frequently less free, as they say, and the general standard is very low.

STENHOLM Do you regard Soviet society today as a class society?

SAKHAROV A society with a tremendous lack of internal equality, at any rate. . . But whether one can call it a class society is hard to say. To a certain extent it's a question of terminology.

STENHOLM But the inequality then?

SAKHAROV There is inequality at many, many levels. Inequality between the rural and urban populations, where you have the collective farm worker with no passport, to all intents and purposes chained to his place of residence, his collective farm. He can only leave the farm if they agree to release him (which they usually do, I grant them that). There's inequality between different areas, Moscow and the large cities, which are privileged in terms of supply, life-style, cultural facilities, and all the other places. And the passport system reinforces, as it were, these divisions, this territorial heterogeneity.

STENHOLM What privileges do you think party workers enjoy in the Soviet Union?

SAKHAROV They have enormous extra-financial privileges. All sorts of things – a network of sanatoria, a medical service. . . There are very real privileges arising from (personal) connexions, various personal factors. Privileges in one's work, one's career. All managerial posts of any standing are either . . . well, a factory manager or a chief engineer, for example, only a party member can get the job. Exceptions are very rare. So your career depends very much indeed on your party membership, your position in the party structure. But as well as this, there's the traditional attitude to party cadres implied in the concept of 'nomenklatura'. According to this, even if a person is a failure in his job, so long as he has been a leading party worker, he is transferred to some other job with very similar material advantages. The whole business of nomination and promotion in one's job is very closely linked with certain interrelationships within this system. Every big administrator has, of course, people who are his personal associates and who transfer with him from one place to another when he moves. There is absolutely no way of overcoming this; it's obviously become a sort of law in the state structure. But talking of material perks, the main ones form an isolated and more or less clearly defined group which applies especially to the administration. They are assigned on the basis of party membership, but there are very big internal distinctions within the party itself also. It looks as though something rather like Orwell's inner party does exist in our country in a certain sense. The people who belong to this inner party, then, enjoy tremendous material privileges. There's a system whereby they are paid extra wages in (special) envelopes. It's a practice that comes and goes. I don't know what the situation is at the moment, but it looks as if the custom has been revived in some places. Then there's the system of closed retail distribution shops where the goods are not only more varied and of higher quality, but even the prices are different, which means that the same currency buys these people goods at a different price in a different shop. In other words, the real amount of their wages is not particularly indicative either.

STENHOLM We have talked a great deal about the defects (in society). Now, of course, there is the problem of what can be done to rectify them.

SAKHAROV What we *can* do and what we should *aspire* to are different matters. I feel there is hardly anything that *can* be done, but. . .

STENHOLM Why not?

SAKHAROV Because the system is intrinsically a very stable one. The more unfree a system, the more intrinsically it is preserved, as a rule.

STENHOLM But can external forces not do anything?

SAKHAROV We don't understand sufficiently well what the outside world is doing. It looks perhaps more as if the outside world is accepting our rules of the game. Which is a very bad thing. But there is another side to the matter. The fact that we are now breaking out of our fifty years of isolation may in time even have a beneficial influence. But it's very difficult to forecast how all this will come about. As far as the West is concerned, we can never make out whether it is a desire to help us or, on the contrary, a sort of capitulation, a game based on western domestic interests, where we are merely the small change.

STENHOLM But those are forces acting abroad. What about inside the Soviet Union?

SAKHAROV There are certainly some processes at work inside the Soviet Union, but for the moment they are so indistinct and so deeply hidden that it's almost impossible to forecast anything positive, any changes at all, any positive ones. . . We realise that a state as huge as ours can never be internally homogeneous, but in the absence of information, in the absence of contact between different groups of people, it is almost impossible to understand what is going on inside it. We know that nationalist tendencies in the peripheral areas of the state are very strong. But whether they are positive or not in each individual case is rather difficult to say. In some cases, the Ukraine for instance, they have become very closely interwoven with democratic trends. It's the same in the Baltic states: religious and nationalist matters merge easily and naturally with democratic ideas. But perhaps in other areas this is not so. We don't know the details.

STENHOLM So you are in fact extremely sceptical.

SAKHAROV On the whole I'm sceptical about socialism in general. I do not see that socialism offers us anything new on the theoretical level, so to speak, for a better way of organising society. It simply seems to be that although there may even be a few positive variants – life is diverse enough – the development of our state as a whole has exhibited more destructive than constructive features. Or rather, the constructive features have been due to general human factors: there may have been quite a number of them, but they were general human factors which could have arisen in any other environment; while in our society there has been such an accumulation of fierce political struggle, destruction, and bitterness, that we are now reaping the sad fruits of exhaustion, apathy, cynicism, . . . which we are having the greatest difficulty in shaking off. In what ways our society will develop is very hard to forecast from inside. Perhaps it's easier from outside, but one must do so with the minimum of preconceptions.

STENHOLM But Andrei Dmitrievich, you say you doubt whether anything at all can be achieved in the way of reforming the Soviet system, and yet you yourself go on doing what you do, writing statements, protesting. Why?

SAKHAROV One always needs to create ideals for oneself, even when one can see no direct way of realising them, because if one had no ideals one would no longer have any hopes, and then one would really feel one was groping in the dark, in an impasse.

Moreover, we are not sure if there are any possible ways in which our country can interact with the outside world. If we don't get any indication that this situation in our country is unfavourable . . . then we shall not even be able to take advantage of the chances we may have, because we shall not know what it is that needs rectifying, or if there is any need at all to rectify anything.

Then there is another factor, the history of our country, which ought to serve as a warning. It ought to restrain the West and the developing countries from making mistakes on the scale of those our country has made during its historical development. A man may not keep silent, but that doesn't mean he hopes to achieve anything. The two propositions are not synonymous. He may not hope to achieve anything at all, but he speaks out all the same because he simply cannot, cannot remain silent.

In almost every concrete instance of repression we never expect to achieve anything, and almost always we have been sadly lacking in any results whatsoever.

STENHOLM But if you think that socialism in the Soviet Union has not displayed its advantages, does that mean you think that in order to remedy the situation here the whole state must be reorganised, or can something be done within the existing system to improve and eliminate its defects?

SAKHAROV I really don't feel able to answer that question. To reorganise the state completely would be unthinkable, there must always be some continuity, some gradualness, otherwise there would be a repetition of the dreadful destruction that we have already gone through several times, total collapse. So naturally I seek gradual change, I'm a liberal, a 'gradualist', if you like.

STENHOLM Well, what is the first thing that must be done?

SAKHAROV Well, I realise that our present system can do nothing, or at least very little, about its own intrinsic qualities. What ought to be done? The ideological monism of our society should be liquidated. It's an ideological structure which is essentially anti-democratic and it is a tragedy for the state. Our isolation from the outside world, for example, the absence of the right to leave the country and return to it, is having an extremely pernicious effect on domestic life. In the first instance it is profoundly tragic for all those people who wish to leave for personal and national reasons. But it is also tragic for those who stay in the country, because a country which cannot be freely left or returned to is, for that reason alone, defective, it's a closed volume where processes develop in quite different ways from those in an open system.

STENHOLM You know that the right of free exit. . .

SAKHAROV . . . is one of the most important preconditions for return, free return.

STENHOLM And what else?

SAKHAROV It is one of the necessary preconditions for our country somehow to develop along more healthy lines. Then there are things of a more economic nature which are also certainly very important. The extremely developed state socialisation in our country has led to a situation in which private enterprise has been closed down in the very spheres in which it is most effective, as it has in large scale industry and in transport, where state control is perhaps the rational (form of management).

And as well as this, it has simply placed severe constraints on the individual initiative of citizens, as it has upon their personal freedom. This is having a bad effect on the living standards of the population and merely makes life more drab and dreary for many people than it might otherwise be. I'm thinking of private initiative in the fields of consumer goods, services, education, medicine. I am quite certain it would all play a very positive role in loosening the extremely monopolistic structure of the state. There are things relating to the administrative monopoly; the fact that the party's monopoly of the administration has reached such proportions here that . . . it must be apparent even to the party bosses that the whole thing is intolerable in principle. It has begun to affect the efficiency of the administration.

Well, what do we need? We need a great deal of openness and publicity in the work of the administrative machinery. And the single-party system is probably excessively and unnecessarily rigid. Even in the conditions of a socialist economy it is possible to do without the single-party system. As a matter of fact some elements of the multi-party system do exist in some of the people's democracies, though admittedly they look very much like half-caricatures.

We need elections with large numbers of candidates for the organs of state. Generally speaking, a series of measures which would have very little effect individually but which when combined might be able to shake the monolith we have created here, this fossilised structure that oppresses the life of the entire country.

The press must change its character. It's so standardised now that it has lost most of its information value. And when it does reflect any facts this is done in such a way that they are intelligible only to the initiated and give a distorted picture of the realities of life in this country; as for the intellectual life, it just doesn't exist, so it's not really something that can be distorted, there's no variety in intellectual life.

One thing in particular I must comment on is the role of the intelligentsia in society. The intelligentsia is kept down in a way that is quite unlawful. Materially it is very badly provided for, even compared with manual labourers. But its absolute living standard is very low, of course, if you compare it with western countries which have reached roughly the same stage of economic development. This oppression of the intelligentsia – it is economically depressed too – means ideological depression as well, creates a sort of general anti-intellectual atmosphere in the country, in which the intellectual professions – teachers, doctors – don't enjoy the respect they should. And another expression of this anti-intellectualism is the way the intelligentsia itself is beginning to retreat either into narrow professional specialisation or into a dual intellectual life at work and at home; in the narrow circle of their friends people begin thinking in different ways, and this split mentality leads to hypocrisy and further moral and creative decline. Of course, it's the artistic, not the technical intelligentsia that is most distressingly affected by this. They already feel that they have reached a total impasse. And as a result tthe literature that does come to the surface is terribly grey, conventional and generaly tedious.

STENHOLM Can I put one final question to you? You have been very active indeed (in the human rights movement) over the last few years. Have you never feared for your own health and liberty?

SAKHAROV Not very much, I personally have never been afraid for myself, but that's partly my nature, and partly because I started out from a very high social position; such fears would have been quite unjustified and irrelevant. What I fear at the moment are the kinds of pressure that don't affect me personally but may be exerted on the members of my family and my wife's family. That is the most painful thing, because it's very real and it's already happening, getting closer and closer to us. Things like what happened to Levich, his son[1] being picked up; it shows you how they go about these things.

[1] Corresponding Member of the Academy of Sciences Veniamin Levich, whose son Evgeny, an astrophysicist, was picked up on the street by the military authorities on 16 May 1973 and called up into the army.

DMITRI SHOSTAKOVICH – Excerpts from his Memoirs

In the first of these two excerpts Shostakovich describes the atmosphere of repression under Stalin, in which creative artists struggled precariously not only to make a living, but to survive.

The new lifestyle brought so many new and fresh conflicts. The exclusive distributor; the communal apartment. In previous eras a man might wander around a castle with a sword looking for a ghost. In our times a man wanders around a communal apartment with an axe in his hands, keeping watch for the resident who doesn't turn out the light in the toilet. Imagine a novel of secrets and horrors of the new era: here's my hero, axe in hand, threatening to chop up the sloppy resident if he catches him in the act. I feel that I didn't sing his praises enough, that is to say, that I didn't portray him enough.

I'm not indulging in irony now. For some reason, people think that music must tell us only about the pinnacles of the human spirit, or at least about highly romantic villains. But there are very few heroes or villains. Most people are average, neither black nor white, but grey. A dirty shade of grey.

And it's in that vague grey middle ground that the fundamental conflicts of our age take place. It is a huge anthill in which we all crawl. In the majority of cases, our destinies are bad. We are treated harshly and cruelly, and as soon as someone crawls a little higher, he's ready to torture and humiliate others.

That is the situation that needs watching in my opinion. You must write about the majority of people and for the majority. And you must write the truth – then it can be called realistic art. Who needs the great tragedies? There's an Ilf and Petrov[2] story about a sick man who washes his foot before going to the doctor. When he gets there he notices that he washed the wrong one. Now that's a real tragedy.

To the best of my ability I tried to write about these people, about their completely average, commonplace dreams and hopes, and about their suspicious tendency toward murder.

I regret that I wasn't consistent enough, perhaps, in that regard. I didn't have Zoshchenko's[3] determination and willpower. Zoshchenko plainly rejected the idea of a Red Leo Tolstoi or a Red Rabindranath Tagore, and that sunsets and dawns had to be described in flowery prose.

But I do have one great excuse. I never tried to flatter the authorities with my music. And I never had 'an affair' with them. I was never a favourite, though I know that some accuse me of it. They say that I stood too close to power. An optical illusion. What was not, was not.

It's simplest to look at the facts. Lenin, as it is easy enough to surmise, never heard my music. And if he had, I doubt that he would have liked it. As far as I can tell, Lenin had specific tastes in music. He had a rather distinctive approach to it, more peculiar than is usually imagined. Lunacharsky[4] used to speak of it in this way: Lunacharsky often invited Lenin to his house to listen to music, but Lenin was always busy and refused. Once, tired of Lunacharsky's invitations, he said directly, 'Of course it's very nice to listen to music. But can you imagine, it depresses me, I find it hard to bear.' You see, poor Lenin was saddened by music. A telling fact, if you think about it.

Chief of Petrograd Zinoviev didn't become a fan of my music. Zinoviev was replaced by Kirov,[5] and I had no luck with him either. In his time Zinoviev ordered all the opera houses in Leningrad to be closed. He explained it something like this: The proletariat doesn't need opera houses. They are a heavy burden for the proletariat. We Bolsheviks can't carry the heavy burden any more. (Lenin, if you recall, also called opera 'a piece of purely upper-class culture'.)

Kirov, on the contrary, often attended the opera. He liked being a patron of the parts. But that didn't help my opera *The Nose*. Kirov had a strongly negative reaction to *The Nose* and the opera was taken out of repertory. They blamed it on the fact that it needed too many rehearsals; the artists, they said, got tired. At least they didn't shut down the theatre. They had planned to squash the opera house completely over Krenek's operas.

I don't need to speak of Stalin, Zhdanov, or Khrushchev here. Everyone knows of their dissatisfaction with my music. Should I have been upset? It seems a strange question. Of course not! That would be the simplest answer. But the simple answer isn't enough. These weren't mere acquaintances, men on the street. They were men wielding unlimited power.

And the comrade leaders used that power without thinking twice about it, particularly if they felt that their refined taste was offended. An artist whose portrait did not resemble the leader disappeared forever. So did the writer who used 'crude words'. No one entered into aesthetic discussions with them or asked them to explain themselves. Someone came for them at night, that's all.

These were not isolated cases, not exceptions. You must understand that. It didn't matter how the audience reacted to your work or if the critics liked it. All that had no meaning in the final analysis. There was only one question of life or death: How did the leader like your opus. I stress: life or death, because we are talking about life or death here, literally, not figuratively. That's what you must understand.

'Formalism' has been a cant word in Soviet art and literature since the 1920s. As history has shown, this word has almost no real aesthetic content. It has been an epithet for the most varied creative figures and tendencies, depending on the political line and personal tastes of the leaders of the Soviet Union at a particular time. Let us quote one typical Soviet definition of formalism:

> Formalism in art is the expression of bourgeois ideology that is hostile to the Soviet people. The Party did not cease its vigilant struggle even for a moment against any even minute manifestation of formalism.

It therefore is not strange that all kinds of punishments were brought upon those branded as 'formalists', up to and including extermination.[6]

In 1948 a widespread campaign against 'formalism' in Soviet music became one of the most important issues of the day. Shostakovich lays the initial blame for this wholesale artistic destruction at the feet of Vano Ilyich Muradeili (1908–1970), a composer whose opera *Great Friendship* had displeased Stalin. In his efforts to regain Stalin's favour, Muradeli claimed he had been prevented from writing truly melodious music by a formalist conspiracy.

> They gathered the composers, and they began hanging one another. It was a pathetic sight that I would rather not recall. Of course, almost nothing surprises me, but this is one thing that's too repugnant to think about. Stalin designated to Zhdanov[7] the task of compiling a list of 'the main offenders'. Zhdanov worked like an experienced torturer – he set one composer against the other.
>
> Of course, Zhdanov didn't have to work too hard, the composers chewed one another up with glee. No one wanted to be on the list; it wasn't a list for prizes but for possible extermination. Everything

had significance here – your position on the list, for instance. If you were first, consider yourself gone. Last – there was still hope. And the citizen composers knocked themselves out to avoid the list and did everything they could to get their comrades on it.[8] They were real criminals, whose philosophy was, You die today, and I'll go tomorrow.

Well, they worked and worked on the list. They put some names on, crossed others off. Only two names had the top spots sewn up: my name was number one, and Prokofiev's number two. The meeting was over, and the historic resolution appeared. And after that. . .

Meeting upon meeting, conference upon conference. The whole country was in a fever, the composers more than anyone. It was like a dam breaking and a flood of murky dirty water rushing in. Everyone seemed to go mad and anyone who felt like it expressed an opinion on music.

Zhdanov announced, 'The Central Committee of Bolsheviks demands beauty and refinement from music'. And he added that the goal of music was to give pleasure, while our music was crude and vulgar, and listening to it undoubtedly destroyed the psychological and physiological balance of a man – for example, a man like Zhdanov.

Stalin was no longer considered a man. He was a god and all this did not concern him. He was above it all. The leader and teacher washed his hands of it, and I think he did so consciously. He was being smart. But I only realized this later. At the time it seemed as though my end had come. Sheet music was reprocessed. Why burn it? That was wasteful; by recycling all the cacophonic symphonies and quartets they could save on paper. They destroyed recordings at the radio stations. And Khrennikov[9] said, 'There, it's gone forever. The formalist snake will never rear its head again.'

All the papers printed letters from the workers, who all thanked the Party for sparing them from the torture of listening to the symphones of Shostakovich. The censors met the wishes of the workers and put out a blacklist, which named those symphonies of Shostakovich's that were being taken out of circulation. Thus I stopped personally offending Asafiev,[10] that leading figure of musical scholarship, who complained, 'I take the Ninth Symphony as a personal insult'.

From now unto forever, music had to be refined, harmonious, and melodious. They wanted particular attention devoted to singing with words, since singing without words satisfied only the perverted tastes of a few aesthetes and individualists.

Altogether this was called: the Party has saved music from liquidation. It turned out that Shostakovich and Prokofiev had wanted to liquidate music, and Stalin and Zhdanov didn't let them. Stalin could be happy. The whole country, instead of thinking about its squalid life, was entering mortal combat with formalist composers. Why go on talking about it? I have a musical composition on that theme, which says it all.[11]

There were further developments. Stalin was rather deflated by the reaction in the West to the historic resolution. For some reason, he thought they'd be tossing their hats in the air as well, or at least be silent. But they weren't silent in the West. During the war, they had come to know our music a little better, and thus they saw that the resolution was the delirium of a purple cow.

Naturally, Stalin didn't give a damn about the West, and the Western intelligentsia in particular. He used to say, 'Don't worry, they'll swallow it.' But the West did exist and he had to do something with it. They had started a peace movement, and they needed people for it. And Stalin thought of me. That was his style completely. Stalin liked to put a man face to face with death and then make him dance to his own tune.

I was given the order to get ready for a trip to America. I had to go to the Cultural and Scientific Congress for World Peace in New York. A worthy cause. It's obvious that peace is better than war and therefore struggling for peace is a noble effort. But I refused; it was humiliating for me to take part in a spectacle like that. I was formalist, a representative of an anti-national direction in music. My music was banned, and now I was supposed to go and say that everything was fine.

No, I said, I won't go. I'm ill, I can't fly, I get airsick. Molotov[12] talked to me, but I still refused.

Then Stalin called. And in his nagging way, the leader and teacher asked me why I didn't want to go to America. I answered that I couldn't. My comrades' music wasn't played, and neither was mine. They would ask about it in America. What could I say?

Stalin pretended to be surprised. 'What do you mean, it isn't played? Why aren't they playing it?'

I told him that there was a decree by the censors, that there was a blacklist. Stalin said, 'Who gave the orders?' Naturally I replied, 'It must have been one of the leading comrades.'

Now came the interesting part. Stalin announced, 'No, we didn't give that order.' He always referred to himself in the royal plural – 'We, Nicholas II'. And he began rehearsing the thought that the censors had over-reacted, had taken an incorrect initiative: we didn't give an order like that, we'll have to straighten out the comrades from the censors, and so on.

This was another matter, this was a real concession. And I thought that maybe it would make sense to go to America, if as a result they would play the music of Prokofiev, Shebalin, Miaskovsky, Kachaturian, Popov and Shostakovich again.

And just then, Stalin stopped going on about the question of the order and said, 'We'll take care of that problem, Comrade Shostakovich. What about your health?'

And I told Stalin the pure truth. 'I feel sick.'

Stalin was taken aback and then started mulling over this unexpected bulletin. 'Why do you feel sick? From what? We'll send you a physician, he'll see why you feel sick.' And so on.

So finally I agreed, and I made the trip to America. It cost me a great deal, that trip. I had to answer stupid questions and avoid saying too much. They made a sensation out of that too. And all I thought about was: How much longer do I have to live?

NOTES

1. *Testimony – The Memoirs of Shostakovich*, as related to and edited by Solomon Volkov, Hamish Hamilton, London (1979)
2. Ilya Ilf (Ilya Arnoldovich Fainsilberg, 1897–1937) and Yevgeny Petrov (Yevgeny Petrovich Kataev, 1903–1942), popular satirists and collaborators. Sentences and jokes from their novels *The Twelve Chairs* and *The Golden Calf* are widely quoted in Soviet life; several characters from these novels were taken on the aura of folklore.
3. Mikhail Mikhailovich Zoshchenko (1895–1958), satirist and playwright, a friend of Shostakovich. A brilliant stylist, he gained unheard-of popularity while still quite young. Zoshchenko noted dryly: 'I write with compression. My sentences are short. Accessible to the poor. Perhaps that's why I have so many readers.' After the Second World War, Zoshchenko was viciously attacked by the Party; 'thoroughly rotten and decayed sociopolitical and literary physiognomy', 'vile, lustful animal', 'unprincipled and conscienceless literary hooligan', were a few of the official descriptions of him. 'Let him get out of Soviet literature,' a Party leader demanded, and the order was carried

out. Zoshchenko's original literary style had a decided influence on Shostakovich's manner of expressing himself.

4. Anatoly Vasilyevich Lunacharsky (1875–1933), a Communist Party leader, People's Commissar of Education. The first and last educated Soviet 'culture boss', he wrote many lively articles on music and would never have given orders, as did a later minister of culture, to organize 'a quartet of ten men'. In 1921, on Lunacharsky's personal orders, young Shostakovich was awarded food rations.
5. Sergei Mironovich Kirov (1886–1934), a Communist Party leader, the 'boss' of Leningrad. He was killed by a terrorist (the murder is now thought by most historians to have been engineered by Stalin), and Stalin used this terrorist act as an excuse for a wave of massive repressions, long remembered by Leningraders. In 1935 the famous Maryinsky Theatre of Opera and Ballet was renamed after Kirov.
6. Solomon Volkov: footnote to Chapter 3 of *Testimony*.
7. Andrei Alexandrovich Zhdanov (1896–1948), Communist Party leader. The term 'Zhdanovism' is well-known in the East. It refers to the harsh regimentation of literature and art in post-war Russia. It is not clear whether or not Zhdanov was merely carrying out Stalin's orders in his 'aesthetic' pronouncements, but as a result of them Zhdanov acquired so much prominence that Stalin began envying him. It is now thought that Stalin had Zhdanov killed and then cast blame for his death on the Jewish doctors.
8. The reference is in part to the desperate attempt by Dmitri Borisovich Kabalevsky (b. 1904) to replace his name on a blacklist, prepared by Zhdanov, of composers 'who held formalistic, anti-people tendencies' with that of Gavriil Nikolayevich Popov (1904–1972). The attempt was successful. The final text of the Party's 'historical resolution' does not mention Kabalevsky. The talented Popov eventually drank himself to death.
9. Tikhon Nikolayevich Khrennikov (b. 1913), composer, head of the Composers' Union of the USSR from the time of its Third Congress (1948). He was appointed to the post by Stalin (as were leaders of the analogous unions of writers, artists, etc.). In the Stalinist years, the duties of the head included approval of lists of the Union's members marked for repression. Khrennikov is the only original leader of the 'creative' unions to retain his post to this day. For many years he attacked Shostakovich and Prokofiev viciously. He has received all the highest Soviet orders and prizes.
10. Boris Vladimirovich Asafiev (1884–1949), musicologist and composer. It would be no exaggeration to say that Asafiev is the most important representative of Russian thought on music throughout the country's musicological history. (His work is only now becoming known in the West.) Unfortunately, high scruples were not among the character traits of this brilliant scholar and critic. Some of the best pages ever written

about Shostakovich belong to Asafiev, though the two men's relationship varied at different times. Shostakovich could not forgive Asafiev for the position he took in 1948, when he allowed his name to be used in an attack on the formalist composers.

11. A reference to a still unpublished satiric vocal work of Shostakovich mocking the anti-formalism capaign of 1948 and its main organizers.
12. Vyacheslav Mikhailovich Molotov (1890–1986), Soviet government leader. In 1949 Stalin sent Molotov's wife Polina Zhemchuzhina, to the camps for 'Zionist activities'. Molotov's career ended in 1957, when Khrushchev had him removed from power as a member of an 'anti-Party group'.

A LETTER TO THE SOVIET BUREAUCRATS

ALEXANDER SOLZHENITSYN

This ideology that fell to us by inheritance is not only decrepit and hopelessly antiquated now; even during its best decades it was totally mistaken in its predictions and was never a science.

A primitive, superficial economic theory, it declared that only the worker creates value and failed to take into account the contribution of either organizers, engineers, transport or marketing systems. It was mistaken when it forecast that the proletariat would be endlessly oppressed and would never achieve anything in a bourgeois democracy – if only we could shower people with as much food, clothing and leisure as they have gained under capitalism! It missed the point when it asserted that the prosperity of European countries depended on their colonies – it was only after they had shaken the colonies off that they began to accomplish their 'conomic miracles'. It was mistaken through and through in its prediction that socialists could only ever come to power by an armed uprising. It miscalculated in thinking that the first uprisings would take place in the advanced industrial countries – quite the reverse. And the picture of how the whole world would rapidly be overtaken by revolutions and how states would soon wither away was sheer delusion, sheerr ignorance of human nature. and as for wars being characteristic of capitalism alone and coming to an end when capitalism did – we have already witnessed the longest war of the twentieth century so far, and it was not capitalism that rejected negotiations and a truce for fifteen to twenty years; and God forbid that we should witness the bloodiest and most brutal of all mankind's wars – a war between two communist super-powers. Then there was nationalism, which this theory also buried in 1848 as a 'survival' – but find a stronger force in the world today! And it's the same with many other things too boring to list.

Marxism is not only not accurate, not only not a science, has not only failed to predict a *single event* in terms of figures, quantities, time-scales or locations (something that electronic computers today do with laughable ease in the course of social forecasting, although never with the help of Marxism) – it absolutely astounds one by the economic and mechanistic crudity of its attempts to explain that most subtle of creatures, the human being, and that even more complex synthesis of millions of people, society. Only the cupidity of some, the blindness of others and a craving for *faith* on the part of still others can serve to explain this grim humour of the twentieth century: how can such a discredited and bankrupt doctrine still have so many followers in the West! In *our* country there are fewest of all left! *We* who have had a taste of it are only pretending willy-nilly. . .

We have seen that it was not your common sense, but that same antiquated legacy of the Progressive Doctrine that endowed you with all the millstones that are dragging you down: first collectivization; then the nationalization of small trades and services (which has made the lives of ordinary citizens unbearable – but you don't feel that yourselves; which has caused thieving and lying to pile up and up even in the day-to-day running of the country – and you are powerless against it); then the need to inflate military development for the sake of making grand international gestures, so that the whole internal life of the country is going down the drain and in fifty years we haven't even found the time to open up Siberia; then the obstacles in the way of industrial development and technoligical reconstruction; then religious persecution, which is very important for Marxism, but senseless and self-defeating for pragmatic state leaders – to set useless good-for-nothings to hounding their most conscientious workers, innocent of all cheating and theft, and as a result to suffer from universal cheating and theft. For the believer his faith is *supremely* precious, more precious than the food he puts in his stomach.

Have you ever paused to reflect on why it is that you deprive these millions of your finest subjects of their homeland? All this can do you as the leaders of the state nothing but harm, but you do it mechanically, automatically, because Marxism insists that you do it. Just as it insists that you, the rulers of a super-power, deliver accounts of your activities to outlandish visitors from distant parts – leaders of uninfluential, insignificant communist parties from the other end of the globe, preoccupied least of all with the fortunes of Russia.

To someone brought up on Marxism it seems a terrifying step – suddenly to start living without the familiar ideology. But in point of fact you have no choice, circumstances themselves will force you to do it and it may already be too late. In anticipation of an impending war with China, Russia's national leaders will in any case have to rely on patriotism, and patriotism alone. When Stalin initiated such a shift during the war – remember! – nobody was in the least surprised and nobody shed a tear for Marxism: everyone took it as the most natural thing in the world, something they recognized as Russian. It is only prudent to redeploy one's forces when faced by a great danger – but sooner rather than later. In any event, this process of repudiation, though tentative, began long ago in our country, for what is the 'combination' of Marxism and patriotism but a meaningless absurdity? These two points of view can be 'merged' only in generalized incantations, for history has shown us that in practice they are always diametrically opposed. This is so obvious that Lenin in 1915 actually proclaimed: 'We are anti-patriots'. And that was the honest truth. And throughout the 1920s in our country the word 'patriot' meant exactly the same as 'White Guard'. And the whole of this letter that I am now putting before you is patriotism, *which means* rejection of Marxism. For Marxism orders us to leave the North-East unexploited and to leave our women with their crowbars and shovels, and instead finance and expedite world revolution.

Beware when the first cannons fire on the Sino-Soviet border lest you find yourselves in a doubly precarious position because the national consciousness in our country has become stunted and blurred – witness how mighty America lost to tiny North Vietnam, how easily the nerves of American society and American youth gave way, precisely because the United States has a weak and undeveloped national consciousness. Don't miss the chance while you've got it!

The step seems a hard one at first, but in fact, once you have thrown off this rubbishy ideology of ours, you will quickly sense a huge relief and become aware of a relaxation in the entire structure of the state and in all the processes of government. After all, this ideology, which is driving us into a situation of acute conflict abroad, has long ceased to be helpful to us here at home, as it was in the twenties and thirties. In our country today *nothing constructive rests upon it*, it is a sham, cardboard, theatrical prop – take it away and nothing will collapse, nothing will even wobble. For a long time now, everything has rested solely on material calculation and the subjection of the people, and not on any upsurge of ideological enthusiasm, as you perfectly well know. This ideology does nothing now but sap our strength and bind us. It clogs up the whole life of society, minds, tongues, radio and press – with lies, lies, lies. For how else can something dead pretend that it is living except by erecting a scaffolding of lies? Everything is steeped in lies and *everybody knows it* – and says so openly in private conversation and jokes and moans about it, but in their official speeches they go on hypocritically parroting what they are 'supposed to say', and with equal hypocrisy and boredom read and listen to the speeches of others: how much of society's energy is squandered on this! And you, when you open your newspapers or switch on your television – do *you yourselves* really believe for one instant that these speeches are sincere? No, you stopped believing long ago, I am certain of it. And if you didn't, then you must have become totally insulated from the inner life of the country.

This universal, obligatory force-feeding with lies is now the most agonizing aspect of existence in our country – worse than all our material miseries, worse than any lack of civil liberties.

All these arsenals of lies, which are totally unnecessary for our stability *as a state*, are levied as a kind of tax for the benefit of ideology – to nail down events as they happen and clamp them to a tenacious, sharp-clawed but dead ideology: and it is precisely because our state, through sheer force of habit, tradition and inertia, continues to cling to this false doctrine with all its tortuous aberrations, that it needs to put the dissenter behind bars. For a false *ideology* can find no other answer to argument and protest than weapons and prison bars.

Cast off this cracked ideology! Relinquish it to your rivals, let it go wherever it wants, let it pass from our country like a storm-cloud, like an epidemic, let others concern themselves with it and study it, just so long as we don't! In ridding ourselves of it we shall also rid ourselves of the need to fill our life with lies. Let us all pull off and shake off from all of us this filthy sweaty shirt of ideology which is now so stained with the blood of those 66 million[1] that it prevents the living body of the nation from breathing. This Ideology bears the entire responsibility for all the blood that has been shed. Do you need me to persuade you to throw it off without more ado? Whoever wants can pick it up in our place.

I am certainly not proposing that you go to the opposite extreme and persecute or ban Marxism, or even argue against it (nobody will argue against it for very long, if only out of sheer apathy). All I am suggesting is that you rescue yourselves from it, and rescue your state system and your people as well. *All you have to do* is to deprive

Marxism of its powerful state support and let is exist of itself and stand on its own feet. And let all who wish to do so make propaganda for it, defend it and din it into others without let or hindrance – but outside working hours and *not on state salaries*. In other words, the whole *agitprop* system of agitation and propaganda must cease to be paid for out of the nation's pocket. This should not anger or antagonize the numerous people who work in *agitprop*: this new statute would free them from all possible insulting accusations of self-interest and give them for the first time the opportunity to prove the true strength of their ideological convictions and sincerity. And they could only be overjoyed with the new twofold commitment: to undertake productive labour for their country, to produce something of practical value on weekdays in the daytime (and whatever work they chose in place of their present occupation would be much more productive, for the work they do now is useless, if not positively detrimental), and in the evenings, on free days and during their holidays, to devote their leisure to propagating their beloved doctrine, revelling selflessly in the truth! After all, that is exactly what our believers do (while being persecuted for it, too) and they consider it spiritually satisfying. What a marvellous opportunity, I will not say to test but to prove the sincerity of all those people who have been haranguing the rest of us for decades.

NOTES

1. An approximate total of people exterminated in the Soviet Union as a result of internal political policies, calculated by a former Leningrad professor of statistics, I.A. Kurganov.

THE PRIVATE ELEMENT IN THE SOVIET ECONOMY AND ACCOMPLICES IN THE PUBLIC SECTOR

A Study of the Underground Aspects of Economic Life in the USSR

ROMAN REDLIKH

The principle of socialism 'from each according to his ability, to each according to his labour', which is the basis upon which, under Article 14 of the Constitution of the USSR, the State 'exercises control over the measurement of labour and consumption', should permeate the entire structure of Soviet society. In fact this is not so, and social and economic life in the Soviet Union is no more reflected in its official description than are the private thoughts of the Soviet citizen in his public utterances.

Although the socialist planned economy is not a fiction, it does mean that it is distorted by fictions. Measures taken by the authorities encounter the opposition of the most elemental economic forces. There are two economies in the Soviet Union, although these are naturally closely interwoven. The first is the socialist economy, which meets military requirements and ensures the launching of satellites, the second is an economy of private gain, one which adapts itself in a distorted way to the conditions imposed by the economic dictatorship of the Party. The former is reflected in the impressive reports of the Central Statistical Board and the grandiose schemes of the State Plan; the latter completely bypasses socialist statistics and socialist legality.

The former is capable of satisfying anyone who can agree to accept gross output as reality, and the USSR at the valuation that the Soviet Communist Party wishes to place upon it. The latter is a significant factor in the life of the people, although there are no numerical data relating to it. The Soviet authorities are inclined to deny its existence. But it surfaces as modest additional earnings from a personal plot of land or from additional work carried out in free time, or as cunning schemes often involving misappropriation, bribery, speculation and corruption.

When we come to consider Soviet life, we are bound to note that a good half of the population of the country has additional earnings, and that the whole of the socialist economy is shot through with speculation and corruption, ranging from that of the soft drinks vendor who adds a short measure of syrup to the soda water and the conductor who 'forgets' to take the ticket from the receipt-book, to the manager of an industrial trust or the director of a factory who organizes exchange deals with those around him, as a by-product of which he builds himself a country cottage and acquires hunting and shooting rights.

The Private Element

It might seem that there could be no provision for any sector of private ownership in the socialist economy, especially now, on the threshold of communism. All remains of the capitalist order have long since been destroyed, and survivals of capitalism ought rather to be sought among individuals more than 70 years old, since Soviet citizens who are younger cannot remember any form of capitalism, even its surviving traces in the period of the New Economic Policy.

Nevertheless, private initiative, private property, and even private capital exist in the USSR and play a not unimportant part in the social and economic life of the country. There is not and cannot be any statistical reflection of this role. 'Those working on their own account and accomplices', if we may be permitted to use the humorous, but absolutely accurate term of the satirical writers Ilf and Petrov, slip through any statistical network. It is just as if they did not exist.

Yet there are whole areas of economic life whose operation would be quite unthinkable without private initiative. Try to imagine Soviet life without the cultivation of individual allotments, the collective farm market and dealing in odds and ends. The Soviet man in the street has to turn to both in order to satisfy his most pressing needs. For good or ill, private initiative offsets the monstrous imperfections of the public economy, and has shown a persistent tendency to expand in the years since Stalin. It may be difficult to estimate its volume, but its function is perfectly clear, that is to *do what the State is incapable of doing*, to fill the gaps in socialist supply and adjust its rhythm.

Because private initiative is a phenomenon that is theoretically inconceivable in Soviet society, it is outside the law. In practice, however, it has always been tolerated, with the proviso that it periodically expands or contracts in scale, depending on the whim of the authorities. It also penetrates into spheres of the socialist economy that might seem to be monopolised by the State. The State has its free medicine and free education, but teachers are not unwilling to give private lessons, and doctors receive patients at home after the dispensary or clinic, and the income of a manager, even the manager of an armaments factory, like that of party workers at all levels, is certainly not confined to what is a fairly modest salary. Let us, however, begin with private economic activity, the principal manifestations of which are land ownership, house ownership and house building, the exercise of a craft or skill, and trading.

Land ownership and house ownership

The bulk of Soviet agricultural output is produced by collective farms and State farms. However, this is a statement that needs considerable qualification. Firstly, virtually the whole of the rural population and a good half of the population of small towns have personal plots, ranging in size from one-tenth of a hectare to half a hectare, which they use as vegetable plots, for fruit growing, and for cowsheds and chicken runs.

These personal plots of land play no part in the production of grain and industrial crops, but their contribution to cattle breeding and sheep farming is far from negligible. The USSR volume of the third edition of the *Great Soviet Encyclopaedia*, which was published in 1977, is reticent on the matter, but the similar volume of the previous edition, which appeared in 1957 at the time of the thaw under Khrushchev, informs us (pp. 330 and 334) that 55.5% of cows, 85.8% of goats, 23.9% of sheep and 37.7% of pigs in 1956 belonged to private owners, and that there were 6,360,000 hectares of private plots devoted to fruit farming and the production of vegetables, melons, and potatoes, as against 7,380,000 hectares used for similar purposes on collective farms and State farms. The productivity of these areas may be illustrated by the following exerpt from a classic description of country life, the *Country Diary of Yefim Dorosh:*

All the private plots hereabouts are given over to onion growing.

> There isn't a tree, there isn't a shrub, there isn't anything in any way evocative of what is usually associated with the word 'farmstead'. . . They are in fact not farmsteads. They are plantations raising cash crops on a commercial basis. Were they all to be combined, the total area might prove to be greater than the onion-growing area on the collective farm. But the yield is far and away greater, because the onions are better cultivated on the plots: they are watered and weeded at the right times, and better manured; although there is a drought this summer, the onions on the plots are green and fresh, whereas the onions on the collective farm are poorer, the tops have begun to wither, and they are heavily overgrown with weeds. . . What we have is not so much personal plots attached to a collective farm, but a collective farm attached to personal plots.

The ownership of a plot of land is often linked to the ownership of a house. The article on Housing and Communial Services in the appropriate volume of the *Great Soviet Encyclopaedia* (third edition, 1977) contains the information that 70% of all dwellings in the country are public property. The remaining 30% are apparently wooden huts and country cottages, which do little more than give their owners a roof over their heads, although the renting of room space and rooms is an additional quite considerable source of income to house owners around large towns and in the vicinity of holiday resorts. What is at issue is not, however, the form of the property. Living space that is quite definitely in public ownership is bought and sold in Soviet cities, is passed on by inheritance and transferred from person to person primarily by a deed of registration, specifying the right of a given individual to live in a given locality. Marriages are entered into or dissolved purely in order to obtain or transfer dwelling space, and thousands of roubles are paid out in key money and bribes. Individual private building is a truly insatiable consumer of building materials in short supply, most of them illegally acquired, and of the subsidiary labour of what are known as 'Sunday workers', skilled craftsmen who work 'off the record', frequently with their own materials stolen from somewhere or other.

Private exercise of a craft or trade

The existence of craftsmen working on their own account is not admitted in socialist society. The most recent edition of the *Great*

Soviet Encyclopaedia does not give the number of registered craftsmen. Nor is there any reason why it should, since it is clear that no Soviet citizen would register as a self-employed craftsman, other than in a case of extreme need, but would prefer to be listed under some other category, as a fireman, a watchman or a doorkeeper, in an occupation providing plenty of free time. Even the Soviet authorities do not know how many people in Russia currently derive extra income from 'Sunday work', nor for how many of them it is in fact only supplementary income, and for how many it is the main means of subsistence. However, if your flat needs repairs, if your furniture needs renovating, if you want to instal a television, or have your shoes repaired quickly, you will inevitably have to avail yourself of the services of such a worker. Furthermore, privately owned houses and country cottages are not built by State organizations, but by the very bricklayers and carpenters whose unavailability is such a cause of delay in the erection of socialist dwellings. Any experienced collective farm chairman who needs a bath house, a cowshed or even a power station will go to the district purely in order to agree on how to handle the bookkeeping entry for payment to the group of 'Sunday workers' or the clandestine entrepreneur who will undertake the order.

A similar situation exists as regards trade. There are no registered private traders in the USSR, and the buying of anything with the object of reselling it at a profit is regarded as speculation, punishable by law. At the same time, it is officially recognized that 'collective farm trade is a third form of Soviet trade' and it is clear to any unprejudiced observer that city dwellers would eat far less well but for this third form of trade.

'Non-traders' also trade on the officially permitted 'second-hand market', or in common parlance the 'junk market'. Here you are able to get, admittedly not cheaply, but at prices that reflect the extent of the risk for those involved in the transaction, everything that you need, from a copy of *The Gulag Archipelago* to the razor blades and fish hooks which it is difficult to find in the shops. Spare parts for cars, tools, and components for colour television sets, for example, find their way invisibly onto this market. But the junk market is only the tip of the iceberg. Many more transactions are concluded in places ranging from gateways to the offices of party leaders. It is these transactions which are the underwater part of the iceberg of the socialist economy, and which we must now consider.

Accomplices

Accomplices are those people who take part in this alternative economic life, whether through private plots, trade on the collective farm market and the junk market, or undertaking Sunday work. These bourgeois values are also reflected in the private ownership of a country cottage, and in the actions of the owner, whether or not he be a member of the party, to acquire both the cottage and the furnishings.

Irrespective of the social structure under which people live, they have needs, and the higher the position of a person in the social hierarchy, the greater are his needs. A high Soviet official of the present day cannot abide to wear a rough shirt and live in a communal dwelling. He pays only lip service to the ideas of the Communist Manifesto, to the true meaning of which he has probably never given serious consideration. His ideal is a bourgeois one: a flat of his own in town, his own country cottage for Sunday relaxation, his own, preferably imported, stylish furniture, colour television, dishwasher and car. He would like to be able to will all this property to his children. He will, if necessary, pay quite considerable amounts for a school-leaving certificate or a diploma from an institution of higher education not merited by the performance of his offspring; he will give presents of dresses, carpets, complete services of china, scarves and watches to teachers and educational administrators. Even the worker and the collective farmer do not aspire to live in a hostel or to eat in a canteen, and every Soviet housewife has her dream, if not for a washing machine, then at least for a good galvanized washing trough.

The socialist economy, which provides miserly salaries that do not meet man's natural needs, is unable to suppress them, and they grow in a distorted way, like a seedling under the weight of a stone. Speculation and corruption of every type, string pulling, humbug and falsification of accounts are all products of the socialist order, distorted correctives made by life itself to the economic monopoly of the State, mutilated manifestations of the indestructible human aspiration to achieve what one wants. It is not only the Soviet collective farmer who derives a considerable part of his income from his private plot. One of the jokes that circulate among Soviet citizens, known as 'Radio Free Armenia', runs as follows. Question: 'Is it possible to live on one's salary in Armenia?' Answer: 'We don't know. Ask around in Georgia.' The income pattern of

Soviet citizens is not simple enough to be assessable on the basis of statistical data.

Every inhabitant of the Soviet Union is well aware that corrupt private interests are well to the fore in the provision of goods and services. Losses ascribed to leakage, shrinkage and spillage, short measure, short weight; clever schemes in which first grade goods are classified as seconds and seconds are sold as perfect goods, illicit and under the counter trading, simple barter and, lastly, downright theft, known as the plundering or squandering of socialist property, have become so much a part of life that no one is seriously disturbed by them any more. It would be superfluous to give examples.

We'll give you, if you'll give us

Private interest and private initiative, permeate the socialist economy. The capitalist profit principle is squeezing out the party idea of the plan. In an economic review of the year 1938, at the height of the Stalin period, it was reported in the newspaper industry on 31 December 1938 that 50% of deliveries in Stalingrad, 33% in Dnepropetrovsk and 30% in Moscow had been illegally obtained. Twenty years later, in its issue of 17 July 1959, the newspaper *Izvestiya* carried an article dealing with the delivery situation with the revealing title We'll give you, if you'll give us. The principle of mutually advantageous exchange, which is as old as man's economic dealings, is described in this article in its socialist form with particular reference not to some co-operative workshop producing consumer goods, but to the Vyksa metallurgical plant:

> Metal was distributed right and left. A black market was set up on which metal was exchanged for every imaginable kind of article and material: electric cable, plywood, cement, fire hoses, paint, glass, tarpaulin, measuring instruments and vehicle trailers. Economic agreements were concluded in order to give these transactions the appearance of legality. In some instances, the pretext was the manufacture of equipment, in others the production of semi-finished goods. In particular, the 335th Building Administration undertook under such an agreement to manufacture 15 tons of airblowers and 40 tons of assorted piping for the factory. The agreement was fictitious. The managers who signed it were pursuing their own local interests. In fact, the builders, who received tens of thousands of gas pipes and

quantities of roofing iron from the factory, paid for the metal goods with ceramic wares and measuring instruments, in short with output released strictly from allocated stocks. It was not only with the Vyksa factory that the head of the Building Adminsitration, V.V. Poygin, conducted exchange operations. Some of the material was used for other transactions. For example, the Building Adminsitration paid for the use of the vehicles of a neighbouring enterprise with metal goods from the Vyksa factory. When news of what was happening at Vyksa got around, some industrial executives began to load lorries with their own goods and send them to Vyksa for exchange. Comrade Sukhoruchkin, the head of the supply section at the Yaroslavl tyre factory, acted in this way. 'Availing myself of a passing lorry', he wrote to Comrade Seregin, the deputy-director of the Vyksa factory, 'I am sending you some rubber. Please let us have in return gas piping as specified in the attached list. It couldn't be clearer "We'll give you, if you'll give us".'

Twenty one years later this principle has finally and irreversibly displaced the communist ideal of 'from each according to his ability'. Most of the Vyksa transactions and those currently involving Soviet enterprise are, of course, of assistance to it in carrying out its production tasks. But this is not the whole story. 'Gas pipes are specified in the attached list' are not only needed by a tyre-producing factory. They are also used, for example, to provide a gas supply for a not inconsiderable number of houses and country cottages for which State building offices will not supply any material. We might further ask ourselves where the parts for colour television sets and motor car spare parts on the second hand market come from, if they are not acquired through a far from short, but quite commercial, chain of commodity exchanges.

Private owners have their accomplices, and the *interests of the enterprise are now indissolubly linked with the interests of its directors.* Irrespective of the salary paid, there are some posts in the Soviet Union that are lucrative and others that are not, and lucrative posts have themselves become something that can be bought and sold. Not the salary, but the actual income of a soft drinks seller or hawker, a railway ticket inspector or a chauffeur is usually considerably in excess of the earnings of a rank and file engineer or a teacher. The incomes of those who occupy favourable positions in the State or party apparatus, in inspectorates and supply bodies, and in production itself, provide the material basis on which, as has already been noted by Djilas, the ruling class in Soviet society builds its prosperity.

The system within the system

The following excerpt from a story by the Soviet author I. Solov'yev, *The House in Palace Street* illustrates the relationship of this alternative economic system to the State and the plan:

> A system may be created within any system; all that matters is to pick the right people. Inspectors? Well, what interests them is. . .' and he lightly patted the left side of his jacket, indicating an inner pocket. 'And what about the Department combating Misappropriation of Socialist Property and Speculation? It just keeps you on your toes. No', he paused on the word, 'if you set about things in the right way, you can live. Your buts don't bother me, the holes in the scheme are what I thrive on. Amazing things happen on earth. Just imagine', and he became animated, 'you get saddled with producing more than your planned output, but you're given only 20 to 25% of the material that you need for it, all the rest is local initiative! If you fail to fulfil the plan by the end of the quarter they'll shake you off the tree like a good pear in a year when there are so many that they are not worth picking. Where and how you get your raw material, and how much you pay for it are nobody's business. Those who can get raw materials and extend the plan are worth their weight in gold. What's all this got to do with legality? If you have fulfilled the plan you're their darling, even if you obviously got the material illegally. If you haven't, you'll be looked upon as worse than the devil himself, even if you are an innocent as a newborn babe under the criminal code. Nobody judges the winners. The most principled management will always stick up for the plan. That's how things are. . .

But for this economy, which operates on a purely commercial basis and is directed toward the satisfaction of private interests, the bureaucratic system of the party and State economy would probably seize up like an unoiled machine. And what does it matter if those who operate this second corrective economic system, party members or no, sometimes end up in the dock? The risk is a calculated one, which they have to take if they are to operate at all under the conditions in which they are placed.

This form of alternative economic life had begun to take shape under Stalin, but its scope was considerably extended by the relaxation of the terror in the post-Stalin period. Despite repeated attempts to do away with 'idlers', people have acquired more time to work on their own account, even spending more or less lengthy periods without working at all. There is also increased opportunity to enrich oneself, to invest money in a house, in land or in a car, to build up one's own undertaking and to pass it on to one's children. It is not only party officials and the captains of socialist industry who are becoming rich, but also shop managers, and workers in industrial co-operatives, building organizations and the provision of services. To these we must add performers, artists, scientific workers and even doctors with private practices and lawyers deriving income from legal advice.

The private element in the present Soviet economy stems from two roots, one of which is undoubtedly Philistine; the other is socialist. Both are indestructible; both will carry on into communism; both are deeply submerged in the economy. The first gives rise to the collective farm market and the junk market; the second to commodity exchange between the Yaroslavl and Vyksa factories: 'I am sending you rubber, and ask you to supply gas pipes in accordance with the attached list'.

Market gardening, small scale livestock rearing, a few chickens, a sow and litter, skilled crafts of every conceivable kind and individual retail trade are in the hands of country and city dwellers, ostensibly collective farm members, weighers or firemen. Private initiative at this level is suppressed but stubbornly refuses to die. It is nevertheless of assistance both to the country and to the authorities, since it satisfies some of the most elementary needs of the people, needs which the authorities are unable to satisfy.

There is also initiative on an almost wholesale scale, handling quite large affairs and serving State organizations rather than the individual consumer. It is at this level that raw materials, semi-manufactured goods and finished goods are exchanged between factories and that assignments on a self-financing basis are handed out to research institutes. It is at this level that flats, furnishings, cars, trips abroad and visits to holiday resorts are paid for, and not only these, but positions and titles giving access to places from which income is derived. Those who take these initiatives are workers in the State and party apparatus who know the real nature of socialism and have been able to adapt themselves to it.

The whole of the Soviet people, and the managerial class in particular, are now involved to a greater or lesser degree in illegal economic operations. Exchanges, mutually advantageous deals and combined arrangements are entered into in all enterprises. They involve directors, party organizers, workshop foremen and, naturally, planners and book-keepers. Observance of State and party interests, to which lip service is paid, is fully offset by the care taken for the personal well being of each individual involved, without any consideration either for hypocritical bourgeois morals or for the moral code of Soviet man.

An Economic Blind Alley

The private element in the Soviet economy and accomplices operating illegally in the Soviet economic process are not in themselves enemies of socialism, although they are certainly not its friends. Real socialism on the Soviet model is their natural environment, just as the tropical forest is the natural environment of the Papuan. They do not as yet dispute the economic monopoly of the party. Commercial transactions entered into in contravention of State plans and the articles of the criminal code, for personal gain are also ultimately the salvation of the State economy. Whatever may be said in solemn speeches and in seminars on Marxism-Leninism, the task facing the leaders of the Soviet economy is not now to kill off private initiative, but to face up to the need to live with it, since the well being of the ruling class, the only social support of the Soviet system, is built on elemental private ownership.

How to control this elemental force is a question that clearly cannot be solved by the equivocating and vacillating policy operated since the time of Lenin, alternately allowing people to keep their own cows and goats, then bringing livestock breeding under public ownership, pretending not to see the speculative dealings of some individual in charge of a State procuring office, and then prosecuting him. All the difficulties encountered by the party in managing the economy since Stalin's time arise from its inability to make use of the creative force of personal initiative for which the plan can make no allowance, which is placed outside the law and is therefore driven into the desert of speculation, self-seeking and corruption. 'If you want to live, learn how to dodge!': under these conditions the incomes of private traders and others in the private sector, and especially of accomplices, are truly hard earned, although not from work. *What is rewarded is not work but risk, and what is distributed is not production but loot.*

Under these conditions honest productive toil loses its sense. With every year that passes, Soviet citizens work less and less and worse and worse. The gap between the rate for what is often also quite useless work and the yield from private economic transactions becomes so great that skilled engineers are often to be found driving taxis, while teachers are beginning to turn to illegal barter and trading with foreigners or to the breeding of white mice for medical experiments.

The spontaneous rejection of work for the party State, and working half-heartedly wherever there is no obvious possibility of additional income, are already beginning to reduce not so much the share of the people in the social product as the share of the State, and to compel the party to pay for the retention of its economic monopoly by a reduction in economic strength. But that is another subject, one that needs separate consideration.

THE NATURAL SCIENCES AND MARXISM

BEVERLY HALSTEAD

'Dialectical materialism is the world outlook of the Marxist – Leninist Party,' so begins J.V. Stalin's 1938 article *Dialectical and Historical Materialism*.

The main tenets of dialectical materialism were formulated by Friedrich Engels in *Anti-Dühring* and the posthumously published *Dialectics of Nature* and it was to the natural sciences that Engels looked for support. Dealing with the materialism aspect, Engels wrote in *Anti-Dühring*

> the materialistic outlook on nature means no more than simply conceiving nature just as it exists, without any foreign admixture. The material, sensuously perceptible world to which we ourselves belong is the only reality. Our consciousness and thinking, however suprasensuous they may seem, are the product of a material, bodily organ: the brain. Matter is not a product of mind, but mind itself is merely the highest product of matter.

According to V.I. Lenin in *Materialism and Empirio-criticism*,

> natural science positively asserts that the earth once existed in such a state that no man or any other creature existed or could have existed on it. Organic matter is a later phenomenon, the fruit of a long evolution. Matter is primary, and thought, consciousness, sensation, are products of a very high development. Such is the materialist theory of knowledge, to which natural science instinctively subscribes.

This is undoubtedly the case, and there is, not surprisingly, a deeper and more widespread sympathy for Marxism among scientists than could ever be gleaned from their publications or public utterances. C.H. Waddington in *The Scientific Attitude* summed up a view of many when he wrote

> the basic notions of Marxist philosophy are then almost, if not quite, identical with those underlying the scientific approach to

nature; there is nothing in them which could cause scientists to reject the rest of the Marxist system out of hand.

The dialectical approach which characterises Marxism and distinguishes it from materialism alone was developed by the philosopher Hegel and stemmed ultimately from the Greek *dialego*, to debate or discourse. This involved arriving at the truth by the clash of opposing opinions, disclosing contradictions and overcoming them. When the natural world is viewed from this standpoint, it can be seen that it is characterised by constant change and that this development can be interpreted as a consequence of the interaction of opposites. Hence for every action there is a reaction. In the metabolism of every living thing, there are at work processes that build up and those which break down; it is hardly possible to have one without the other and still remain a living being.

The key tenets of dialectical materialism included the realisation that it is not possible to understand a phenomenon in isolation; that it must be viewed in the context of its universal interconnections. It is all too easy to study a subject in itself but a much deeper insight and understanding will be achieved if it is viewed in the context of its interrelations.

The second basic approach is that it is not sufficient to study a phenomenon as it is observed at any one moment in time. It is important to be able to recognise its stage of development, whether it is a phenomenon arising or dying away, whether the structure is in its youth, has reached its maturity or is on its way out. The identification of stages of development is likely to provide a significant insight into any understanding of the natural world.

The third and perhaps most important premise is the recognition that from small imperceptible quantitative changes there can arise qualitative changes. The notion of change from quantity to quality is perhaps the key concept that dialectical materialism has contributed to the natural sciences. This serves as a useful conceptual antidote to the attempts to reduce everything in the universe to fundamental particles, for example trying to reduce biology to chemistry and physics alone. It clearly accepts that there is something qualitatively different between man and the rest of the animal kingdom and between living and non-living things. Indeed between these two extremes of the evolutionary spectrum there are numerous examples of other changes in quality.

All these basic premises that together are encompassed in the approach of dialectical materialism hardly seem to be matters capable of engendering much controversy. All they are likely to do is to enable the working scientist to achieve a deeper and more rewarding insight into his own discipline. In many areas the influence of such an approach has been undoubtedly on the credit side and there are certainly no political overtones that can be discerned in this.

On top of this wholly sensible and admirable methodology, there is imposed a further premise, which is concerned with the nature of qualitative change. This is the fundamental aspect of dialectical materialism and on this all the rest hangs. Again culling examples from the natural sciences, Engels in *Anti-Dühring* states that 'at definite nodal points, the purely quantitative increase or decrease gives rise to a qualitative leap'; in *Dialectics of Nature* he speaks of 'a development in which the qualitative changes occur not gradually but rapidly and abruptly, taking the form of a leap from one state to another'.

Here then is the recipe for revolution. If this is the observed rule in the history of life, then when translated into human history and political action, it would serve as a scientific justification for accentuating the inherent contradictions within society, so that the situation can be hurried towards its appropriate 'nodal point', and a qualitative leap will supervene.

Such a policy, which characterises all the Marxist parties is, it is claimed, based on the scientific laws of history. That there are qualitative changes recorded in the history of life on Earth cannot be denied. The question at issue is whether these changes are gradual or sudden, whether the fossil record, which documents this history, portrays a gradual evolutionary pattern or a revolutionary one.

Perhaps the major advance in human thought during the last century was the general recognition that the physical world was one of gradual change through time and that the processes by which this came about were still in operation and could be examined at first hand. The acceptance of this notion of a dynamic world as against a static one was due in no small measure to the brilliant advocacy of Sir Charles Lyell in his book *Principles of Geology*, a book, moreover, which accompanied Charles Darwin during his voyage round the world on H.M.S. Beagle. Darwin's great contribution was to establish beyond all measure of doubt that the history of life too had been one of constant change. Darwin in 1859 in *On the Origin of Species by Means of Natural Selection or the Preservation of Favoured Races in the Struggle for Life* amassed such a wealth of evidence that the idea of change through time, indeed that life had had a long gradual history, became firmly established in men's minds. The way in which the fossil record illustrated the succession of forms and the replacement of faunas by more advanced forms, put paid once and for all to the long held notion of life having been created at a stroke.

By the end of the 18th century it was widely recognised that the geological record was not in agreement with the Mosaic account of creation, but it was not until the advent of Darwin that the importance of progressive change through time became the accepted philosophy of the day.

The significance of these ideas on society and the established order was not lost on the ecclesiastical authorities nor indeed on Marx and Engels. Engels in *Anti-Dühring* discussed Darwin's work at some length and with, moreover, considerable perceptiveness. The study of the history of life even in its broadest outline established that change was the order of the day in the natural world, and, furthermore, that there had been important qualitative changes during this history. On these two issues Engels could call upon the natural sciences in his support with complete confidence.

However, Engels was concerned with the nature of qualitative change, with leaps:

> In spite of all gradualness, the transition from one form of motion to another always remains a leap, a decisive change . . . and this is even more clearly the case in the transition from ordinary chemical action to the chemism of albumen we call life. Then within the sphere of life the leaps become ever more infrequent and imperceptible.

To Engels the biological and geological sciences provided incontrovertible evidence of change and, moreover, of qualitative changes. However, Engels in *Dialectics of Nature* was constrained to write,

> hard and fast lines are incompatible with the theory of evolution. Even the borderline between vertebrates and invertebrates is now no longer rigid, just as little is that between fishes and amphibians, while that between birds and reptiles dwindles more and more every day. Between *Compsognathus* and *Archaeopteryx* only a few intermediate links are wanting, and birds' beaks with teeth crop up in both hemispheres. Either or becomes more and more inadequate. For a stage in the outlook on nature where all

> differences become merged in intermediate steps and all opposites pass into one another through intermediate links. . .

This same opinion was echoed by Lenin

> dialectical materialism insists on the approximate, relative character of every scientific theory of the structure of matter and its properties, it insists on the absence of absolute boundaries in nature, on the transformation of moving matter from one state into another.

With great good sense Engels did not insist upon leaps in the history of life. Darwin had only just succeeded in winning the battle for evolution against the ecclesiastical geologists who interpreted the fossil record as a sequence of separate creations. The idea of sudden catastrophes or leaps in this context would have had such an archaic and anti-scientific air about it, that it is not surprising that Engels made no attempt to insist upon the notion of leaps in this context. In this instance he was content with gradual change through time, that was sufficient for his purposes.

Dialectical materialism when transferred to human society and history and especially into political action has as its centrepiece the firm belief in sudden qualitative leaps. The irony of all this is that at the very place where dialectical materialism would be expected to obtain its most solid backing, from the study of evolution and the fossil record, that support was not forthcoming.

Some of the major qualitative changes in the evolution of the vertebrates such as the transition from water to land, the evolution of the amniote or closed egg, the acquisition of warmbloodedness and the origin of man himself can be traced over periods of millions of years. Indeed Engels in his brilliant essay *The Part Played by Labour in the Transition from Ape to Man* makes no attempt to insist upon sudden leaps. He even writes

> at first, therefore, the operations, for which our ancestors gradually learned to adapt their hands during the many thousands of years of transition from ape to man, could only have been very simple.

There are certainly qualitative differences but whenever the transitions are examined in detail, a pattern of gradualism supervenes.

This was the point at which the matter should have been allowed to remain, but for the nagging problem of the gaps in the fossil record.

One of the criticisms levelled against Darwin and clearly faced by him was

> why then is not every geological formation and every stratum full of such intermediate links? Geology assuredly does not reveal any such finely graduated organic chain; and this, perhaps, is the most obvious and gravest objection which can be urged against my theory. The explanation lies, as I believe in the extreme imperfection of the geological record.

Darwin discusses this question at length and accepted

> our not finding in the successive formations infinitely numerous transitional links between the many species which now exist or have existed; the sudden manner in which whole groups of species appear in our European formations on which evidence other geologists of the time have unanimously, often vehemently, maintained the immutability of species.

Darwin for his part maintained that the evidence established that

> new species have appeared very slowly, one after another both on the land and in the waters. If then the geological record be as imperfect as I believe it to be, and it may be asserted that the record cannot be proved to be much more perfect, the main objections to the theory of natural selection are greatly diminished or disappear. On the other hand, all the chief laws of palaeontology plainly proclaim, as it seems to me, that species have been produced by ordinary generation: old forms have been supplanted by new and improved forms of life, produced by the laws of variation still acting around us, and preserved by Natural Selection.

Darwin's view was a gradualist one and he remarked on more than one occasion that all the evidence tended to confirm the old naturalists' adage *Natura non facit saltum*, Nature does not make leaps.

Anyone who has collected specimens in the field for research purposes is only too well aware of the incompleteness of the record. If one takes the evolutionary history of the dinosaurs, which spanned 140 million years, less than a thousand different types are known from throughout the world and these are confined to relatively few geological horizons in a few dozen major locations. It goes without saying that the greatest concentration of knowledge of the fossil record is coincident with the greatest concentration of geologists. Indeed the general consensus has been that the appearance of jumps or leaps in the fossil record was simply due to the accidents of preservation and discovery. The attitude was exactly that of Charles Darwin: that evolution was a gradual process and that the appearance of saltation or leaps was an artifact. The belief was that the processes that could be observed taking place at the present day appertained also in the past. The combination of the scientific data from geneticists and palaeontologists allowed a comprehensive synthesis to be put forward by G.G. Simpson in his two seminal works *Tempo and Mode in Evolution* in 1944 and *The Major Features of Evolution* in 1953.

All the evidence was consistent with a gradualist pattern and Simpson was aware of the gap problem and dealt with it in the following terms:

> At best, paleontological data reveal only a very small proportion of the species that have lived on the earth, and the known fossil deposits do not and never can represent anything distantly approaching adequate sampling of the diverse facies of the various zoological realms throughout geological time.
>
> A great deal is known – an amazing amount in view of these limitations – and it would be pointless to emphasize once more the general incompleteness of the paleontological record, except to stress that this incompleteness is an essential datum and that it, as well as the positive data, can be studied with profit. When the record does happen to be good, it commonly shows complete continuity in the rise of such taxonomic categories as species and genera and sometimes, but rarely, in higher groups. When breaks or apparent saltations do occur within lines that are true or structural phyla, frequently they can be shown to be due to one of the two causes now exemplified: to hiatuses in the time record caused by nondeposition of middle strata or fossils and to sampling of migrants instead of main lines. Continued discovery and collecting have the constant tendency to fill in gaps. The known series are steaily becoming more, never less, continuous. It cannot be shown that discontinuity between, let us say, genera has never occurred, but the only rational conclusion from these facts is that no discontinuity is usually found and that there is no paleontological evidence that really tends to prove that there is

any. On these levels everything is consistent with the postulate that we are sampling what were once continuous sequences.

The general consensus among palaeontologists was that species evolved gradually and that when different species were recognised in a continuous sequence this involved the drawing of arbitary lines across a continuum. Gaps in the fossil record in fact facilitated this, as they could often be drawn most conveniently at an appropriate gap. The really important contribution which Simpson made was to establish the concept in the minds of palaeontologists that their fossils were samples of populations which exhibited a range of continuous variation and that many important evolutionary changes could be accounted for by gradual shifts of the mean towards one extreme or the other. Organisms at the different ranges of the population could become adapted to different environmental conditions. Occasionally a new environment would become available for exploitation and there could be a major evolutionary radiation until the available niches had become suitably filled. Indeed all the evidence as it accumulated was clearly consistent with a gradualist mode of evolution rather than with one of sudden leaps; the very antithesis of a revolutionary framework for the history of life and by extrapolation of man and hence human society.

This was the generally accepted view of the fossil record during the 1950s and 1960s and is still probably held by the majority of palaeontologists. During the 1970s an articulate and vociferous minority has mounted a major assault against the concept of gradualism; indeed Darwin, Simpson and gradualism are used virtually as terms of abuse. It is difficult to avoid the conclusion that the current intemperate language against gradualism, the fanatical fervour with which the campaign is conducted and the rampant evangelism with which the alternative concepts of sudden leaps are being promoted are an attempt to establish the Marxist approach in the natural sciences. If the concept of gradualism in evolution can be badly shaken and the alternative revolutionary ideas of sudden leaps can be established, then the latter-day Marxists will have succeeded where Engels and Lenin singularly failed. If gradualism can be shown not to be the process in the history of life then the one fundamental flaw in the edifice of dialectical materialism would have been finally surmounted. In these circumstances, it would indeed become possible to claim that Marxism was now consistent with the scientific laws of history as revealed by the study of evolution and the fossil record.

One of the most curious phenomena to have hit the palaeontological and evolutionary studies world in recent times is an evangelical cult known variously, as Hennigism or Cladistics.

Cladistics or phylogenetic systematics is a method of delineating the relationships of organisms and is based on a set of rules adumbrated by the late Willi Hennig in his book *Phylogenetic Systematics* (1966, republished 1979). This approach is now being actively promoted by the British Museum (Natural History) London and is presented with great clarity in two exhibitions and their accompanying booklets *Dinosaurs and their Living Relatives* (1979) and *Man's Place in Evolution* (1980)[1], which avoid any discussion of the gradual evolutionary *versus* the revolutionary leap concepts, by simply accepting the basic assumptions of the latter and ignoring those of the former. Hence it is assumed that new species arise when one species splits into two; it is assumed that no species gradually evolves into another. It is further assumed that no fossil species is an ancestor of another. The gradual evolution of one species into another is denied. By the deliberate construction of such rules the concept of gradual evolution through time is excluded by definition and one is left only with the notion of sudden qualitative leaps, new species appearing suddenly by the splitting of pre-existing species.

When considering any three closely related species, it is assumed by the cladists that two will share a common ancestor not shared by the third. This allows degrees of relationships to be portrayed in the form of a dichotomously branching diagram or cladogram. With three species three different cladograms can be constructed and compared directly with one another. By considering the available data it is possible to test which of the three alternatives is the more likely the principle of parsimony. This testing is claimed to be 'scientific' according to the precepts enunciated by Karl Popper. At the same time it is claimed, again on the supposed authority of Popper, that evolutionary theory is not scientific and moreover that the study of palaeontology, being concerned with the historical record of unique events, must also by definition be outside of science[2]. In parenthesis it should perhaps be noted that Popper[3] has recently (1980) commented on this matter:

> I fully support this purpose [to defend the scientific character of the theory of evolution and of palaeontology] . . . it does appear that some people think that I have denied scientific character to the historical sciences such as palaeontology, or the history of the

> evolution of life on Earth. This is a mistake, and I here wish to affirm that these and other historical sciences have in my opinion scientific character: their hypotheses can in many cases be tested.
>
> It appears as if some people would think that the historical sciences are untestable because they describe unique events. However, the description of unique events can very often be tested by deriving from them testable predictions or retrodictions.

The situation at present is that the public galleries of the British Museum (Natural History) London are being used as a propaganda vehicle for a Marxist interpretation of the history of life, which is being foisted onto the public not by argument or discussion, but simply by official decree.

There is a further attack on Darwinism and gradualism currently being mounted but which is at least scientifically respectable. This scientific attack is two pronged. Stephen Jay Gould has recently (1980) resurrected the notion of 'hopeful monsters' which was promoted by R. Goldschmidt in 1940 in his book *The Material Basis of Evolution* in which he considered that new species can arise by single large macromutations, hence the concept of 'hopeful monsters'. In this way the sudden jump from species to species in the fossil record could be explained as a reflection of the underlying genetic saltation or sudden leaps. Again this would obviate any recourse to the concept of gradualism. Goldschmidt's curious ideas were discussed in detail by Simpson and apart from Gould no-one has taken them particularly seriously.

The other current concept that has become something of a fashion is associated with Gould and his collaborator Niles Eldredge who published a seminal paper in 1972 entitled *Punctuated Equilibria: an Alternative to Phyletic Gradualism.*[4] Apart from a vehement attack on gradualism, the idea of punctuated equilibria postulates that new species arise in small isolated geographical regions and then re-invade the previously occupied habitat. In this way species in the fossil record appear suddenly and the seemingly saltatory nature of the fossil record is again claimed to be simply a reflection of the underlying reality. The fossil record portrays a pattern of sudden leaps between which there are long periods of equilibrium which exhibit little or no change.

Much of the fossil record, it must be admitted, can be interpreted in terms of punctuated equilibria. Wherever there is a morphological gap in a sequence of forms a sudden act of speciation can be invoked – the beauty of this theory is that the changes always take place in isolated areas which are always unlikely to leave any evidence of their existence in the fossil record. They are not expected to be found so there is little point in even looking. Following my oft repeated aphorism 'evolution always occurs somewhere else' the late P.C. Sylvester-Bradley advocated that palaeontologists should travel to resolve this problem. C. Patterson (1980) has commented

> travel they do, yet still they have to offer the same excuse as Darwin (gaps in the record) for their failure to demonstrate evolution. This is fair enough, for it gives palaeontology a splendid programme for full employment – let's just keep splitting rocks until we find the place where evolution is going on.

This humorous jibe puts its finger on the crux of the matter. If one is intent on speculating upon the details of the changes through time of any particular group, the first task is surely to examine all the available material. This is generally considered to be impractible but no meaningful conclusions can be drawn until this is in fact done.

The classic historic case concerns the evolution of the horse. This was first presented in outline by W. Kowalevsky (1874) when he demonstrated several major steps of horse evolution preserved in the rocks of the Old World. The objection to this story was that here were a series of jumps, there was no evidence of transitions between the different forms. It was not until the discovery of the vast and continuous record of fossil horses in North America that such connecting forms became known. It is today accepted that the evolution of the horse took place in North America, and that there were successive waves of migration across to Asia and Europe. The evolution of the horse as protrayed in North America supports a gradualist interpretation. Indeed it falsifies the saltationism, punctuational or leap explanation. On the other hand the sequence of Europe fossil horses in isolation could have been used to 'falsify' a gradualist interpretation had not the American fossils been discovered. The leap model is argued from the standpoint of negative evidence and hence is exceedingly vulnerable to annihilation by new discoveries.

Recent researches by Gingerich (1979) on early primates and primitive herbivorous mammals from the beginning of the age of mammals in North America have established incontrovertible evidence of gradual evolutionary changes through time, including the gradual evolution of new species both by changes within a single population, phyletic evolution, and by splitting or speciation. It is evident that the evolution of these primitive mammals was taking place in the areas where fossils have been discovered.

One of the difficulties that any worker encounters in attempting to study a single group of organisms on a global scale is that generally speaking the representatives of the group when studied in the scientific literature will belong to different genera and species in the different parts of the world. If one takes the ostracoderms, armoured jawless vertebrates, from the Devonian (400 million years ago), they have been described from Scotland as belonging to a number of different species, by a Scotsman R.H. Traquair at the end of the last century. Representatives of the same group have been described from the Baltic States and Russia but assigned to different species. When the specimens themselves are directly compared, it is evident that the identical species were represented in the two provinces. If one then examines all the available material from throughout the world, one finds that a succession of species in any one area gives an impression of sudden jumps. But over wide areas the same sequence of species is recorded. It seems likely that we are dealing with repeated migrations from a major evolutionary source area. The punctuated equilibria model would contend that

> the 'somewhere else' of evolution is populations too small to show in the record, and quantum changes, which are instantaneous in geological time (Patterson).

In this particular instance the evolutionary source area was not small but positively huge, comprising the full extent of the Russian Platform, the major part of Western Russia. The Baltic Province was the region in which the evolution of these fishlike animals was taking place and it was from this area that there were periodic waves of migration to other regions[5]. This example is comparable to the record of horse evolution and this seems to be a consistent pattern throughout the fossil record.

It can be asserted with confidence that the gaps in the fossil record are a genuine reflection of the real situation; there is no need to postulate the inadequacy of the fossil record on the one hand nor leaps on the other to explain the observed situation. The fossil record is not as poor as it has been claimed. The geographical location of evolutionary source regions always seems to be in tropical or sub-tropical climatic regimes – the Baltic Province was located at

15°S 400 million years ago. At the present day, the genetic diversity of the tropics is significantly higher than that in temperate and polar latitudes. The latter may support a greater biomass but their diversity is lower. This same pattern seems to be reflected in the fossil record.

The pattern that emerges from a world wide examination of just one group of vertebrates is of gradual evolutionary changes taking place in evolutionary centres from which there emerged successive waves of migrants to other provinces. An invasion or replacement may well have been a sudden event but this seems hardly to qualify as a leap in Engels' sense with regard to the evolutionary process itself.

Wherever the fossil record can be adequately documented, it reveals a slow gradual evolutionary pattern, wherever the evidence is inadequate then it is possible to produce explanations which advocate sudden leaps as required of dialectical materialism. But these arguments are simply special pleading and relying on negative evidence have as much to commend them as invoking the Deity. Only with a paucity of evidence is it possible to postulate some kind of gap theory, either hopeful monsters or punctuated equilibria. Such theories are usually refuted as more and more data becomes available. These arguments although misguided are nonetheless entirely sincere and held honourably; the same can hardly be said for the cladistic construct which seems to be inherently dishonest in its formulation of rules which take as axiomatic the basic assumptions of dialectical materialism. Engels and Lenin had more integrity than this and they made no attempt to prostitute the basic data of evolution and the fossil record to force them into the straightjacket of their political dogma.

Surprising as it may appear, the natural sciences do not have any antagonism towards the approach of dialectical materialism. No natural scientist worthy of the name should be prepared to accept any particular maxim without supporting evidence. At the present time the accumulated evidence of palaeontology gives greater credence to the notions of gradual change through time and does not favour the saltation or leap hypotheses demanded of dialectical materialism.

The natural sciences accept Francis Bacon's admonition:

Naturae enim non imperator, nisi parendo

Nature cannot be ordered about, except by obeying her.

NOTES

1. A major controversy on this subject was initiated in *Nature* (B. Halstead, November 20, 1980) and ran for 9 months. Subsequently the Natural History Museum published in 1983 an excellent scholarly pamphlet *Our fossil relatives: more about Man's place in evolution* which went some way to redress the damage; similarly a completely re-written second edition (1985) of *Dinosaurs and their living relatives* removed most of the objectionable material of the first edition. See, however, my article 'The New Left's Assault on Science – the case of anthropology at the Natural History Museum' (*Salisbury Review*, January 1987, Vol. 5. no. 2. pp. 37–39).
2. C. Patterson. 1978. *Evolution*. British Museum (Natural History) London.
3. K. Popper *New Scientist*, 21 August 1980, p. 611, replying to my article 'Popper: good philosophy, bad science?' (*New Scientist*, 17 July 1980, pp. 215–217).
4. N. Eldredge and S.J. Gould, 1972. *In* T.J.M. Schopf (ed.) *Models in Paleobiology*, Freeman, San Francisco.
5. See L.B. Halstead. 1982. *Hunting the Past*, Hamish Hamilton, London, and references therein.

SCIENCE IN THE USSR

DAVID PEAT

How good is science in the USSR? The simple and immediate answer is that in some fields Soviet science is amongst the best in the world. But when we follow this question by asking how important is research to Soviet industry as a whole, we find an answer that is less encouraging for that nation.

The Soviet Union contains one quarter of the world's scientists located in some 5,000 research institutes. It possesses the world's largest oil reserves, 40% of its iron and large deposits of coal and important minerals. Yet despite the considerable investment that has been made in science and the generally high standards of pure research, much of Soviet industry is backward. High technology, microelectronics and computing are in a particularly poor state.

Why in a nation that has produced exceptional scientific minds should this be so? At the time of the revolution Lenin could offer the excuse that in the past his country had been robbed of the benefits of science, but he was confident that now 'the marvels of science and the gains of culture belong to the nation as a whole.' According to the dictates of dialectical materialism science would flourish in a true socialist state as it had never done before. It is true that space research and nuclear power have been successfully developed in the Soviet Union, but in many other areas the country has been outstripped by the United States and Japan.

Clues to this paradox in Soviet philosophy can be found in the past for, from its beginnings in the eighteenth century to the present day, science in the USSR appears to bhave been plagued by an inefficient and insensitive bureaucracy and poor relationships with the authorities.

From Peter the Great to the Revolution

The Soviet Academy of Sciences is the centre of so much that is of importance in the nation's science. The fundamental research that is carried out in its various institutes is respected, not only within the Soviet block, but throughout the scientific world.

This organization was the dream of Peter the Great, (Czar from 1682–1725) who recognised the importance to his country of good education, particularly in technical areas. Peter set up a number of schools of mining and planned the Academy itself, which was established the year after his death.

From its inception the Academy concerned itself not only with the physical sciences but with all knowledge. In the first years of its existence expeditions were planned to the neglected eastern provinces and this interest survives today in the powerful Siberian branch of the Academy.

In the United Kingdom and the United States the best research generally comes from the universities, but in Russia it is traditionally associated with the Academy's institutes. (This is not to say however that there are not some centres of high quality work in the universities.) A scientist who is elected to full membership is often given an institute of his own and enjoys an elevated social position.

Thanks to the energies of Mikhail Vaxilyevich Lomonosov and others, the eighteenth century saw the birth in 1755 of Russia's first university at Moscow. Lomonosov was poet, scientist and pioneer in linguistics. He corresponded with the greatest Europeans of his day, developed laws of conservation of energy and matter, theories of heat and an anticipation of Dalton's atomic theory. But like many of the intellectuals who followed him, Lomonosov's political views were to land him in trouble, and following his death his collected writings were censored before publication.

Under the 1762–1796 reign of Catherine II an Austrian educational system was imported, and following her death the universities of Vilna, Dorpath, Kazan, Kharov and St Petersburg were founded.

The nineteenth century saw a number of high points in Russian science but the impact of research work on the nation's economy was not particularly strong. Nikolay Ivanovich Lobachevsky (1792–1856) not only founded a famous school of mathematics at the university of Kazan but developed a new and important mathematical field – Non-Euclidian geometry. His ideas were particularly advanced and not fully appreciated until the German mathematician Bernhard Riemann entered the same field several decades later. Lobachevsky and Riemann's work was later to provide the mathematical basis for Einstein's General Theory of Relativity.

Lobachevsky's energies were not only focused on teaching and research but in defending his university against the attacks of M.L. Magnitsky of the Ministry of Education, a man whose personal vendetta went so far as demanding that the institution should be publicly destroyed.

In St Petersburg Dmitri Ivanovich Mendeleyev (1834–1907) was making important contributions to chemistry including his famous Periodic Table of the Elements. Largely ignored by Russian chemists, the Periodic Table placed chemistry on a rational basis by exploring the family relationships between the elements. In the twentieth century, Niels Bohr's theoretical explanation of why the Periodic Table worked was one of the triumphs of the emerging Quantum Theory.

Although Mendeleyev received foreign honours, including fellowship of the Royal Society, he was never made an Academician. Within his own country he was damned as 'progressive' and after passing a student petition to the Ministry of Education, he was forced to resign his chair at the St Petersburg Technical Institute.

Mendeleyev's treatment is just one example of nineteenth century Russia's suspicion of intellectuals. Towards the end of that century, the university entrance had been restricted to members of the elite class and although scientists like Mendeleyev were to make technical suggestions based on their knowleedge of .S. and European manufacturing, new factories were imported wholesale from outside Russia.

Other neglected scientists include Ilya Illich Mechnikov (1845–1916) whose advances in microbiology earned him the 1908 Nobel Prize, yet he was forced to leave Russia to complete his work. Konstantin Edvardovich Tsiolkovski (1857–1935) was the first pioneer of space travel and designed rockets, experimented with liquid fuel systems and demonstrated the importance of closed biological cycles for long space voyages. Although he was elected to the Academy, his work drew little official support.

At a technical school in Kronstadt, Alesandr Stepanovich Popov (1859–1906) carried out early work on radio and, in March, 1896, demonstrated wireless transmission. Two years later he designed a ship to shore radio for the Russian navy but the authorities showed little interest in his work. Today, the Soviet Union credits Popov with the invention of radio.

Winning the Science Race

The Soviet claims to priority such as radio and the first piloted aero flight are usually greeted with derision in the West. After all, the layman may argue, if the Russians really invented so many things, then our own scientists must have been lying to us.

Science, of course, does not work in this way – it is not a race in which the first researcher to break the tape is the winner. (But this is not to say that scientists are not the worst offenders in the cry of priority. Even Isaac Newton was not above some dirty tricks in pressing his claim to have invented the calculus before Leibnitz.)

Roughly speaking a new discovery moves through three phases; at first the insight or observation followed by careful development and, finally, technical exploitation. Ideas are often 'in the air' and it is not unusual for more than one person to make the same intuitive leap. For example, W.K. Clifford in 1870 anticipated aspects of Einstein's General Theory of Relativity. But it remained to Einstein to work out the rigorous theoretical foundations of the theory.

While Charles Darwin was working on the fine details of his evolutionary arguments, he received a letter from Alfred Russel Wallace that contained essentially similar ideas. Both men reached the gentlemanly compromise of presenting a joint paper to the Linnaean Society but, thanks to the publicity attracted by *On the Origin of Species*, Darwin is today regarded as the author of the theory.

The case of penicillin illustrates all three aspects of a discovery. While Flemming discovered the mold's power as an antibiotic, he discontinued his research for what he felt to be good scientific reasons and it was left to H.W. Florey and E.B. Chain to purify it in large quantities and demonstrate its effectiveness on human beings. Finally, when it came to commercial exploitation, wartime Britain had to look to the U.S. to manufacture the drug.

The history of science is full of examples where more than one scientist independently comes across a new idea, effect or process and it is important that the Soviet claims should be viewed in this light. Popov was certainly a pioneer in radio, but so was Nikola Tesla who was prepared to press his claims against Marconi through the U.S. courts. When one considers how much Russian science of the nineteenth century was unknown in the West, it is not surprising that Russians co-pioneered in so many areas. But even today, when Soviet scientists lead in the first stage of innovation, they are often left behind in the third – industrial development.

After the Revolution

At the time of the revolution only 25% of the Russian population could read and write. Industry was often old-fashioned with pockets of modernisation brought about through foreign interests. In terms of research the Russian scientist was often isolated or alienated from his society.

Lenin's objectives were education, exploitation of natural resources, improvements in farming and the modernisation of industry. Heavy investments were made in science and research workers were encouraged to tackle the technological problems of the state.

Lenin was confident of success for it was his philosophical belief that science could only operate fully in a socialist state. Marxist-Leninism claims that nature consists only of matter maintained in motion by its 'internal contradictions'. The evolution of human consciousness and the force of history are likewise material manifestations of the dialectical process. The Soviet philosopher A.G. Spirkin later wrote, 'Dialectical materialism is the universal methodology and a basis for the knowledge of nature and social sciences.'

From the perspective of this curious philosophy the state could not help but advance along the royal road of scientific knowledge towards absolute truth. In the early years this certainly looked true. By 1939 the Academy had expanded to direct 3,000 scientists in eighty institutions and a series of Five Year plans called for the enrichment of industry by scientific research. Mining was improved, a massive electrification program set up and a number of hydroelectric generating stations built. Shortly after World War II new institutes were established to counteract the traditional bias of Moscow, Leningrad and Kiev. In particular, the Siberian Branch of the Academy flourished and the scientific town of Akadem Gorodok was built.

Under Stalin the glorious march towards absolute truth caught a case of the staggers. Future Nobel Prize winners like Pyotr Kapitsa and Lev Landau were jailed or placed under house arrest, and the geneticist Nikolay Ivanovich Vavilov was hounded to death. But throughout this dark period the Academy retained a measure of independence. The country needed high quality science and for this it was dependent on the Academy. For this reason, although scientists did suffer under Stalin, they did not fare as badly as other intellectuals.

After the Soviet thaw this 'party line' in science withered and, depending on the temperature of the cold war, scientists from the USSR were seen at international conferences, scientific exchanges were encouraged and references to Marx and Lenin disappeared from Soviet scientific publications. Today the Soviet Union has distinguished itself in a number of areas.

The Space Programme

If we date the start of the Russian space programme with Tsiolokovski, then it is certainly the first in the world. Following Tsiolokovski's early work, rocket experiments were made throughout the 1920s largely on an amateur basis but with limited government support.

Towards the end of World War II the authorities kept their eyes on Dornberger and Von Braun's V.2. rocket laboratory at Peenëmudde. The complex itself, and many of its technicians, fell into Soviet hands but many top scientists had already fled to surrender to the advancing U.S. army. Following a time of secrecy, the world next heard of the Soviet space effort with the launching of Sputnik 1 on October 4, 1957 and later Yuri Gagarin's trip into space on April 12, 1961.

Clearly the Soviets had won the first stage in the race for space and the U.S. government responded by pouring funds into its own space programme. In retrospect the Soviet lead was given by the very powerful rockets it had built for the arms race. While the U.S. had successfully reduced the size of their H bombs and could, therefore, deliver them with smaller rockets, the Soviets had concentrated on large rockets to deliver heavier, but not necessarily more destructive, H-bombs.

The USSR space effort continued with such milestones as Lonokhod-1, the robot lunar laboratory, and the Venera series which transmitted data from Venus. Its manned voyages included single trips by cosmonauts from Soviet block countries with a French guest-astronaut in 1982. For their part, the U.S. triumphs included manned expeditions to the moon, data gathering on Mars, and the Voyager trips to Saturn, Jupiter and the outer planets.

On June 12, 1975, U.S. astronauts and USSR cosmonauts linked their respective craft in space. This co-operative experiment also underlined the differences in technology between the U.S. and

USSR. The latter's equipment appears crude and 'heavy-duty' when set beside that of the west. The reason lies in the Soviet failure to miniaturise equipment, a deficiency that plagues much of their experimental science. Computers, microelectronics and solid state devices that are taken for granted in the West seem beyond Soviet technology.

Although new designs are on the drawing board the USSR has lost the lead in the size of its rockets. Between 1969 and 1972, experimental superboosters capable of carrying a 100 tonne payload into orbit were built but test failures led to the abandonment of the project. With the U.S. Skylab representing a 77 tonne payload, the biggest Soviet (Proton) rockets can carry only half that weight.

In terms of manned flight the U.S. has focused on reusable vehicles, like Columbia, which will carry 30 tonne payloads into orbit, manipulate them with the Canadian 'space-arm' and then return to earth. By contrast the Soviet mission uses modules which are shot into space by rockets. The linking of Cosmos 1267 to Salyut 6 in 1981 is probably an experiment in the production of a larger space station. 'Salyut 7', launched in 1982, may represent a section in this super-station. Various modules will include living quarters, scientific laboratories and areas where technological processes are investigated. Cosmonauts have already prepared glasses, alloys and semiconductors in space.

Nuclear and Particle Physics

The Soviet nuclear programme has its origins in the pure research on cosmic rays carried out in the 1920s. In the following decade research on the interactions of elementary particles and matter continued with scientists like S. Vavilov, A. Ioffe, D. Skobeltsyn, I. Kurchatov, N. Semynov, G. Flerov, A. Alikhanov and A. Alexandrov who also kept their eyes on European developments such as Hahn and Strassman's discovery of nuclear fission in 1938. In the following year Yakov Frenkel of the USSR, along with J.A. Wheeler in the U.S. and N. Bohr in Denmark, developed the theory which lies at the heart of the nuclear reactor and the atomic bomb.

While several nations recognised the strategic importance of the atom's energy, it was the U.S. who first built, tested and used a fission bomb (A-bomb). However, the Soviets were the first to test the more powerful fusion bomb (H-bomb).

In addition to throwing their energy into the arms race, Soviet scientists also worked on the powerful applications of atomic power along similar lines to Western countries. Isotopes were produced for research, medical and industrial use. Reactors were designed for electricity production and to power shipping. In 1958 a Nobel Prize was awarded to P.A. Cherenkov, I.M. Frank and I.Y. Tamm for their theory of the 'Cherenkov effect', the blueish-green glow that occurs when radioactive materials are immersed in water.

Igor Tamm himself was the senior scientist who, with Andrei Dmitrievich Sakharov was responsible for the Soviet H-bomb. Sakharov's own contribution earned him the title of Academician at the unprecedented early age of 32 and following the development of the bomb he concentrated on the peaceful use of fusion energy.

The major problem involved in harnessing fusion power (the energy that powers the sun) is that of containing a plasma at several million degrees of temperature long enough for energy production. Sakharov's solution was an improvement on a 'magnetic bottle', and his Tokamak design is used today in fusion laboratories throughout the world.

Sakharov's other work included an attempt to explain the curvature of Einstein's space-time in quantum mechanical terms but his criticism of the Soviet authorities led to the removal of his security clearance in 1968 and his exile to a town in Gorki in 1980.

Research into fusion power has been well funded in the Soviet Union and their results are internationally important. In 1980, the USSR, Japan, the U.S. and European scientific community held workshops on the problem of controlled fusion. One plan, drawn up at these meetings, is for INTOR, an international laboratory to be built by 1990 for research into the first years of the 21st century.

The nuclear laboratories at Dubna are also active in investigating the structure of the elementary particles. In general, Soviet research follows the same lines as that in the West, of building elementary particle accelerators to test such theories as the quark structure of matter or the Grand Unification theory. A 10 GeV accelerator is in use at Dubna and a larger 70 GeV model at Serpukov. At one time the latter was the largest in the world but it has now been surpassed by machines at CERN in Geneva and the Fermilab in the U.S. New Soviet accelerators are now being planned.

Some experiments on the 70 GeV accelerators are the result of international collaboration, mainly with the European physics community but also with U.S. input. Important work has also been done on the interactions between electrons and positrons using a different accelerator and the name of B. Pontecorvo is associated with research on the Weak Interaction. Soviet elementary particle physics is good and, while the USSR contribution is internationally important, it is probably fair to say that no truly fundamental discovery has come from that country. As in other fields it seems difficult for them to move with the necessary speed into a new area or to follow a discovery with a weight of back-up research.

Physics in Other Areas

Above all, Soviet scientists excel in their theoretical and mathematical work, although there have also been exceptional experimentalists like Kapitsa working in the USSR. Pyotr Leonidovich Kapitsa won the 1978 Nobel Prize for his work on superfluidity, an interest that began when he studied with Rutherford at the Cavendish Laboratory, Cambridge. Kapitsa was put in charge of the Low Temperature Laboratory and elected to the Royal Society. In the 1930s he returned to Russia as head of the S.I. Vavilov Institute of Physical Problems in Moscow. Not only was Kapitsa responsible for a body of work on liquid helium near absolute zero but he worked on controlled nuclear fusion and the Sputnik program.

Kapitsa chose Lev Davidovich Landau to head the Theoretical Physics section of his institute. Born in 1908, Landau became one of the outstanding theoretical physicists of the century. His research extended across the whole of physics and his Nobel Prize was awarded for his theory of superfluidity. Landau was also a great teacher and his series of textbooks, co-authored with E.M. Lifshits, *A Course in Theoretical Physics*, are widely used in the west.

Although Soviet scientists are active in experimental solid state physics, their greatest contribution has been in theory. To understand the properties of metals, alloys, glasses, semiconductors and the like, scientists must understand the detailed motion and interaction of the enormous number of electrons and ions that go to make up these substances. During the 1950s and 1960s, theoreticians such as A.A. Abrikosov, N.N. Bogolyubov, V.L. Bonch-Bruevich, and L.P. Gor'kov made important contributions in this field (using techniques such as Green's Functions). More recently, theoreticians such as V.E. Zkharov, A.B. Shabat and others have been working in the fashionable field of 'solitons' and non-linear differential equations.

The lack of good computers has made itself felt in many areas of Soviet physics. Theoreticians such as L.D. Faddeyev have been forced to invent ingenious solutions and clever numerical approximations to solve their problem. In many areas Soviet theoreticians and mathematicians also seem to take their problems more directly from nature and their approach is less abstract. E.I. Arnold, M. Minorsky, S.L. Sobolev, A.N. Tihorov, M.M. Vainberg and I.M. Gelfand are other distinguished names. In recent years such mathematicians and mathematical physicists have been turning to engineering problems and 'control theory' to understand the behaviour of automatic and robotic systems.

In the experimental field N.G. Basov and A.M. Prokhorov shared the 1964 Nobel Prize with the American C.H. Townes for the invention of the laser and maser. Up to the mid 1970s, the USSR carried out some of the leading research in this field but more recently they have been hampered by the difficulty in obtaining the sort of back-up equipment that is routine in Western laboratories.

Unlike the U.S. the Soviets are not actively pursuing controlled nuclear fusion using lasers. There have, however, been rumours of powerful Soviet particle beams and lasers – 'death rays' that can shoot missiles out of the sky. If such stories are true, however, it would mean that military research is in considerable advance of published Academy work.

In the field of astronomy, the Academy has built good quality optical and radio telescopes with additional instruments on the drawing board.

Chemistry

Russian chemistry boasts a number of distinguished names and institutes, nevertheless, to Western contemporaries Soviet chemistry appears behind the times with few truly outstanding names. The story of Electron Paramagnetic Resonance (EPR) is a good illustration of why this is so.

In 1944 Yeugeny Konstantinovich Zavoysky, working at the university of Kazan, discovered a technique that could be used to probe the chemical environment around electrons in various substances. EPR proved to be of exceptional value to chemists since it told them directly about the inner structure of molecules. By the 1960s an EPR 'boom' had swept across the world but by now the Soviets had lagged far behind. The reason is that EPR machines (and their important cousins Nuclear Magnetic Resonance Machines (NMR) which are also hard to obtain in the USSR) are high technology equipment with carefully designed magnets and sophisticated electronics. While such devices can be easily produced in Japan, the U.S. and Europe, the Soviet versions were of poor quality. In the end the larger Soviet laboratories could only compete in research by buying their EPR (and NMR) machines from the West.

This problem of manufacturing and obtaining laboratory equipment plagues every area of Soviet science. Computers are hopelessly inadequate and solid state electronics is out of date. Even where equipment is manufactured it becomes difficult to get it from the factory to the laboratory bench. None of those informal, profitable contacts between scientist and high technology industry exist and the business of ordering equipment involves mountains of forms and a Dickensian bureaucracy.

As a result, Western researchers find that much of Soviet science lacks the flexibility to follow new experimental lines. In addition, when breakthroughs are reported in Soviet scientific papers, it takes too long before all the necessary background research follows.

But Soviet chemistry does have its successes. N. Semynov's work on reaction kinetics earned him a 1956 Nobel Prize. M. Zinin established an important school of organic chemistry at Kazan. A. Favorsky and S. Lebedev did important work on synthetic rubber and N. Beketov in organic chemistry. But often, top quality work is outweighed by much that is second rate or by research which simply follows the Western lead.

As with other areas of Soviet science the development of a new discovery into a full industrial process is slow and inefficient. The petrochemical industry, for example, is weak and any innovations and advances are as likely to be imported from the West as from Soviet laboratories. On the other hand, investments are being made in the new field of gas hydrate technology where the USSR leads the world. Soviet scientists argue that vast deposits of natural gas are trapped in the Soviet and Canadian permafrost inside molecular cages and can be released by special techniques. Indeed, they go further and claim that gas, in excess of one hundred times the world's known reserves, is trapped in similar hydrate cages at the bottom of the ocean. Canadian scientists are also interested in this field but find that technological information is more easily exchanged within the Soviet Union than in the West where industrial secrecy is important.

Biology

To Western scientists biology in the USSR is linked to the name Trofim Denisovich Lysenko. As head of the Lenin Academy of Agricultural Sciences and supported by Stalin, Lysenko promoted his eccentric views on the development of plant and animal hybrids and his rejection of genetics. Biology, and biologists, suffered under Lysenko, in particular the brilliant Vavilov. Nikolay Ivanovich Vavilov (1887–1943), studied genetics at Cambridge under William Bateson and on his return to the Soviet Union established research institutes, led scientific expeditions and made important contributions to the understanding of plant evolution. For his pains he was hounded and, in 1941, sent to a concentration camp in Saratov.

In 1965 Lysenko was exposed as a fraud within the USSR and Russian biology has yet to recover from this stain. Western colleagues estimate that research is between five and ten years out of date and is making no significant contribution to the rapidly expanding field of genetic engineering. In an effort to catch up a number of new institutes are being built outside Moscow and, in the field of protein production from single cells, an industrial plant is in operation.

East-West Contracts

Contact between scientists generally begins after they have read each other's research publications. All the major Soviet journals are regularly translated and published by the West with less important journals being reported by title and short abstract. The various annual reviews of scientific work in specialised fields also includes information on research in Soviet institutes and in recent years, some scientists from the USSR have even published in Western scientific journals.

Anyone who has had contact with the USSR reports that its scientists are eager for contact with the West; they want to talk over new ideas and approaches, engage in co-operative research projects, exchange students, visit conferences and invite senior scientists to spend time at their institutions.

But inviting a Soviet scientist to speak at a meeting can be a considerable headache for, until the moment that the guest steps onto the podium, no-one is certain that he will actually arrive. Applications for travel outside the USSR can be made a year in advance, will involve considerable paperwork and levels of approval, yet the scientist may not receive his visa until the day before he plans to leave.

Western scientists who travel to the USSR speak of the warmth of their reception, the many small gifts and large drinks that are pressed on them and the active scientific discussions they encounter. Science is obviously important in the USSR and it is not unusual to see a street poster praising its virtues. Seminars and lectures lead to lively and productive discussions with criticism being freely made.

Experimental scientists appear to work the same long day as their Western scientists but the theoreticians only turn up for lectures and seminars and, generally having no offices, work at home or in a library. The ratio between theoreticians and experimentalists is larger than in the West.

The Academician has considerable power and prestige, enjoying special restaurant services, superior medical attention and a car and chauffeur. To be the guest of the Academy is to assume social privileges unknown by most Western scientists. At their best the Academicians are brilliant scientists, good teachers and inspiring leaders of their large research teams. However, those who have become old and inflexible, still find it easy to retain their positions and power. They have been described by visitors as 'robber barons' or 'slave drivers' for they direct armies of young research scientists along chosen lines of research. Initiative is discouraged but the young research worker's only hope for advancement is to catch the eye of his patron.

Laboratories themselves are often poorly supplied with the type of equipment that is considered standard in the West – desk computers, or terminals, high quality oscilloscopes, Polaroid photography, photocopying and the like. New research projects move more slowly from their inception and ordering new equipment or laboratory space is a discouraging procedure. A common remark made by Western scientists on their return is 'If you thought it was bad here, well, it's a hundred times worse in the USSR.'

Personal experiences of the Soviet Union vary. Some visitors feel themselves under surveillance, approached by suspicious characters and believe that their rooms are electronically 'bugged'. They note that while their hosts are eager to talk about scientific matters they pretend not to understand when political questions are raised. They are irritated by the constant need for passes in entering institutes and may be told that certain scientific laboratories are closed to outsiders.

By contrast, others do not feel themselves under surveillance, see little evidence of political interference in science and ascribe any difficulties they encounter to a stupid and old fashioned bureaucracy. They may also be amused when their hosts boast that they never believe anything that Soviet politicians tell them.

Dissidents and Refusniks

Not every Soviet scientist is free to publish and pursue his research. Dissidents and Refusniks are often deprived of their scientific positions, unable to publish in Soviet journals and afraid of the repercussions of sending a paper to a Western scientific journal.

The Refusniks (many Jews) are those who have been refused exit visas from the USSR. Unable to work in orthodox institutions, they have banded together to form the famous Moscow Sunday Seminars. Around one hundred Refusniks from twelve Soviet cities may take part in these unofficial meetings together with distinguished Western visitors who make it a point to lecture at these seminars.

Dissidents, who have criticised the Soviet political machinery, will have been deprived of their jobs, placed under house arrest or exiled. Western scientists, individually or through their professional organisations, maintain contact and monitor their treatment through a regular programme of mailing letters and scientific papers together with 'Advice of Delivery' cards. Reports in the professional journal of the American Physical Society, *Physics Today*, suggest that in some instances this mail has been delayed, censored or undelivered.

Education

In 1966 a major educational reform took place in the Soviet Union with an increased emphasis being placed on science and mathematics. Soviet school children now receive a wider scientific education than do their Western counterparts with mathematics being taken to a more advanced level.

In the universities a higher proportion of engineers and applied scientists take degrees than in the U.S. and this is reflected in the large number of factory managers with engineering degrees. However, Soviet students at the doctoral level who come to the West for additional experience are generally considered hardworking but with a more old fashioned background.

Science Policy and Control

Through its various institutes the Academy controls much of the nation's pure research. By comparison the smaller universities and ministry research institutes are often poor cousins. Military research, however, is probably of a high quality.

As a centre of excellence, respected throughout the scientific world, the Academy has managed to preserve a measure of autonomy throughout the fluctuations of post-revolutionary history. The country, which recognises the need for high quality research, also realises that this depends on the economy.

However, politicians are never too happy when control lies in other hands, particularly in the Academy's case where it has tended to close ranks to protect its dissident members. Attempts have been made in the past to 'infiltrate' the Academy but have not met with particular success. Research scientists, like writers, artists and composers, have an allergy to directives and policies, and prefer to choose their own professional pathways. From time to time the scientist reaches a crossroads from which may branch several paths of research. One may lead to an important discovery while the others result in months or years of fruitless work. At such a juncture the scientist has only his intuition and experience to guide him and it is highly unlikely that he will give up control to a policy planner or external directive.

On the other hand, since the nation invests considerable funds in science, it also likes to call the tune. In recent years a lagging economy has emphasised the importance of improving industry and getting scientific innovations from the laboratory bench to the factory floor. The State Committee for Science and Technology, answerable to the USSR Council of Ministers, was created to encourage the applied sciences and assist the transfer of new technologies. In practice, along with the State Planning Committee which determines science policy, it also acts as a counterbalance to the Academy.

In terms of basic research, the arms race and space exploration, the Soviet people have been given good returns for their investment in science. But high technology, petro-chemicals and modern industry remain weak. To some extent this is the fault of the pure scientist, who from his privileged position is reluctant to become involved in applied research. But this is not the whole story for in the USSR it is particularly difficult for a young scientist with a bright idea to get it adopted by industry. Personal contacts between laboratories and industry are weak and no good government programmes exist to encourage such exchanges. As with other facets of Soviet life an obsession with centralisation, bureaucracy and levels of approval act to hamper initiative and atrophy innovation.

The factory manager, for his part, is ruled not by profits and efficiency but by quotas and directives and it is more than his job is worth to compromise these. For this reason, he will be suspicious of any innovation which may have the effect of disrupting his factory. Where directives are concerned, they will be drawn up by anonymous authorities in Moscow who may have no first hand experience of local problems or the quirks of a technological process. The factory manager, located possibly thousands of miles away, is then expected to carry out these plans to the letter. No wonder considerable hostility towards Moscow exists in the more remote regions.

Summary

In a number of fields Soviet science is of high quality and boasts some top quality minds. In other areas, mediocre and out of date work flourishes like weeds. Even in the best areas experimentalists are hampered by an absence of good equipment which makes it difficult for them to move into new fields.

In a number of areas Soviet industry is badly in need of an injection of new technology but the machinery of the government at its many levels makes this difficult to do. Research scientists are not always willing to turn to applied problems and those that do find it difficult to get their ideas adopted by industry. Directives and centralised control tend to hamper initiative and discourage industry from exploring new approaches.

To some extent none of this is new. Soviet science has made great strides in the twentieth century, yet when it comes to industrial applications or the ability to move into new and exciting fields, the rusty machinery of the state continually gets in the way. In this respect the scientist at his laboratory bench in the 1980s is no different in position from Mendeleyev, Tsiolokovski or Popov a century before.

MARX, THE FALSE PROPHET

JONATHAN GUINNESS

The word prophet has two meanings. It means one who foretells the future, and also one who tells people what they ought to do. Karl Marx set out to be a prophet in both senses. As a forecaster, he proved to be largely wrong, though the situation is confused by the fact that the political and military elites which control the countries of the East style themselves Marxist parties, defining their own rule as being that of the working class, and thus as being in accordance with Marx's predictions. This re-definition is accepted by many people out of self-interest, *naivété* or simple inattention.

However, it is not primarily as forecaster that I am describing Marx as a false prophet, but as teacher. His assertion was that the good society would ultimately come through the action of cause and effect if everyone followed their selfish class interests, and this in effect excused people from any general personal obligation to behave well. He saw all individual kindness, and all the improvement that in fact took place in society without revolution, as being either irrelevant or due in reality to self-interest. What looked like morality was in fact a class weapon.

> What could be more characteristic of the capitalist mode of production than the fact that it is necessary, by Act of Parliament, to force upon the capitalists the simplest appliances for maintaining cleanliness and health?

he asked, (*Capital I*, p. 611) But, one might reply, Parliament did at least pass such laws. Aha! – Marx would undoubtedly retort: that just shows how ingenuous you are. Parliament passed such laws because it was at that time under the control not of the industrial, but of the landed interest.

> There is an old English proverb to the effect that when thieves fall out, honest men come into their own, and in fact the noisy and passionate dispute between the two factions of the ruling class as to which of them exploited the workers more shamelessly was the midwife of truth on both sides of the question. (*Capital* I, p. 830/1.)

Marx's cynicism, which was pervasive and systematic, derives both from his version of Hegel's 'dialectical' idea of progress through the conflict and combination of opposites, and from his notions of political economy drawn from Ricardo and Adam Smith. Hegel's view that progress resulted from thought-processes bringing about the political realisation of a transcendent 'Idea' could, as Schopenhauer saw, be made to justify any existing state of affairs: and Hegel was, sure enough, politically a conservative. But many of his successors, the 'Young Hegelians', were radicals and socialists. Marx adapted Hegel's scheme by relating human history and progress to changes, not in thought-processes, but in methods of production. Each stage in the development of production methods was typified by, and necessitated the dominance of a particular type of ruling class. Marx himself thought that he had demystified Hegel. He said his dialectic

> is not only different from the Hegelian, but is its direct opposite. . . With me . . . the idea is nothing less than the material world reflected by the human mind, and translated into forms of thought.

In fact, though this did constitute a difference, it was hardly so great a difference as Marx claimed. The Italian Marxist Antonio Gramsci implicitly agreed with this assessment when he denied that Marx was in fact materialist. Whether or not one goes as far as this, it is certain that Marx's type of materialism works in a way that makes it uncommonly like idealism. True, he says 'What individuals are depends upon the conditions of material production.' (*The German Ideology*) This is of course a sound half-truth, the only trouble with which is the fact that Marx makes conditions of production the only important influence – a little earlier he even says that what individuals are *coincides* (my italics) with what they produce. But in that case, and if material forces are the only ones which exist, what can have started the evolution of production methods? What made man into the producing animal? When analysed, the Marxist hypothesis requires a mystical force to set the process in motion; and as to its subsequent guidance, the 'material world reflected by the human mind and translated into forms of thought' is not, really, all that far from Hegel's 'idea' which it replaces.

Already in Hegel there is, as we have seen, a tendency to moral relativism, to a denial of absolute standards of right and wrong. He saw moral standards not as existing independently of conditions, but as being *generated* by the historical process as he conceived it. From the undoubted fact that, in the real world, the enforcement of the moral order depends largely on the authorities, he deduced that the State was, or could be, above moral criticism. Marx inherits Hegel's moral relativism, but in a greatly enhanced and coarsened form. This is first because he injects into the scheme the fundamental amorality of political economy as expounded by Adam Smith and developed by Ricardo. For the doctrine derived from political economy, *laissex-faire* liberalism (which is what is being reintroduced now under the misleading name of 'monetarism') is essentially amoral; it is in fact an assertion that the greatest collective benefit is secured by the mechanical, and inevitably in places ruthless, operation of the market. It is an assertion that ethics do not apply in economics. Marx, to be sure, was not backward in using this argument to discredit the liberals of his day, as witness the sarcastic passage at the end of the second part of the first book of *Capital*. His objection, however, is not to the amorality as such, but to its operating in the interests of the bourgeois, rather than the working, class; the superiority of which in the last analysis resides, not in its merit, but in its predicted power as predestined victor. Marx merely, as it were, transfers *laissez-faire* to a different level where it is the strongest collective force, rather than the most efficient individual, who wins. (And under liberalism the winner, ruthless though he may be, has at least produced or sold goods that people want.)

Again, the transmutation of Hegel's intellectual dialectic into a pre-determined class struggle implies that selfishness is not just condoned, but actually enjoined. For altruism, if it occurred on any serious scale, would stop the ruling class fulfilling its historic function of oppressing and provoking, and thus interfere with the painful, but ultimately beneficient, process. This is why Marx welcomed what he regarded as the destructive behaviour of the British in India: it would hasten the Revolution. (British Rule in India, article, 1853, in *Marx, Surveys from Exile*.)

It is true that the proletarian victory which was to end the class dogfight was in turn to lead to a classless society ruled by kindness, and the withering away of the coercive state; but the expectation that those who had taken power on behalf of the proletariat would, unlike any other power group, obligingly bow out, was entirely a matter of faith. Up to that vaguely glimpsed future point, Marx was explicitly and in the very worst sense Machiavellian. The use of the word is in fact a libel on Machiavelli who, though he advised rulers to put practical considerations before moral ones, did possess what might be described as a political aesthetic, a view that crimes ought to be limited to what was necessary to the purpose in hand. Nothing of the sort can be discerned in Marx. Again, Machiavelli's ultimate good, the ordered and tranquil state enforcing consistent laws where people can live their lives in peace, has at intervals arisen, if temporarily; whereas Marx's classless society is chimerical.

My thesis is not that Marx lacked compassion, or good personal impulses. One must be chary of unsupported remarks about him like this assertion of Leopold Schwarzschild, 'It was rather the future humiliation of the rich than the future elevation of the poor which seemed to attract him'. The quotation is from an otherwise interesting and well-documented study of Marx called *The Red Prussian* which certainly shows him up as uncharitable, devious, and vituperative in controversy; but such evidence is not a proof of fundamental motive. The point is not in his personality but in his doctrine, and it is that the evil in Marxism has more vitality than the good because it is integral to its structure. The humanitarian sentiments, present mainly in his currently fashionable earlier works, may for all we know have seemed to him to constitute the ultimate point of the whole exercise; but they are incidental and easily omitted. In this, Marx is the exact converse of Christ. Several of Christ's sayings have unfortunate implications in isolation, as for instance the parable of the unjust steward, which can easily be interpreted as an endorsement of dishonesty. However, the general sweep of the Gospel message is such that one is justified in reinterpreting or disregarding such passages. The dynamic of Marx's philosophy works in the opposite direction.

This characteristic of Marx's thought is not just a theoretical point; it has had a pervasive effect in corrupting the reasoning, the style of argument, and finally also the political practice of those under his influence. In the first instance, it affected his own development as a thinker. We have mentioned the fact that there are more humanitarian and compassionate passages in his early works than in his later ones, notably *Capital*; within *Capital* itself, too, passages that can be given such an interpretation are mostly concentrated in the first volume. This progression in itself argues the existence in Marx's mode of thinking of an interior dynamic working from the comparatively humane towards the inhumane, related to a shift in emphasis from advocating revolution as desirable to predicting it as inevitable. This is only, to be sure, a shift in emphasis; at all stages in

Marx's development the revolution is presented as both desirable and inevitable. But the question as to which aspect is uppermost is nevertheless important as determining the moral assumptions, and ultimately the behaviour in power, of socialists.

The change from advocacy to prediction is to be seen in most people whom Marx influenced, both among contemporaries and successors. Take for example his slightly older contemporary Moses Hess, an important figure because it was he who converted Friedrich Engels to socialism; he may even have been partially responsible for the conversion of Marx himself. Hess believed that the root of all human evil was competition; the removal of competition would allow the development of a communistic society ruled by mutual love. His initial view was that the condition for achieving this was psychological; a transformation of hearts and minds. It is perhaps the residual influence of Marx's cynicism on all of us that prevents us realising that this is, in fact, not less but more realistic than Marx's view that the moral transformation would occur through purely material, economic, forces. The Welfare State in Britain and Europe came about in great degree through a gradual refinement in the sensibility of public opinion; a psychological change under which conditions for the poor which had been generally accepted by the rest of the population were no longer considered tolerable.

However, Hess did not stick to these views. He came, temporarily, very strongly under Marx's influence, and an essay he wrote in 1847 – a year before Marx and Engels promulgated their Communist Manifesto – could almost have been by Marx himself. In this essay, *The Results of the Revolution of the Proletariat*, he describes the creation of the proletariat by mass industry, the inevitability of crises through over-production, and the revolution as the result of these factors. This did not save him from violent attacks by Marx, who possibly discerned a rival for the leadership of the world revolutionary movement. At the end of his life, Hess became one of the earliest advocates of the return of the Jews to Palestine.

A tougher and more rumbustious figure than Hess was the anarchist leader M.A. Bakunin. Far from coming under Marx's influence, he reacted against him. He clearly foresaw from Marx's thought just what a Marxist state would be like. In his book *Statehood and Anarchy*, he said that in the Marxist state, as in all other states, a minority would govern the majority.

> But, the Marxists say, this minority will consist of the workers. Yes, no doubt – of former workers, who, as soon as they become governors or representatives of the people, cease to be workers and start looking down on the working masses from the heights of state authority. . .

Milovan Djilas was later to call the resulting elite the New Class. The fact that a contemporary of Marx could already spot the way Marxism would turn out helps to dispose of the facile view, common among those who want to assimilate such an influential figure as Marx to the company of world moral teachers, that Lenin and Stalin and Mao and Castro and Pol Pot somehow perverted Marxist doctrine. They did not; they carried it out, each in his own way, which bore to that of the others a strong family likeness. Lenin did not invent, but made explicit and systematic, a view that is already inherent in Marx, that the Communist Party should constitute itself as the leader of society, the elite; in effect a new, collectively self-conscious, aristocracy, rendered legitimate by its expertise in Marxist 'science.'

However, it is not only in the East that Marx's false prophecy debases the thinking and practice of his adherents. The squalid treatment of the idealistic socialist George Orwell by the Communists during and after the Spanish Civil War is a case in point. Orwell had fought bravely on the side of the Republic; the biography by Bernard Crick makes clear just how bravely. But he had fought in a unit that was classified as Trotskyist, and the Stalinist Communists were at the time purging such 'elements.' So he barely escaped arrest in Spain itself, and the pro-communist Left, including the *New Statesman* under Kingsley Martin, did its very best to limit the publicity given to his views. One minor incident stands out as particularly unpleasant. *The Daily Worker* – predecessor of the *Morning Star* – published a review of Orwell's *The Road to Wigan Pier* by the Communist Party General Secretary, Harry Pollitt, which among more generalised smears contained the remark: 'I gather that the chief thing that worries Mr Orwell is the 'smell' of the working class. . .' In fact what Orwell had said was that middle class people had been brought up to believe that the working classes smelt. He wrote a letter of complaint to Victor Gollancz, who was at that time – though not later – a close Communist fellow-traveller, complaining about Pollitt's review, and threatening to reveal to the public something John Strachey – another 'thirties fellow-traveller who later became one of Attlee's ministers – had said, relevant to the 'smell' of the working class. Gollancz forwarded this to Pollitt with a note saying: '. . . You should see this letter from Orwell. I read it to John over the telephone and he assures me that he is quite certain that he said nothing whatever indiscreet.' That is, there was no hint on Gollancz's part of any concern about the lie, still less any reproach; implicitly, the right to smear in the cause is accepted. The point is that Gollancz was not a natural cynic but, as his post-war record of concern for the sufferings of European children showed, a good and compassionate man. He was simply, at that period, caught up in Marxist moral habits.

Orwell's personal experiences of the Communists were obviously a factor in the creations of his masterpieces, *Animal Farm* and *1984*. But it is also Orwell, like Bakunin a dedicated revolutionary though an anti-Marxist, who very shrewdly noted: 'Marxists are not very good at reading the minds of their adversaries'. Again and again this has proved true, especially in the politically sophisticated countries of the West. They mishandled the rise of Mussolini and Hitler and the Spanish Civil War, and they frittered away their position of strength in Europe after the Second World War, for just this reason. It comes down to this: the moral aesthetic, the fact that (to put it no higher) people find truth and kindness inherently more attractive than lies and cruelty, is an important attribute of humanity. As Crick comments, Orwell was probably led to make his remark because he had heard Marxists argue, 'forever categorising their opponents, rarely grasping their authentic motives'. The moral aesthetic is by no means all that they ignored; their mistake in pre-Hitler Germany was to ignore the desire, exploited by Hitler, for national self-respect. The reductionism inherent in Marx's thinking extends well beyond the moral sphere, even though it is this with which I am dealing here.

In fact one of the tragedies of the spread of Marxist views among the young, especially students, is a personal blighting and crippling of this outlook. To the extent that Marxism 'takes' in a person's thinking, it induces a kind of tunnel vision, or colour-blindness. The imperative to harden the heart would of course be an acute danger for the rest of us if these students achieved their aim of power over our country; but in the meantime my own feeling for them is rather one of compassion, in the sense that there is so much that they miss. A perhaps extreme, but not untypical, example is a student who wrote to me some time ago. He objected to a letter I had written to the *Guardian* asking for free speech in universities; the National Union of

Students had started its policy, analogous to that of the South African Government in its Suppression of Communism Act, of 'naming' people as fascists or racists and banning them from speaking to students. I had suggested that the achievement by these people of State power would bring general suppression of freedom. The student said, in effect, that freedom was phoney because it did not apply to ordinary people whom he called the 'peasants'. These, he implied, were the majority of the country, and they were miserably oppressed and ground down, 'forced into leading a disgustingly boring existence of neo-slavery'. He added: 'Peasants can own their own homes these days but they only sleep in them because they have to work the rest of the time.' The implication was that the country consisted only of such people and an 'abhorrent upper crust.' Feeling sorry for him, I wrote a long reply, which remained unacknowledged, pointing out something of the real variety of our society; asking, for instance, who tended all those gardens if all the workers could do at home was sleep, and mentioning some of the hobbies and leisure activities and sports that go on.

To be sure, the student had clearly not read a line of Marx, whose sociology bears no relation to this grossly simplified model. He had nevertheless, at second or third hand, absorbed the essential evil; the reductionism which makes production methods, social conditions, class relationships, and relative incomes into the only basic reality – the 'basis' – and all else, religion, morality, love, loyalty, beauty, into the 'superstructure.' He carried around with him his own internal concentration camp.

For before the Gulag Archipelago was thought of, let alone the Berlin Wall, this grey gloom had already taken shape in the strange brain of this powerful, proud, and disappointed man. He was right, and not alone, in seeing some form of socialism, in the sense of solidarity within society, and greater equality, as being the assumption of the future. But he perverted and debased it. Socialism without Marx, private enterprise tamed and exploited for society, is by and large what Britain and Western Europe have achieved since 1945. If, through the successful infiltration of the Labour Party, Marxism prevails, then we shall progress from this untidy but basically humane consumer society with welfare to something like the Eastern system of collective feudalism.

Gramsci, interestingly, calls the Communist party in power the 'Collective Prince', meaning Machiavelli's prince, and means this of course as a compliment. He believed that the leaders of the working class once they had achieved power, could drop the materialism of their revolutionary phase and take over the idealism of established ruling classes, adopting a viewpoint of '*noblesse oblige*'. This is a possible way forward for Communist parties in the Soviet Union and other Eastern countries; but it would require the whole Marxist cast of mind to be rejected. (Gramsci would have disputed this, but it is the case.) Otherwise one envisages the nightmare of 'perpetual revolution', the mad and sinister dream of the ageing Mao who could not accept any established élite, however recent; present revolutionary status was the only legitimacy he accepted. Or, less dramatically, ruling Communist parties might simply carry on as at present, morally shackled in perpetuity by the dismal genius of Karl Marx. We must hope that the natural good in humanity breaks these shackles over the years, as the roots of an oak can finally break concrete.

THE RELATION BETWEEN ECONOMIC FREEDOM AND POLITICAL FREEDOM*

MILTON FRIEDMAN

> Freedom is a rare and delicate plant. Our minds tell us, and history confirms, that the great threat to freedom is the concentration of power.

It is widely believed that politics and economics are separate and largely unconnected; that individual freedom is a political problem and material welfare an economic problem; and that any kind of political arrangements can be combined with any kind of economic arrangements. The chief contemporary manifestation of this idea is the advocacy of 'democratic socialism' by many who condemn out of hand the restrictions on individual freedom imposed by 'totalitarian socialism' in Russia, and who are persuaded that it is possible for a country to adopt the essential features of Russian economic arrangements and yet to ensure individual freedom through political arrangements. My thesis is that such a view is a delusion, that there is an intimate connection between economics and politics, that only certain combinations of political and economic arrangements are possible, and that in particular, a society which is socialist cannot also be democratic, in the sense of guaranteeing individual freedom.

Economic arrangements play a dual role in the promotion of a free society. On the one hand, freedom in economic arrangements is itself a component of freedom broadly understood, so economic freedom is an end in itself. In the second place, economic freedom is also an indispensable means toward the achievemement of political freedom.

The first of these roles of economic freedom needs special emphasis because intellectuals in particular have a strong bias against

* An excerpt from Chapter 1, Capitalism and Freedom.

regarding this aspect of freedom as important. They tend to express contempt for what they regard as material aspects of life, and to regard their own pursuit of allegedly higher values as on a different plane of significance and as deserving of special attention. For most citizens of the country, however, if not for the intellectual, the direct importance of economic freedom is at least comparable in significance to the indirect importance of economic freedom as a means to political freedom.

The citizen of Great Britain, who after World War II was not permitted to spend his vacation in the United States because of exchange control, was being deprived of an essential freedom no less than the citizen of the United States, who was denied the opportunity to spend his vacation in Russia because of his political views. The one was ostensibly an economic limitation on freedom and the other a political limitation, yet there is no essential difference between the two.

A citizen of the United States who under the laws of various states is not free to follow the occupation of his own choosing unless he can get a licence for it, is being deprived of an essential part of his freedom. So also is the farmer who cannot grow the amount of wheat he wants. Clearly, economic freedom, in and of itself, is an extremely important part of total freedom.

Viewed as a means to the end of political freedom, economic arrangements are important because of their effect on the concentration or dispersion of power. The kind of economic organisation that provides economic freedom directly, namely, competitive capitalism, also promotes political freedom because it separates economic power from political power and in this way enables the one to offset the other.

Historical evidence speaks with a single voice on the relation between political freedom and a free market. I know of no example in time or place of a society that has been marked by a large measure of political freedom, and that has not also used something comparable to a free market to organise the bulk of economic activity.

So long as effective freedom of exchange is maintained, the central feature of the market organisation of economic activity is that it prevents one person from interfering with another in respect of most of his activities. The consumer is protected from coercion by the seller because of the presence of other sellers with whom he can deal. The seller is protected from coercion by the consumer because of other consumers to whom he can sell. The employee is protected from coercion by the employer because of other employers for whom he can work, and so on. And the market does this impersonally and without centralised authority.

Indeed, a major cource of objections to a free economy is precisely that it does this task so well. It gives people what they want instead of what a particular group thinks they ought to want. Underlying most arguments against the free market is a lack of belief in freedom itself.

The existence of a free market does not of course eliminate the need for government. On the contrary, government is essential both as a forum for determining the 'rules of the game' and as an umpire to interpret and enforce the rules decided on. What the market does is to reduce greatly the range of issues that must be decided through political means, and thereby to minimise the extent to which government need participate directly in the game. The characteristic feature of action through political channels is that it tends to require or enforce sustantial conformity. The great advantage of the market, on the other hand, is that it permits wide diversity. It is, in political terms, a system of proportional representation. Each man can vote, as it were, for the colour of tie he wants and get it; he does not have to see what colour the majority wants and then, if he is in the minority, submit.

It is this feature of the market that we refer to when we say that the market provides economic freedom. But this characteristic also has implications that go far beyond the narrowly economic. Political freedom means the absence of coercion of a man by his fellow men. The fundamental threat to freedom is power to coerce, be it in the hands of a monarch, a dictator, an oligarchy, or a momentary majority. The preservation of freedom requires the elimination of such concentration of power to the fullest possible extent and the dispersal and distribution of whatever power cannot be eliminated – a system of checks and balances. By removing the organization of economic activity from the control of political authority, the market eliminates this source of coercive power. It enables economic strength to be a check to political power rather than a reinforcement.

One feature of a free society is surely the freedom of individuals to advocate and propagandise openly for a radical change in the structure of the society – so long as the advocacy is restricted to persuasion and does not include force or other forms of coercion. It is a mark of the political freedom of a capitalist society that men can openly advocate and work for socialism. Equally, political freedom in a socialist society would require that men be free to advocate the introduction of capitalism. How could this freedom be preserved and protected in a socialist society?

In order for men to advocate anything, they must in the first place be able to earn a living. This already raises a problem in a socialist society, since all jobs are under the direct control of political authorities. It would take an act of self-denial for a socialist government to permit its employees to advocate policies directly contrary to official doctrine.

But let us suppose this act of self-denial to be achieved. For advocacy of capitalism to mean anything, the proponents must be able to finance their cause – to hold public meetings, publish pamphlets, buy radio time, and so on. How could they raise the funds? There might and probably would be men in the socialist society with large incomes, perhaps even large capital sums in the form of government bonds and the like, but these would of necessity be high public officials. It is possible to conceive of a minor socialist official retaining his job although openly advocating capitalism. It strains credulity to imagine the socialist top brass financing such 'subversive' activities.

The only recourse for funds would be to raise small amounts from a large number of minor officials. But this is no real answer. To tap these sources, many people would already have to be persuaded, and our whole problem is how to initiate and finance a campaign to do sso. Radical movements in capitalist societies have never been financed this way. They have typically been supported by a few wealthy individuals who have become persuaded – by a Frederick Vanderbilt Field, or by a Friedrich Engels, to go further back. This is a role of inequality of wealth in preserving political freedom that is seldom noted – the role of the patron.

In a capitalist society, it is only necessary to convince a few wealthy people to get funds to launch any idea, however strange, and there are many such persons, many independent foci of support. And, indeed, it is not even necessary to persuade people or financial institutions with available funds of the soundness of the ideas to be propagated. It is only necessary to persuade them that the propagation can be financially successful; that the newspaper, book or other venture will be profitable. The competitive publisher, for example, cannot afford to publish only writing with which he personally agrees; his touchstone must be the likelihood that the market will be large enough to yield a satisfactory return on his investment.

In this way, the market breaks the vicious circle and makes it possible ultimately to finance such ventures by small amounts from many people without first persuading them. There are no such possibilities in the socialist society; there is only the all-powerful state.

Let us stretch our imagination and suppose that a socialist government is aware of this problem and composed of people anxious to preserve freedom. Could it provide the funds? Perhaps, but it is difficult to see how. It could establish a bureau for subsidising subversive propaganda. But how could it choose whom to support? If it gave to all who asked, it would shortly find itself out of funds, for socialism cannot repeal the elementary economic law that a sufficiently high price will call forth a large supply. Make the advocacy of radical causes sufficiently remunerative, and the supply of advocates will be unlimited.

Moreover, freedom to advocate unpopular causes does not require that such advocacy be without cost. On the contrary, no society could be stable if advocacy of radical change were cost-less, much less subsidised. It is entirely appropriate that men make sacrifices to advocate causes in which they deeply believe. Indeed, it is important to preserve freedom only for people who are willing to practise self-denial, for otherwise freedom degenerates into licence and irresponsibility. What is essential is that the cost of advocating unpopular causes be tolerable and not prohibitive.

But we are not yet through. In a free market society, it is enough to have the funds. The suppliers of paper are as willing to sell it to the *Daily Worker* as to the *Wall Street Journal*. In a socialist society, it would not be enough to have the funds. The hypothetical supporter of capitalism would have to persuade a government factory making paper to sell to him, the government printing press to print his pamphlets, a government agency to rent him a hall in which to talk, and so on.

What is clear is that there are very real difficulties in establishing institutions that will effectively preserve the possibility of dissent. So far as I know, none of the people who have been in favour of socialism and also in favour of freedom have really faced up to this issue, or made even a respectable start at developing the institutional arrangements that would permit freedom under socialism. By contrast, it is clear how a free market capitalist society fosters freedom.

THE UNACCEPTABLE FACE OF MARX

(The distasteful theories behind the creation of an ideal world)

ROBERT MILLER

Even among his opponents, Karl Marx has earned the reputation of a selfless if misguided idealist who dedicated his life to improving the lot of the human race.

Dedicated Marxist scholars have spent much time and energy on presenting him as supporting a world revolution to free the oppressed of all nations and races and to initiate a new order of equality and universal felicity. Even if we do not share his view of the need for violent revolution, surely everyone can share or at least admire his humane ideal of a Communist society?

But non-Marxist scholars have shown that this is not the whole story; Marx's view of the revolution and the Communist society that was to succeed it was quite different. In the first place Marx and Engels were convinced that the Communist revolution could only take place in advanced industrial societies and that after the revolution the leaders of the proletariat in advanced countries would rule by a sort of consortium the primitive ahistorical parts of the world such as Africa, India, China and Russia.

This view of the post-revolutionary world is not dissimilar to the Nazis – it will be remembered that Hitler was quite prepared to share out the rule of colonial territories with Britain.

Marx believed that there were reactionary peoples as well as classes and that they were both due to disappear in a series of horrifyingly destructive wars. It is not surprising that the reactionary peoples were the traditional objects of German territorial ambition – the Slavs and the Latins.

As Marx wrote:

> The general war that will then begin will . . . destroy all these little, bull-headed nations so that their very name will vanish. The coming world war will cause not only reactionary classes and dynasties, but entire reactionary peoples too, to disappear from the face of the earth. And that will also be progress.

Hitler could not have put it better.

In addition to reactionary peoples and classes, Marx's fiercest hatred was reserved for the Jews although his father was a Jewish convert. Marx claimed in true Heinrich Himmler style that the Jews were the essence of capitalism.

Marx's essay *On the Jewish Question* is a nauseating effort in the style of *Der Stürmer:*

> What is the secular basis of Judaism? Practical need, self-interest. What is the worldly cult of the Jew? Haggling. What is his worldly God? Money . . . money is the jealous god of Israel before whom no other god may exist. Money degrades all the gods of mankind and converts them into commodities. . . What is contained abstractly in the Jewish religion – contempt for theory, for art, for history, for man as an end in himself. . . The social emancipation of the Jew is the emancipation of society from Jewishness.

Marx even anticipated the 'Jewish conspiracy' claim of the Nazis.

> Thus we find every tyrant backed by a Jew, as is every Pope by a Jesuit. In truth the cravings of oppressors would be hopeless and the practicability of war out of the question, if there were not an array of Jesuits to smother thought and a handful of Jews to ransack pockets. . .

Some of Marx's comments about Jews are so unpleasant that they do not bear repetition but the argument of some of his apologists that Marx was using Jewishness as a synonym for capitalism is refuted by the savagery with which he referred to individual Jews in his correspondence with Engels. For example, he referred to Ferdinand Lassalle as 'a Jewish nigger'.

If Marx had a low opinion of Jews, it was nothing to his view of negroes. He believed that negroes were 'degenerate' human beings and he claimed that the author of this preposterous theory, the French enthnologist Pierre Trémaux, had made a discovery greater than Darwin's. He frequently referred to them as 'niggers' – a term which, as we have seen, he used to abuse his enemies, and he had no compunction in sneering at his son-in-law because he had negro ancestry.

He informed Engels that 'idiots' and 'niggers' are 'closely related'. Marx's view of the inferiority of negroes fitted neatly with his theory of historical peoples; in his scheme negroes in North America had much the same position as the Slavs in Europe. This explains Marx's ambiguity about the emancipation of the American slaves, which for a time he opposed on the grounds that it would slow down revolutionary developments – not, it should be said, for the unfortunate negroes but for the white working class.

Even towards the end of his life he copied out a remark of Sir Henry Maine with evident approval:

> Modern research conveys a stronger impression than ever of the separation between the Aryan races and races of other stocks.

If Marx despised Jews and negroes, he had no very high opinion of women and was by no means an exemplary husband. For many years he kept his family in squalor and fathered an illegitimate son by one of his wife's maids. He was not the last Hampstead intellectual to get the au pair into trouble!

Even in his writings Marx gives indications of extreme male chauvinism. According to the *Economic and Philosophical Manuscripts* of 1844, Marx claimed that bourgeois marriage made women the property of their husbands. But as with all private property, Marx thought that the owners ought to be expropriated and their property nationalised.

This, as Marx declared, would make all women prostitutes.

> In the same way as women are to abandon marriage for general prostitution, so the whole world of wealth, that is, the objective being of man, is to abandon the relation of exclusive marriage with the private property owner for the relation of general prostitution with the community. Such was to be the status of women under Communism.

Yet perhaps the most horrifying part of Marx's doctrine is that which its supporters claim requires no apology. This is Marx's enthusiasm for the revolution and civil war which he thought were both necessary and desirable to usher in the new age.

Marx had no illusions about the horrors that were to be expected:

> We have no compassion and ask no compassion from you. When our time comes, we shall not make excuses for terror.

> There was only one way in which the murderous death agony of the old society can be shortened and that way is revolutionary terror.

It is this claim rather than his ridiculous racial theorising which makes him still one of the great enemies of civilisation.

IN DEFENCE OF FREEDOM

by Margaret Thatcher

Introduced by
COLIN WILSON

When Margaret Thatcher agreed to be represented in this volume, the editors asked her whether there was any point in her life when she suddenly became aware of her rejection of Marxism. Had she, for example, any contact with Marxists at Oxford, or taken part in debates on socialism? The answer was no. Although she had joined the Conservative club at university, most of her energies had been devoted to science. Her rejection of socialism was not some kind of conversion, but a basic part of her mental outlook.

The reason for this becomes clear from Patricia Murray's biographical profile[1] of Mrs Thatcher. The major influence on her outlook was her father, who ran a grocer's shop in Grantham; and this was not so much because he preached the principles of conservatism as that he embodied them. Although the income from the grocery business was merely adequate, Alfred Roberts was a member of the town council, the library committee, the Rotary Club, the Chamber of Trade and the local Methodist congregation, as well as being a lay preacher, a school governor and an indefatigable voluntary worker. He was a born individualist.

> My father constantly drummed into me, from a very early age: You make up your own mind. You do not do something, or want to do something, because your friends are doing it. . . You do not follow the crowd because you're afraid of being different – you decide what to do yourself, and if necessary lead the crowd.

Her ability to put this hard advice into practice was demonstrated when she became Conservative candidate for Dartford at the age of 23. Dartford was a Labour stronghold, so her chances of capturing it for the Tories were minimal. And since she worked during the day at a laboratory in Hammersmith, she had to do her canvassing at evenings and weekends. Inevitably, she lost; but she campaigned to such good effect that she reduced the Labour majority by a third and increased the Tory vote by 50%. Undaunted by her failure, she stood again in 1951, and again lost. But she had the consolation of knowing that she had left behind a great deal of affection in Dartford – even the winning Labour candidate took her to lunch in the House of Commons.

More than a quarter of a century later, when she was leader of the opposition, Mrs Thatcher expressed her own version of her father's philosophy in a letter to the *Times*:[2]

> Ms Sandra Pontac rightly questions why some people should have to work out their own salvation in a slum. Yet beware of being patronising. For millions on millions have worked out their salvation in every sense of the term from just such beginnings, just as others have wasted their opportunities. I look forward to a day when there will be no slums. But I believe that we shall achieve more by helping people to help themselves than by trying to relieve them of their own responsibilities and thereby of their own dignity and self-respect.

This paragraph probably contains the essence of Margaret Thatcher's conservatism and of her anti-Marxism. She is aware that there are no easy options. What bothers her about socialism is that it gains its converts by insisting that there *are* easy options; and, moreover, delivering these unredeemable promises in the name of altruism and love of humanity. Her own political philosophy is, in essence, a simple matter of realism.

The letter to the *Times* was written in July 1977, as a contribution to a correspondence brought about by her Iain Macleod Memorial Lecture of July 4, 1977. This lecture contains her most closely-reasoned attack on the philosophy of socialism and Marxism. After speaking of the history of the Tory party, and its links with the Church of England, she goes on:

> Our religion teaches us that *every human being is unique* and must play his part in working out his own salvation. So whereas socialists begin with society, and how people can be fitted in, we start with Man, whose social and economic relationships are just part of his wider existence.
>
> Because we see man as a spiritual being, we utterly reject the Marxist view, which gives pride of place to economics. However

much the Marxists and their fellow-travellers new and old may try to wriggle and explain away, this was Marx's stated view and a linch-pin of his whole system.

The religious tradition values economic activity, how we earn our living, create wealth, but warns against obsession with it, warns against putting it above all else. Money is not an end in itself, but a means to an end.

The letters to the Archbishop of Canterbury received in reply to his 'call to the nation' were recently published. One of them was from a country vicar: 'I am concerned,' he wrote, 'that I haven't enough to do my job properly. I am concerned because my parishioners, some of them at least, are not receiving what I ought to be able to provide and be glad to give them, i.e. a visit in emergencies, just because there is no petrol in the tank and no money in the pocket to buy more; or that there is petrol only sufficient to provide transport for my wife to work'.

That vicar knew that he needed money, not for itself, but for what he could do with it.

The increased involvement of government with economic life has coincided with a marked worsening of economic performance.

It has heightened tensions between different groups of workers, some struggling to keep differentials, others trying to override them; between producers and consumers, landlords and tenants, public services and the public.

To observe these things is not to deny a role to government in economic life; it is not to preach *laissex-faire*. That was preached two centuries back when manufacturers and commerce were fighting to free themselves from state monopoly and interference which were holding back their development.

There is much that the state should do, and do much better than it is doing. But there are also proper limits which have long since been passed in this country.

To understand the reason and how these limits can be adduced, we must come back to the nature of man. This is a matter where our understanding and our case, based on religion and commonsense, are so much sounder than that of the socialist doctrine. Yet the socialist travesty has succeeded in gaining wide acceptance by default, even among our own people. I refer to the question of self-interest as against the common good. The socialists have been able to persuade themselves and many others that a free economy based on profit embodies and encourages self-interest, which they see as selfish and bad, whereas they claim socialism is based on, and nurtures, altruism and selflessness.

This is baseless nonsense in theory and in practice; let me explain why. Let us start from the idea of self. There is not and cannot possibly be any hard and fast antithesis between self-interest and care for others, for man is a social creature, born into family, clan, community, nation, brought up in mutual dependence. The founders of our religion made this a cornerstone of morality. The admonition: love thy neighbour as thyself, and do as you would be done by, expresses this. You will note that it does not denigrate self, or elevate love of others above it. On the contrary, it sees concern for self and responsibility for self as something to be expected, and asks only that this be extended to others. This embodies the great truth that self-regard is the root of regard for one's fellows. The child learns to understand others through its own feelings. At first its immediate family; in course of time the circle grows.

Our fellow-feeling develops from self-regard. Because we want warmth, shelter, food, security, respect, and other goods for ourselves, we can understand that others want them too. If we had no desire for these things, would we be likely to understand and further others' desire for them?

You may object that saintly people can well have no personal desires, either material or prestigious; but we do not legislate for saints.

Now since people in their day-to-day lives are motivated by this complex of attitudes, self-regard and fellow-feeling, group and sectional interests, personal and family responsibility, local patriotism, philanthropy, an economy will be effective only insofar as it can contain and harness all these drives. Perhaps Archbishop Temple had it right when he said: 'The art of Government, in fact, is the art of so ordering life that self interest prompts what justice demands'.

Adam Smith, who came to economics via philosophy, (sociology – as we should now call it) and history, described how the interplay between the self-interest of many can further the mutual interest of all. I urge you to read him, both for what he said and for what he did not say, but is often ascribed to him. He did not say that self-interest was good per se; he saw it as a major drive which can be a blessing to any society able to harness it and a curse to those who cannot harness it.

He showed how the market economy obliges and enables each producer to serve the consumers' interest by serving his own.

People must be free to choose what they consume in goods and services. When they choose through the market, their choice is sovereign. They alone exercise their responsibility as consumers and producers. To the extent that the fruits of their efforts are appropriated by the state, or other coercive bodies, they not only have responsibility taken away from them, but the ability to make their wishes felt. Power accrues more and more to the politician, bureaucrat, state-owned or subsidised providers of goods and services.

Choice in a free society implies responsibility. There is no hard and fast line between economic and other forms of personal responsibility to self, family, firm, community, nation, God. Morality lies in choosing between feasible alternatives. A moral being is one who exercises his own judgement in choice, on matters great and small, bearing in mind their moral dimension, i.e. right and wrong. Insofar as his right and duty to choose is taken away by the state, the party or the union, his moral faculties, i.e. his capacity for choice, atrophy, and he becomes a moral cripple in the same way as we should lose the faculty of walking, reading, seeing, if we were prevented from using them over the years.

In a letter from a person who responded to the Archbishop of Canterbury's 'call to the nation', this point was beautifully put:

'We wish to be self-reliant and do not want to be dependent on the state, nor do we want the state to take so great a proportion of our money in rates and taxes to decide for us what we shall have and not have. . .*I may be wrong, but I think it weakens character when little by little our freedom of choice is taken from us.*'

And another person said:

> I am a middle-aged woman, wife of a lower-paid worker. We have struggled through the years to buy our own house, old though it may be. We have asked for nothing. We only had one child, so no child allowance. What we have achieved we did ourselves. *When we look round and see all the handouts people are getting from this welfare state, we sometimes feel so sad that what should be a wonderful thing has really turned out to sap the goodness and initiative from so many of our people.*

So let there be no mistake: economic choices have a moral dimension. A man is now enabled to choose between earning his living and depending on the bounty of the state, a choice which comes about because benefits rise and remain tax-free, while earnings rise more slowly if at all, and tax is high at very low income levels.

A man must choose between spending and saving, between housing himself and depending on the state to house him at his fellow-citizen's expense, between paying for his children's education and accepting whatever the state provides, between working for a wage or salary and setting up on his own, between longer hours of work or study and spending more time in leisure with his family, even between spending more of his money on himself and more on his family, between joining a union and not joining, even if it means persecution by union and state.

The Socialists would take away most or all of these choices. A man would do what he was told by the state and his union, work where work was 'found' for him, at the rate fixed and degree of effort permitted. He would send his children to school where the education authority decided what the children are taught and the way they are taught. Irrespective of his views, he would live in the housing provided, take what he could get, give what he was obliged to give.

This does not produce a classless society; on the contrary it produces the most stratified of all societies, divided into two classes: *the powerful and the powerless*; the party-bureaucratic elite and the manipulated masses.

And are these rulers better fitted to make choices on our behalf or to dispose of resources? Are they wiser, less selfish, more moral? What reason have we for supposing that they are? As the French economist and critic of socialism, Claude Frederic Bastiat, asked a century and a half ago, how can the socialists, who have such a low opinion of the people's ability to choose have such a high regard for their own?

I quote his own words:

> Since the natural inclinations of mankind are so evil that its liberty must be taken away, how is it that the inclinations of the socialists are good? Are not the legislators and their agents part of the human race? Do they believe themselves moulded from another clay than the rest of mankind? They say that society,

> left to itself, heads inevitably for destruction because its instincts are perverse. They demand the power to stop mankind from sliding down this fatal declivity and to impose a better direction on it. If, then, they have received from heaven intelligence and virtues that place them beyond and above mankind, let them show their credentials. They want to be *shepherds*, and they want us to be their *sheep*.

We know from experience that these self-appointed guardians use their power to perpetuate it. We have seen how the economic considerations which in a market economy are decisive, are increasingly subordinated in a controlled economy to the party political interests of politicians, to the group interest of state employees, and to workers in some nationalised industries. We pay through the nose in prices and taxes and take what we are given. In that sense, *we don't own those industries, they 'own' us.*

And have we not seen at home, and particularly abroad, how some socialist politicians soon come to adopt the very 'ruling life-styles' they rose to power by denouncing?

In the market economy, people are free to give of their money and their time for good causes. They exercise their altruism on their own initiative and at their own expense, whether they give directly and personally through institutions, charities, universities, churches or hospitals. When the state steps in, generosity is increasingly restricted from all sides.

From the one side, the idea is propagated that whatever needs doing is best done by the state.

Since the state knows best, causes it does not support must be of questionable worth. On the other side, since the state takes more and more of people's earnings, they have less inclination to give what money they still have left for those needs which the welfare state fails to meet.

When people give directly, personally or through an institution they respect, they feel that the sacrifices they may make in giving, and the effort in earning is worth while. People have always accepted the responsibility to sustain the young and the old, the unfortunate and the needy. But when the money is taken away and spent by government, the blessing goes out of giving and out of the effort of earning in order to give.

This contrast is borne out by historical experience. The Victorian age, which saw the burgeoning of free enterprise, also saw the greatest expansion of voluntary philanthropic activity of all kinds, the new hospitals, new schools, technical colleges, universities, new foundations for orphans, non-profit making housing trusts, missionary societies.

The Victorian age has been very badly treated in socialist propaganda. It was an age of constant and constructive endeavour in which the desire to improve the lot of the ordinary person was a powerful factor. We who are largely living off the Victorians' moral and physical capital can hardly afford to denigrate them.

You may remember Lord Acton's aphorism that while only a foolish Conservative would judge the present by the standards of the past, only a foolish Liberal would judge the past by the standards of the present. There are many foolish Liberals in the Socialist camp; we can do without them in ours.

Why then you may ask, did socialist thought make so much headway? It is not only a fair question but a vitally important one for us. There are many possible answers. But one obvious reason stands out. Socialists criticised imperfect human reality in the name of a theory. So long as socialism was only a theory, it made criticism of other ways easy for them. They could claim that their way was best. But now we are beyond the days of theory. For decades Socialists have extended their power until they control almost half the world's population. How has the thing worked out in practice? Disastrously. Wherever they have imposed their heavy hand, people are worse off and less free.

The last sentence is an appropriate place to end, for it answers the most important of all questions about socialism: how it succeeds in making so many converts: not merely the poor and needy – who can be expected to vote for a theory that seems to offer something for nothing – but large numbers of the intelligent, talented and wealthy. Man, at his least evolved level, is hardly a social being at all; he is concerned solely with his own needs. At a higher level of development, he becomes concerned with the needs of others, with society in general. And at this stage, he becomes prone to simplistic solutions. Hitler managed to persuade a large number of intelligent Germans that Germany could be turned into Utopia by simply expelling the Jews. In the socialist mythology, the 'privileged' become the equivalent of the Jews – the scapegoats.

Under the circumstances, then, it seems strange that the socialists have not had things entirely their own way, and that they are not swept into office at every election by an enormous majority. The reason is undoubtedly that there are large numbers of people who have achieved a certain amount of security through their own efforts, and who object to a theory that implies that people like themselves ought to be feeling guilty. They exist in slums as well as in semi-detached council houses and suburban villas, and they object to a government that feels it should have absolute control over their lives and pay packets.

The *Times* leader of July 5, 1977, paid less attention to this aspect of Mrs Thatcher's argument than to her remarks about Adam Smith and Karl Marx. For a few days there was an erudite and not-very-lively correspondence about whether Adam Smith or Marx laid more emphasis on economics. Then a correspondent named J. W. Saunders of Cleveland dropped a cat among the pigeons by launching into an impassioned defense of that 'great and humane philosophy' called Marxism. More than half the world's population, he suggested, are now under Marxist governments, and the rest will inevitably follow. 'Can we not be much more sensible', he asks, 'and accept with grace and intelligence our inevitably plural and Marxised future?'

This brought a flood of replies that continued for the next three weeks. And most correspondents took the opportunity to make the same point. (The following sentences are taken from different letters.)

> All attempts hitherto to put Marx's theories into actual practice have only resulted, after much killing, in governments of coopted 'apparatchiks' living in luxury and maintaining themselves in power with the help of an army or a secret police.

> Marxism and fascism are in practice two facets of the same oppressive statist coin.

> If Marxism enjoys the widespread willing support that he implies, why is it so hard to identify even one Marxist state whose government was elected and is maintained by anything resembling a democratic system? And why does the world's leading Marxist state constitute a yardstick for repression and lack of personal liberty by which all the others are judged?

> Marxism is not an adolescent affectation or a debating society diversion: it is a handbook to the concentration-camp state.

The irrepressible Mr Saunders came back with a reply in which he asserted that he was not a Marxist, and that no one need worry about

Marxism because 'oppressive regimes cannot hold for long without mass support'. To which I. Dmytriew, of the Ukrainian Information Service, replied that he had been in Stalin's Russia as well as Hitler's Germany, and that the question of mass support did not arise; after the regime had been in power a short time, it made no difference whether the masses supported it or not; they had no choice.

In a 'Profile' published during this correspondence, Mr Wedgewood Benn went on record as supporting the view that Marxism is a great and altruistic philosophy perverted by wicked men like Stalin. Victor Hill, of Beckenham, Kent, asked whether Mr Benn or other apologists for Marx had actually read the *Communist Manifesto*.

> Let us ignore the seething, violent contempt for the bourgeoisie that characterises this document and is itself an incitement to violence; let us turn to the 10-point programme set out at the end of Chapter II, 'Proletarians and Communists'. So far as I can see, every one of these points, from the abolition of private ownership of land, through the monopolisation by the State of credit and transport, to the State takeover of education, is specifically designed to augment the Power of the State, to suffocate the rights of the individual beneath those of the body politic.

The argument steamed on into August, providing a lengthy and interesting footnote to Mrs Thatcher's comment that socialism succeeds because it 'criticises imperfect humanity in the name of a theory.' All could be summarised in a single sentence: Marx's intentions may have been great and humane; in practice, Marxism has repeatedly and invariably shown itself to be oppressive and inhumane. The essence of a theory is that it should predict the results of experience. By this standard, Marxism has falsified itself.

Let Mrs Thatcher have the last word; it is from the conclusion of her Iain Macleod lecture:

> We are really in no better position to prophesy than preceding generations were, and they always got it wrong; the more scientific they thought they were, the further they strayed. For the unfolding of human history is richer and more complex than our minds can foresee.
>
> Yet by understanding the present and the past, and adducing possibilities and probabilities as best we can, so long as we leave some margin for error, *we can influence the shape of things to come.*

We have learned much from the over-optimism of the post-war era, when we thought Government could do it all. *We need healthy scepticism, but not pessimism.* We are not bound to an irrevocable decline. We see nothing as inevitable. Man can still shape history.

NOTES

1. *Margaret Thatcher: A Profile*, W.H. Allen, 1980
2. 18 July, 1977.

REDRESSING THE BALANCE

MARGARET THATCHER

For fifty years or more now we have lived in an intellectual climate in which we have been led to believe that decisions made by the State on behalf of the people are in some way both more moral and more efficient than decisions taken by the individual himself.

There is no evidence in the history of our century that that is true. On the contrary, all the evidence is that the more you take away from the individual his own powers of decision, the more you increase the risks of tyranny. The more, too, you help to create a shoddy and second-rate society.

The values we stand for are threatened not only from within our societies, but from without. It was very understandable that, once the tensions of the so-called Cold War were relaxed, the peoples of the West greeted the idea of detente with relief. But detente should be a two-way business, and I fear that so far too many of the concessions have been made by the West; few of the undertakings given by the Soviet Union at Helsinki have been observed. But Western countries have almost fallen over themselves in their eagerness to keep their side of the bargain. Originally the series of talks which culminated in the Helsinki declaration were to proceed at the same pace as the exchanges on mutual and balanced force reductions (MBFR) on either side of the Iron Curtain. That was the understanding on which the last Conservative Foreign Secretary in Britain, Sir Alec Douglas-Home, proceeded.

Now MBFR has almost been forgotten, and the might of the USSR increases every year. We must not confuse hope with attainment. Because we earnestly want peace and co-operation we must not assume that it is permanently assured. We must add deterrence and defence to detente, for unless we do, we in the West will find ourselves constantly accommodating ourselves to Marxist values, instead of making the world safe for our own. We should not be timid or uncertain in proclaiming our values; we must build a world in which freedom is on the offensive. No single Western state – not even the United States of America – can stand alone against the power of Russia, nor alone can stem the spread of Communist influence around the world. In this great endeavour we must all stand together. Our alliance, not only military but intellectual and spiritual, is our indispensable shield.

Of all the provisions in the Helsinki agreement, none has been more blatantly ignored than that providing for freer traffic in ideas between East and West. The most minimal effort has been made by the Soviet Union to fulfil its part of the bargain for the simple reason that the Soviet Union dare not allow its society to be invaded by our beliefs and values.

How sad it is, then, that in the last generation the West has so often been lax in fighting the intellectual battle with extreme Socialism. Those of us who believe passionately in a free society know that we must fire the imagination, and enthusiasm of minds *today* if we are to safeguard freedom *tomorrow*.

Sometimes Britain and the free democracies of the West seem to be suffering more from a failure of nerve than from anything else. 'After the fall of Athens, in 404 BC' wrote C.M. Bowra (*The Greek Experience*)

> something was extinguished, not merely a zest for life and a boldness of enterprise and experiment but certain assumptions which had never been seriously questioned now lost their authority and their hold.

The evidence of every kind proves that our free democratic system is superior in technology to the communist one. We are infinitely quicker to take advantage of promising inventions than is the communist system. Since 1945, our system has brought benefits to large numbers. The population of communist countries, on the other hand, has suffered horribly and unnecessarily from the deadening hand which the State has held over them. No communist country, for example, has made a success of collectivised agriculture. Russia, before the Revolution, used to be a great exporter of wheat. She has often recently had to import that staff of life from the USA. The writings of Solzhenitsyn made obvious even to the wilfully blind that it was not simply Stalin who was an evil man, but that communism, in practice, is an evil system, which gave birth to Stalin.

Prosperity in the West can also be measured in direct relation to the role which the State had played in the economy concerned. West Germany and Japan, for example, where the part of the State has been modest, are more successful, measured in terms of output, than are Britain and Italy, where the hand played by the State has been strong. Even so, morale among the free democracies is low. Prominent people have publicly wondered whether democracy can survive. Very few people describe themselves willingly as 'capitalists'.

The reasons for the disillusion or even despair in the West are various. Many suffer from a certain historical shortsightedness. People forget that democracy in the sense of a universal franchise is new. Even in Britain, it is only fifty years old. Thus, our version of democracy is not an old, ramshackle building which, after many generations, is beginning to fall down. It is a system still with growing pains – an infinitely new system in comparison with absolute systems, such as practised by our enemies. A hankering for absolutism, like a hankering for a single leader, is a throwback to the past, not a foreshadowing of the future.

In addition, spokesmen for democracy too often allow their opponents to choose the ground for debate. It is not enough to say that private enterprise gives a better material life, true though that usually is. We should look more to ideas and realise that people respond to them often more than they respond to appeals to their material interests. Communists know the power of ideas, despite their doctrine of historical materialism. We too should show we are aware of their importance despite our material success.

A generation of easy liberal education has accustomed many to suppose that Utopia was soon to be achieved. Such education left the belief that, with the welfare state, all ills would soon vanish and, with the UN, all tyrannies would soon crumble. That has proved an illusion. Each generation has to fight for its own liberties, in whatever way is appropriate. The ideal solutions of one generation may even become, unless refurbished and brought up to date, the cause of bondage, or at least bureaucracy for the next.

The friends of the free society have also too often accepted the argument of their enemies that the dominant issue in politics is a matter of social class. Policies with that as a basis are both divisive and meaningless. Those who, in the nineteenth century, worked out a theory of history based on class did so at a time when there were comparatively few urban wage-earners dependent on a powerful employer. Neither Marx nor Engels could possibly have recognised *their* 'working class' in present-day England or indeed elsewhere. Of course, many workers of the mid-nineteenth century did feel lost, if they were working twelve hours a day, with the protection of neither unions nor social legislation. But modern workers in Detroit, Coventry, the Ruhr, even Moscow, are now primarily citizens of their country, like everyone else. They are not members of an under-privileged and internationally recognisable 'class'. The moral of all this is simple: Marx was wrong about the working-class when he wrote his books; and his prescriptions have as little use today as other mid-Victorian arguments have as to what should, or should not, be done.[1]

NOTES

1. These two excerpts from speeches given by The Rt Hon Margaret Thatcher, PC, MP, were taken from:
   Address to the Christian Democratic Union, Hanover, of 25 May 1976 (published by Centre for Policy Studies).
   'The Ideas of an Open Society': speech to the Bow Group at the Royal Commonwealth Society, London, on 6 May 1978.

IN DEFENCE OF FREEDOM

MARGARET THATCHER

The first word in this symposium was given to Lenin, who expressed his cynicism about 'threadbare Marxist phrases' and 'Marxist hairsplitting.' It seems appropriate to give the last word to Mrs Thatcher.

Politicians' official speeches are seldom remarkable for their intellectual content. But Mrs Thatcher's Donovan Award Speech, made in New York on February 28, 1981, contains a clear and concise summary of the West's objection to Soviet Marxism. It may serve as a reminder that the real enemy is not misguided Utopianism, but the ruthless opportunism Marx advocated to achieve it.

I intend this evening to speak about the defence of freedom. Freedom based on respect for the individual, is an idea whose strength and beauty has remained undimmed down the ages.

We face a group of states whose leaders believe, or profess to believe, that history has predetermined them and us to a relationship of struggle, and preordained that they and not we should be the winners. This new creed of struggle is backed by the old tools of pressure. The Soviet Union itself spends on military purposes about one sixth of the national wealth it produces. To take some recent figures at random, last year the Soviet Union manufactured 1600 combat aircraft, 3000 tanks and some 1500 missiles of intercontinental or intermediate range. Some of this equipment has been sent abroad to swell the Soviet foreign trade – or foreign 'aid' – statistics: but most of it will simply join the already gigantic Soviet arsenals on land, at sea and in the air.

Does this mean that the government of the Soviet Union, a founder member of the United Nations and a permanent member of the Security Council, is contemplating direct aggression against the West? I do not suggest that, and I do not believe that. I see three other motives. Firstly, they seek reassurance for their own fears. Secondly, they hope that knowledge of their sheer might will be enough to split Europe and Japan from the United States. Thirdly, they want to gain influence outside Europe with the aim of out-flanking the West through the South.

The expansion of Soviet military power has therefore been accompanied by repeated attempts to increase Soviet influence in the Third World, by subversion and by active intervention – directly or through proxies. In Angola, in Somalia, in Ethiopia the Soviet Union or Cuba have intervened by force in African conflicts thousands of miles from their borders. In South East Asia Soviet weapons, training and money have enabled Vietnam to impose its will on both Laos and Cambodia. Fourteen months ago the Soviet Union marched into Afghanistan to rescue a regime tottering under the weight of its own unpopularity. One in ten of the Afghan population have since fled the country. Today that new Anschluss is maintained only by the guns of eighty thousand Soviet troops.

This then is the present danger: an unstable world harbouring a super power with a destructive ideology and an expansionist record. But let us not exaggerate the danger: to measure it dispassionately is the first step to meeting it. The Soviet Union has suffered setbacks over the years. For all her efforts, she has made no advances in Europe since 1945. Recent events in Poland have demonstrated the failure of the Soviet system to take root in Eastern Europe. The Soviet Union was thrown out of Egypt and has been unable to re-establish herself in any other major Middle Eastern state. Her relations with China are deeply hostile.

All this suggests the Soviet Union may have a handful of clients but it has few friends or admirers. Which is not surprising – for what is there in the Soviet system to admire? Material prosperity? It does not produce it. Spiritual satisfaction? It denies it. After an uninterrupted monopoly of absolute power lasting 63 years the controlled society has failed. The economy is run on strange principles: *from* each according to his instructions, *to* each according to his party status. The rules of the political system are equally simple: for the *few*, privilege; for the *many*, the part of a studio audience clapping for the cameras.

Recognising this, let us set about the defence of our liberties with confidence. Of course we face economic, social and political problems at home and abroad. But who on our side would exchange our problems for theirs? History is not moving, inevitably or otherwise, in favour of Marxism/Leninism. Its disciples know that their ideas run counter to the deepest and strongest instincts of men. They are destined, sooner or later, to fail.

AFTERWORD

by
COLIN WILSON

By the late 1950s, Hayek was convinced that socialism, as a living historical force, was finished. In *The Constitution of Liberty* he wrote:

> The great change that has occurred during the last decade is that socialism in this strict sense of a particular method of achieving social justice has collapsed. It has not merely lost its intellectual appeal; it has also been abandoned by the masses so unmistakably that socialist parties everywhere are searching for a new programme that will insure the active support of their followers.

The chief reason for this collapse, he thought, was the Soviet Union. 'Marxism was killed in the Western world by the example of Russia.' But the practice of socialism in countries like Britain and Scandinavia had also created disillusionment. There were three main reasons: that socialism was actually less productive than capitalism, that it meant more 'inescapable order of rank than ever before' and therefore less social justice, and that it led to more authoritarianism.

More than two decades later, it seems clear that Hayek was fundamentally correct. It is still unmistakably clear that the masses have no stomach for the kind of socialism preached by the extreme left; every time they have a chance to show their opinion, they decisively reject it. It is also clear that the majority of working people regard the trade unions with cynicism or active hostility; this is inevitable, since most strikes impose inconvenience on the majority of the population. Most strikes nowadays have nothing to do with the class struggle or the liberty of the workers; they are aimed at extorting a few per cent more from employers who feel they have already offered as much as they can afford. Popper had pointed out in *The Open Society* that

> there are . . . groups of workers who pursue their particular group interest even where it is in open conflict with the interest of other workers, and with the idea of the solidarity of the oppressed.

He also pointed out strikes inevitably lead to the strengthening of anti-democratic tendencies in the opponents' camp, since they clearly make democracy unworkable. In this passage (p. 163) Popper takes care to distinguish between political strikes and strikes in furtherance of wage disputes; but these were easier to distinguish in the mid-1940s than they are in the 1980s, when a group like the miners tried to use its 'muscle' to force the Conservative government to halt the closure of loss-making pits, and thus to reverse one of its most basic policies. And here again, it is clearly a case of a group pursuing its own interest 'in open conflict with the interest of other workers', since it is the other workers who must subsidise the loss-making pits with their taxes. The other workers may sympathise with the miners' desire to keep their jobs; but they can hardly enjoy the rise in taxes that would, in fact, be necessary to pay for this 'victory.'

Then for how long can socialism continue? The answer seems to be: for just as long as it can rely on a muddle-headed belief that socialism is 'for' the workers and 'against' their exploiters. My mother remarked on the phone the other day: 'I'll never vote Conservative. I'm working class', and an opinion like this is so simple as to be unbudgeable. It is a question of emotional loyalty, like religion. This was the kind of attitude that Marx and Engels relied upon to bring about the revolution; they saw it as a simple matter of persuading the workers to seize the power that was already within their grasp. And since workers form the majority of the population in most industrial nations, it seems surprising that the kind of revolution they prophesied has never come about. (For, as Popper and Hayek point out, all communist takeovers have been brought about by a non-representative minority.) The answer seems to be that in most country areas, the workers are conservative by tradition, and feel the same basic distrust of bureaucrats that industrial workers feel towards the 'bosses.' Marx was mistaken when he believed that socialism would triumph through sheer weight of numbers. He was forgetting that most of the 'numbers' are influenced by old loyalties rather than by political arguments. By the time socialist traditions became sufficiently established to influence loyalties, its practical disadvantages – such as the inconveniences suffered by the public every time a major union goes on strike – had become obvious enough to tilt the balance the other way.

According to Marx, the ultimate triumph of socialism is historically inevitable. An unbiased look at history tells us that this is simply untrue. No 'commune' has ever worked for long; all – from the French revolution to the Oneida Community – have collapsed as the realities of human nature have asserted themselves over muddled ideals. Communist ideals thrive in an atmosphere of short-sighted emotionalism – the kind of strong emotion that can be found wherever there is poverty or misery. With economic prosperity, communism simply evaporates. Twenty-five years ago, this seemed to be the likeliest possibility: that the communist State would wither away as its emotional ideals were eroded by prosperity and economic realism. The attempted uprisings in Hungary and Czechoslovakia suggested that it might not take as long as that: that human nature itself might revolt long before prosperity made it inevitable. Now, in the 1980s, we become aware of a more startling possibility. Events in Chile, in Afghanistan, in Poland, suggest the possibility of a world in which communism has simply vanished, finally overturned by the masses it is supposed to represent. History is not always gradual. The 'witchcraft craze' collapsed quite suddenly, in Europe and America; at one moment it seemed as strong as ever; in the next, it had disappeared. Matthew Hopkins and the Salem witchcraft trials were too much for human nature to swallow.

In that sense, every trial of a dissident is a hopeful sign. If communism disappears in our generation, it will not be as a result of violent anti-communism, but of the excesses of communism itself. Human commonsense will do the rest.

INDEX

Note: Since the whole book concerns Marx and Marxist doctrines, entries under 'Marx' are confined to biographical details and overall summary of doctrine.